Call for Change

Call for Change

The Medicine Way of American Indian History, Ethos, & Reality

DONALD L. FIXICO

University of Nebraska Press ☾ Lincoln and London

 An earlier version of chapter 2 appeared in *The American Indian Mind in a Linear World: American Indian Studies and Traditional Knowledge* (New York: Routledge, 2003).
Manufactured in the United States of America

♾

Library of Congress Cataloging-in-Publication Data
Fixico, Donald Lee, 1951–
Call for change: the medicine way of American Indian history, ethos, and reality / Donald L. Fixico.
p. cm.
Includes bibliographical references and index.
ISBN 978-0-8032-4356-9 (cloth: alk. paper)
1. Indians of North America—Historiography.
2. Indian philosophy—North America. I. Title.
E76.8.F59 2013
970.004'97—dc23 2012043316

Set in Minion Pro by Laura Wellington.
Designed by A. Shahan.

*To April, ****
who understands all of this.

Contents

Illustrations

Preface

The time for a call for change in American Indian history is now. For too many years the academic discipline has ignored the ethos and reality among Indian people or lacked the open-mindedness to understand these forces. Many years of thinking about the subject are represented in this book. The frustration has been that most scholars writing about Indian people do so with limited understanding. The idea of others writing your people's history naturally deepens the frustration, provoking feelings that "they don't really understand us," or "they just don't get it." Many Indian people would agree with these statements. Hence the task is to address how the discipline of history can be improved by reconsidering the approach toward Native people in order to produce more balanced scholarship. It is for these reasons that I offer observations about how historians have frequently misunderstood Indians.

In response, I provide as a thesis the idea of the Medicine Way of American Indian history, which demonstrates and explains the indigenous ethos and reality. The concept further demands the acknowledgment of a "Natural Democracy" paradigm consisting of what I have called the First, Second, and Third Dimensions, as a cross-cultural bridge for individuals to understand the past of Indian people more comprehensively. This is a new approach to help the history discipline intellectualize indigenous people in the Medicine Way, a standpoint drawn from the ancient postulate that medicine power is all around Indian people, who live the Medicine Way of life. Derived from centuries of studying nature, this approach is both cyclical and circular in philosophy.

Chapter 1 addresses the general historiography of Indian history and considers which academic disciplines have promoted the field. American Indian history is a complex subject due to the need to try to understand and reconstruct Indian historical reality. This chapter also introduces the Indian-white paradigm of Indian-white contact and works retrospectively toward establishing a Native reality. In the process the Medicine Way of history, which begins with binary relationships, is revealed. Chapter 2 is about the two important concepts of "seeing" and Natural Democracy. Seeing is defined as how Native people who are close to their tribal cultures think and how this circular and visual logic has developed into a Native ethos. Natural Democracy is the inclusion of all things to be mutually recognized based on reciprocal respect among all within a totality that the Muscogee Creeks and Seminoles call *Ibofanga*. An earlier version of this chapter on Indian circular philosophy appeared in my book *The American Indian Mind in a Linear World: American Indian Studies and Traditional Knowledge* (2003).

In 1982 I taught an Indian history survey at the University of Wisconsin, Milwaukee. As I described the democratic government of the League of the Iroquois to my class, I included the importance of the Iroquois animal clans in the worldview of life and used the phrase Natural Democracy for the first time. Later I discovered that Nobel Prize–winning author Pearl Buck illustrated in her novel *The Good Earth* a kind of Natural Democracy to describe Chinese farmers' practice of kinship and rural life in a social community. In hearings to repeal the Chinese Exclusion Act in 1943, Buck used a more developed cultural concept of Natural Democracy. Much earlier, Aristotle spoke of civil government as a form of Natural Democracy in Greek society.

While Aristotle and Buck use Natural Democracy as a cultural concept and governmental practice for people, I broaden the usage to include human and nonhuman entities in a totality where all are respected on a lateral basis. In 2000 Native scholar Gregory Cajete described the earth as hosting a Natural Democracy of all things as parts of her body, and each one has a right to live. Other scholars may have used Natural Democracy, and it is my hope that people will become familiar with it as a practical term to include the natural environment as a part of our daily lives so as to avoid disregarding animals, plants, and the natural environment.

Chapter 3 addresses the historical equation of Indian-white relations, examining the primary trends in historical literature written "about" American Indians. The chapter identifies works written about Indians as the First Dimension. Chapter 4 on the Indian-white binary discusses the present scholarship with Indians and whites as equal actors on the historical stage. Such scholarship centers on Indian-white interactions in war, trade, boarding schools, and activism. This interaction in a "shared experience" is the Second Dimension, which has developed since the mid-1980s and is where the current scholarship is mostly practiced.

An earlier version of chapter 5 was presented as "The Metaphysical Reality of American Indian History" at the Twenty-fifth Anniversary of the D'Arcy McNickle Center at the Newberry Library, Chicago, during September 1997. The Third Dimension of American Indian history was conceived in my teaching seminars in ethnohistory at Western Michigan University and was initially introduced in a paper presented at the annual meeting of the American Society for Ethnohistory in 1996. The Third Dimension is Native ethos: how Indian people view history from their own perspective. This chapter explains how historians and other scholars can reconstruct Native reality.

Chapter 6 on transdisciplinary and cross-cultural analysis provides academic tools to build a bridge of understanding to cross to the third dimension and return to the first. Related to this approach is chapter 7, providing the basis of Native culture in oral tradition and its importance in accounting for the past. Chapter 8 emphasizes that the earth and indigenous women are vital to understanding the infrastructure and inner perspective called the Native ethos. This chapter is also about the role of place in providing a sense of Native reality. Chapter 9 reemphasizes the need for a call for change, to rethink Indian history and how it should be reanalyzed for a balanced history of Indian-white relations.

Ten figures are integrated into the first nine chapters to illustrate the development of the model of Natural Democracy via the three dimensions identified. Each figure represents a visual phase, starting with a binary paradigm of Indian-white relations—Creek-white, for example—that demonstrates a reciprocal relationship. Any tribal community can be used and can be represented by a circle. The same tribal community as a circle becomes the focus of a natural environment, surrounded by other circles of human and nonhuman communities. For instance, with the Creeks in the center, we also have the following binary relationships: Creek-white, Creek-Cherokee, Creek-animal, Creek-plant, and so forth. The Creeks have a binary relationship with each community, and they are all connected via their reciprocal relations within a totality that I call Natural Democracy. The one exception is the Creek-metaphysical binary in figure 9. Although the Creek people desire to remain always connected to the metaphysical, it communicates with the Creeks only when it wishes. Finally, the key to this spherical indigenous world, as depicted in multiple reciprocal relationships in figure 10, is that Indians are communal people and are inclusive of all others.

A note on terminology: I have used American Indian instead of Native American. Indians do not typically call one another Native Americans; non-Indians more commonly refer to Native people as Native Americans. People who know Indians well usually use the names of tribes.

Many people have influenced my thinking about how to develop an innovative approach to writing American Indian history. To begin with, the mentors at the University of Oklahoma who trained me as a historian were the late Arrell M. Gibson, H. Wayne Morgan, William H. Maehl Jr., and William Bittel; and Bittel introduced me to anthropology as a useful discipline to understand the interwoven combination of culture and history. Postdoctoral fellowships years ago at UCLA and at the Newberry Library added to my training and exposure to a larger thinking of American Indian history. The seminar discussions at the Newberry Library were invaluable to broadening my perspectives, although at the time they added to my personal frustration as a young scholar. These ideas needed more honing to be developed into sharper concepts and deeper thoughts about American Indian history.

As a young professor at the University of Wisconsin, Milwaukee, I benefited from the influence of Reginald Horsman and Francis Paul Prucha, who was nearby at Marquette University. I listened to their wisdom and interpretative analysis about Indian history. Further words of advice and influences on my thinking came over the years from conversations with Blue Clark, R. David Edmunds, Michael Green, Peter Iverson, Floyd O'Neil, Katherine Osburn, Donald Parman, Margaret Connell Szasz, Gregory Thompson, and John Wunder. I am grateful to all of them and to others not mentioned here. From a distance, I am thankful for the works of Richard White, Phil Deloria, James Axtell, William T. Hagan, William Fenton, Fred Hoxie, Colin Calloway, Calvin Martin, Fred McTaggart, Robert Berkhofer, and Ray DeMallie, whose writings have forced me to think more deeply about how to argue for an *Indian* Indian history.

My former graduate students at Western Michigan University deserve apologies for having had to listen to my ideas and thoughts about history and Indians, especially during the days of building a new doctoral program in the history department. These young people indulged my early concepts in seminars and contributed ideas about how to analyze American Indian history. More than the students ever realized, our exchanges helped me to shape new ideas and ponder convictions. These young scholars are Rob Galler, Mary Younker, Barbara Sears, Michelle Martin, Maribel Izquierdo-Rodriguez, JoAnne Thomas, Tim Willig, and Dixie Haggard. I am thankful to my former history chair at Western Michigan University, Ron Davis, who allowed me to experiment with new graduate seminars focusing on methodology, ethnohistory, and oral history as we built a new doctoral program.

I am also appreciative of my patient graduate students and colleagues in the history department and in the Indigenous Nations Studies Program at the University of Kansas for sharing my ideas and concerns about American Indians and history. At Kansas University, I am grateful for the support from my former colleagues Peter Mancall, Rita Napier, Don Worster, and many others, including the Discussion Club. What I learned from the club was that a sharp mind is always young. I am especially appreciative of my former secretary Fredina Drye, who helped immensely on my arrival to Kansas. The writing for this book began at KU. Graduate students at Kansas University who helped with typing and researching articles were Tom Niermann, Sara Summers, and Viv Ibbett.

I am very grateful to Gary Dunham, former director of the SUNY Press and University of Nebraska Press, who read an early draft of the manuscript and commented fully on it. He knows all about writing from the Indian side of history. At the University of Nebraska Press, I am appreciative of the support from my editor Matt Bokovoy, assistant project editor Kyle Simonsen, and copyeditor Sally Antrobus. They made my ideas easier to understand. I also appreciate the responses from the outside readers, whoever they are, for making this a stronger book.

In addition, I am thankful for the services of Channette Kirby of the Watson Library at the University of Kansas. During the final stages of manuscript development I presented an overall paper on the complexity of American Indian history at the first regional meeting of the Organization of American Historians, held at Iowa State University, and I am grateful to those who listened to my ideas and offered comments. Particular thanks go to Chris Newman of Elgin Community College, who shared his paper with me and offered helpful comments on my work.

After relocating to Arizona State University I took up this manuscript again and revised it with new courage. I am grateful for my Distinguished Foundation Professorship and support from President Michael Crow, Provost and Vice President Betty Philips, Executive Dean Robert Page, and Interim Dean Elizabeth Langland. I appreciate the warm friendships with Matt Garcia, director of the School of Historical, Philosophical and Religious Studies, history faculty head Phil VanderMeer, and the staff of the school as well as my colleagues Peter Iverson, Katherine Osburn, Paul Hirt, and others in history and across the campus, David Martinez, James Riding In, Bryan Brayboy, Diane Humetewa, Eddie Brown, Simon Ortiz, John Tippeconnic, Delia Saenz, Carol Lujan, Patricia Ferguson, Michael Begaye,

Laura Tohe and Rebecca Tsosie. In bringing this project to fruition I also received much help and hard work from my research assistants Clara Keyt and Chelsea Mead. In the final stages, research assistants Brianna Theobald and John Goodwin worked thoroughly to help complete the final draft and I am grateful to them.

As I completed this book, I thought considerably about the past and my parents and grandparents. My mother, Virgina Fixico (Sac & Fox and Shawnee), and my father, John Fixico (Seminole and Muscogee Creek), and their Depression-born generation, including aunts and uncles, remember when much mainstream prejudice went against them, making life harder than necessary. Even earlier, following World War I, my grandparents—Jonas Fixico (Seminole), Lena Spencer Fixico (Muscogee Creek), Glade Wakolee (Sac & Fox), and Rachel Dirt Wakolee (Shawnee)—lived during an even more difficult generation of unwarranted discrimination, all due to misunderstanding, greed, and limited acceptance of Indian people in Oklahoma. Discrimination and ethnocentricism fostered a mainstream attitude in which the ideas of others were denied. For them and other Indian people of their times, this book is intended to help today's generation toward a better understanding of American Indians and their history. I also hope this model of Natural Democracy in the Medicine Way will help other indigenous communities in the world, as we are much alike in a binary system of colonizer and colonized, although in her work on gender and colonialism, Ann Stoler effectively argues that this adversarial model is much more complicated.

Last and most important, I am eternally grateful to my son Keytha and my wife April Summitt for helping bear my personal challenge of trying for a better understanding of Indian people by the history profession and mainstream society. The patience and support of my family have nurtured my confidence and boldness to go out on the limb of putting my ideas into words; I alone, of course, should bear any criticism people may have about this attempt to "see" American Indian history in a new light and with analytical insight. I do not speak in this book for all Indians; but as a full-blood I know that many Indian people feel history has been written "about" us and our people without real awareness of the depths of our Native cultures. I attempt to demonstrate how we see the world and live life in our Native reality while at the same time living and working in the other reality called the American mainstream. Life is seeking the spiritual balance between many challenging opposites and finding the courage to move forward to live.

Donald L. Fixico
Arizona State University

Glossary

Circle of Life means all things are connected within a totality. Via blood or symbolism, kinship provides membership that extends beyond human society to include nonhumans, such as the animals, plants, and all known forms in the earth and heavens.

Cultural bridge of understanding is the equation of Indian-white relations, (read from right to left) consisting of the First Dimension, Second Dimension, and Third Dimension. By passing through these dimensions of kinds of Native history, the bridge enables individuals to reach the Third Dimension and return with an understanding of all three types of Indian history.

First Dimension is the way in which western-trained historians write "about" American Indian history while not properly understanding the cultural reality of Native people from inside Native communities.

Medicine Way is the Native way of "seeing," or the worldview in an indigenous paradigm, whereby American Indians experience physical and metaphysical realities as one.

Natural Democracy is an indigenous paradigm consisting of everything in a totality being mutually respected by all entities within the system.

Nation and *tribe* are interchangeable terms used with the same meaning of a group of people working under one belief or direction that gives them purpose. This understanding of nation includes more than one community speaking the same language.

Other Side is the spiritual dimension in a metaphysical world where the nonliving exists. The spirits from the Other Side make themselves known to the living world.

Second Dimension is the "shared-experience" stage of scholarship in writing American Indian history as western-trained historians are putting Indians at center stage as makers of history with white Americans.

Third Dimension is the Native reality of the physical and metaphysical combined, in which spirits and visions are a major part of the indigenous paradigm and Native worldview, with details varying by tribe.

Call for Change

1

The Complexity of American Indian History

As it began to get dark on April 12, 1991, three Indians stood on a street corner in downtown Louisville, Kentucky. There was no doubt that they looked Indian. Two of them had long black hair. As people walked by, they stared at the Indians. One lit a cigarette and offered a smoke to the other two, but they shook their heads to decline. The smoker mentioned he was going to quit his habit someday. The long day had ended for the annual conference of the Organization of American Historians, meeting that year in Louisville. All three Native friends who attended the conference were historians with doctorates in hand from universities known for Indian history. We were deeply engrossed in conversation about one of the sessions where we had heard papers presented on Indians.

More people walked past us, but we paid them no mind. We criticized the papers, saying that the non-Indians in the session really did not know enough about Indians. We talked about the tribal differences of our people. One Indian historian said, "There wasn't enough scholarly analysis in the papers." The three of us concluded that American Indian history focused on Indian-white relations but that there were many tribal histories that needed to be included as well. We stood there talking for almost an hour; it was dark as we stood under a streetlight. I was hungry, and I told my friends I was going to get something to eat and go back to my hotel room. One of the other Native historians said he had to leave to meet a friend. The third said he had heard there was a blues band playing nearby, and he was going to listen to some blues.

As we left in our different directions, I thought about what the other people were thinking as they walked by us—three Indians standing on the street corner. Instantly all the stereotypes would come to their minds about Indians, and they might feel a bit tense walking past us. They might only ever have known Indians on television, or through the racist presumptions of Indians being dirty, lazy, and uneducated. I would have bet a million dollars that they would never have guessed we were three Indian scholars of history. Three Indian professors, out of fewer than fifteen Indian PhDs in history in the entire country at the time, were discussing the complexity of Indian history on a downtown street corner as the evening began to cool down.

Real Indian history focuses on how Indian people were involved in experiences from their own perspective and also on understanding the views of non-natives who participated. "How" and "why" Native peoples responded as they did in situations typically called events are significant questions for understanding Indian history. In this light, the present study is not just the history of Indian-white relations. This is not a history "about" Indians from a non-Indian point of view. Instead, it is a history of how Native people have been misrepresented, and this study sheds light on being Indian while expressing an indigenous ethos within a Native reality. In order to understand Indian history, it is necessary to attempt to "see" things from the Native perspective of a tribal community's inside.

In addition, "experience" is more significant to Indian people than "event." Native people describe experiences in their daily conversations or when telling about the past. In contrast, mainstream Americans place more emphasis on events as the text of history. Whether it is through experiences or events, Indians and whites have engaged each other throughout history, whether it was written or told via the oral tradition in stories.

Throughout this book, it is essential for the reader to put aside previous notions about history as a collection of events and to think about history in terms of experiences. In this Native ethos, history is a series of experiences recounted by storytellers through the oral tradition.

AMERICAN INDIAN HISTORY

NATIVE AMERICAN HISTORY

AMERICAN INDIANS' HISTORY

Equation of

HISTORY OF INDIAN-WHITE RELATIONS

FIGURE 1. American Indian history is equated with the history of Indian-white relations.

Current American Indian historiography represents the field of literature of historical accounts, including oral history, that non-Indian historians have produced about Indians and their relations with other peoples. This broad inclusion also takes in the works of other scholars and writers who have produced accounts about indigenous Americans as well as the writings of early chroniclers and travelers who kept diaries and journals and made reports about the Native peoples of America. It is crucial to acknowledge the oral history and written accounts produced by Native peoples, as they also produced pertinent records that are a part of American Indian historiography. While more than forty thousand books have been written about American Indians, mostly by non-Indians, there are also tribal accounts, works by Native authors, and oral histories that have added significantly to this historiography, although the mainstream academy has failed to appreciate this contribution.

In the discourse throughout the chapters that follow, American Indian history consists of understanding the *experiences* of Indian-white relations. Indian history is about relationships, including non-human relationships. However, in teaching Indian history one typically ends up teaching the history of Indian-white relations. Whatever the course is called—American Indian History, Native American History, Native Studies, or American Indians' History—the hyphenated Indian-white binary predominates, even if only implicitly.

In this equation, looking from right to left, one can imagine the settlers moving from the east toward the west as many of them re-

HISTORY OF

INDIAN — WHITE

RELATIONS

FIGURE 2. Generally Indian history courses focus on Indian-white relations.

corded their travels and wrote about Indians, keeping diaries, describing Native people in their journals, and telling others later about what they saw. In his introduction to *Bury My Heart at Wounded Knee: An Indian History of the American West*, Dee Brown invites his readers to stand up, and he states, "Americans who have always looked westward when reading about this period [the western expansion] should read this book facing eastward."[1]

The equation of Indian-white relations can be used to illustrate that a First Dimension exists in which non-Indians write "about" Indian people, and it is from this dimension that most Indian history has been written.

A Second Dimension can be theorized of scholars analyzing and writing about the "interactions" between Indians and whites. This second door represents the threshold where the mainstream reality meets Native reality. For example, the United States and Native groups have engaged in more than sixteen hundred wars, battles, and skirmishes. This common ground includes the first encounter with Columbus as well as other historical contact situations, such as trade relations, missionaries among Indians, boarding school experiences, and even intermarriages.

This Second Dimension has always been present, but it was not opened in academic circles until the 1970s. Ironically Native peoples have been using this door to go both ways: to enter white reality and to return to their own world as a part of the government's efforts to assimilate them in the mainstream.

A Third Dimension is proposed, which is actually the First Dimension from the Indian point of view, as indigenous people saw whites approaching from the east. This Third Dimension of Indian-white relations involves researching, analyzing, and writing from the inside

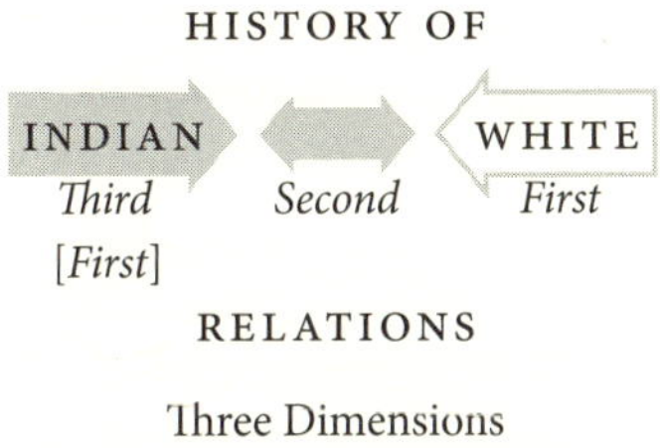

FIGURE 3. Three dimensions of history are illustrated from right to left: history written by non-Indians, history focused on both Indians and whites, and the Third is from a Native approach, which is actually the First from a Native view.

out, based on Indian views of history. Applying the equation of Indian-white history as outlined in the following pages provides a framework and route for enlightening non-Indians about the Indian perspective.

A key consideration in studying American Indians is to understand their reality and learn how it has changed. It is the "real life" of how people lived, what they thought, how they formed their values, and how they viewed the world of medicine power in all things, including the universe, that is most relevant in writing the history of American Indians in the Third Dimension. This perspective is the Medicine Way of Indian history/experiences. This power-in-everything interpretation consists of the three dimensions as described and uses a binary paradigm of Indian-white relations. The interaction of the three dimensions creates a "cultural bridge of understanding" that becomes more familiar with regular usage. Within this indigenous paradigm is a Native reality called a "Natural Democracy" that contains all things (see the glossary for special terms used in this book). For example, medicine is all around Native people, and it is part of the metaphysical component of Native reality called the Third Dimension. This is the Medicine Way of understanding power. And the three dimensions in the equation in figure 3 illustrate a bridge of cultural understanding that can be crossed by mainstream academics from right to left.

In this sense, understanding the "historic" and "traditional" reality at any point in time becomes the task for historians and scholars from other fields in their efforts to explore, understand, and analyze the actual history/experiences of American Indians.

It is imperative to realize that indigenous reality has changed throughout the course of time and that indigenous communities have had various and sometimes conflicting worldviews. The constant in the Indian universe was and remains change due to adaptation for survival against the forces of nature and other powers, including white settlement. Forces of the universe and external pressures from white encroachment caused an acceleration of changes in Indian life, although the rate varied with the control of cultural evolution possessed by Indians themselves. It bears repeating that such external forces acting on Native communities and causing change occurred well before the arrival of Columbus in the Americas in 1492.

Yet continuity persisted as change occurred within the indigenous communities. The continuity consisted of an evolution of change as the people adapted new ideas and new material items from Europeans, such as the horse from the Spanish, guns from the French, and metal items from the British, to improve their societies.

This continuum was aided by the power of "story," the vehicle of oral tradition as generations of people told and retold stories of myths and legends and of experiences that made them a part of the present. Prophetic accounts of experiences to occur in the future were made a part of the present reality so that the past and the future were entertained in one time continuum. This was the Circle of Life for Native peoples, who believed in cycles of events and whose fundamental philosophy and thought functioned circularly (see glossary).

The survival of Indian people has enabled them to rebuild and adapt their communities and cultures. This ability might be called transformation of cultural adaptive systems. American Indians are indeed products of their environments, and their oral traditions of stories and myths corroborate this adaptive ability. Yet Indian history in the Third Dimension of an Indian reality is about understanding the indigenous ethos.

It is foolish to suppose that there is only one canon or one American Indian viewpoint, which presents us with a question—which point of view do we mean? "Indian perspective" means a point of view from a Native reality—not a specific tribal ethos. Within the indigenous context is a Navajo ethos, a Muscogee Creek ethos, a Mohawk ethos; each Native nation has its own way of seeing. All these ways of seeing represent a collective Indian perspective called the Medicine Way.

It is imperative to acknowledge the presence of more than one category of perspectives—or ways of interpreting Indian history. Standpoints range from that of the academic historian to that of the generic category of Native people, some of whom are also professional historians. American Indians who speak of and write history may be academically trained, and/or are trained in oral traditions, and they include those persons who are historians of their tribes, bands, communities, or organizations. Further discussion still needs to be addressed to determine "whose interpretation is it?" That is, Native people have an inherent right to preserve and/or write their own history, although the gatekeepers of Indian academic history who decide what gets to be published largely continue to be non-Indians. In fact, many non-Indian scholars and writers have made handsome careers from writing books about Indians without giving back something to the Native communities. Some scholars have even tried to keep others from studying and writing about "their" Indians. Yet to be fair, since the 1980s growing numbers of young scholars have become more sensitive to Indian views and Native concerns and now include Indian voices in their work.

Indeed, several historians have boldly attempted to write or compile books on the complexity of American Indian history. Historians and other scholars have produced articles on writing Indian history; some scholars have elaborated on the skills of history and how they feel such skills should be broadened. In his anthology *The American Indian and the Problem of History* (1987) Calvin Martin compiled many Indian and non-Indian views in essays on the nature of Indian history, which led to his book *In the Spirit of the Earth* (1992). Martin's anthology consists of essays from various scholars in disciplines that are troubled by bringing together two different kinds of history—one linear from the western thinking and the other circular from the Native consciousness. He called for an Indian perspective in Indian history, while challenging historians to think about history and time beyond their western-mindedness as trained historians. His *In the Spirit of the Earth* was more meaningful in articulating his view of connecting Native people with the earth, which has produced an Indian-earth consciousness. Although this work is insightful, the aspect that various kinds of medicine powers are always present is shortchanged. How this can be understood is addressed in the following chapters.

Colin Calloway's anthology *New Directions in American Indian History* (1988) suggested additional ways for other disciplines to approach Indian history. Calloway argued that we should not rely solely on the discipline of history. My own anthology *Rethinking American Indian History* (1997) left more to be said, although part 1 demonstrated the need for ethnohistory and part 2 argued for scholars to employ additional disciplines in writing Native history. Laurence Hauptman said much about the irony and challenge of writing about Indian people in his *Tribes and Tribulations: Misconceptions about American Indians and Their Histories* (1995). Hauptman argues that Indian people have been inaccurately represented, and these miscues have produced erroneous and harmful stereotypes about American Indians. Peter Nabokov, in *A Forest of Time: American Indian Ways of History* (2002), argues that a history from an Indian viewpoint is too large an undertaking for historians alone and suggests the inclusion of folklorists, anthropologists, linguists, historians of religion, and Indian oral historians. In order to understand the Medicine Way, one must use a transdisciplinary approach to contextualize an indigenous paradigm.

These studies contributed to the need to explore the Native perspective about the Indian version of Indian history. Yet how are non-Indians to engage the Native point of view and its reality for understanding the other side of historical issues, events, and shared experiences? A special edition of the *American Indian Culture and Research Journal* (2010) on contemporary Native communities argues that Native Studies scholars can provide a better understanding of historical and contemporary events.[2] Based on their insights into their own communities, they can yield an approach from the inside out for presenting research and analysis of the infrastructures of tribal nations.

American Indian history in this light is both a paradox and an enormous challenge, and unfortunately it is typically understood from one's personal point of view. Perhaps it is best to consider the paradox first, and then address the deep myriad of American Indian history.

In the twenty-first century, after more than five hundred years of contact, America's scholars and mainstream society persist in largely ignoring the Indian view of the American experience. This is the paradox and a central part of the problem. Although Indians have recorded their own experiences in the oral tradition of myths, legends, and stories and in pictographs, etchings, and paintings, this information is not meaningfully incorporated into academic history. Ironically, this ethnocentrism on the part of American historians, anthropologists, and other experts who study the American experience prohibits a complete record of Indian-white relations. This unfortunate prejudice has produced a one-sided view from mainstream America (fig. 2, right to left), and the other side, from Indian America, still needs to be heard and included as a part of academic history. So rather than try to solve the entire problem of Native peoples in American history or the American experience, it is difficult enough to attempt to clarify the paradox and complexity of American Indian history.

The fiction of the conqueror's version, shrouded in optimistic glory, remained the prevailing narrative of the American experience and the textbook version introducing the American Indian experience for the first half of the twentieth century. Although this rhetorical mythologizing of the past influenced the popular readers of history, after 1970 historians and other scholars began to be more sensitive to including Indian voices in their work. Unfortunately the damage had already been done, as the public consciousness believed the conqueror's approach for most of the rest of the century.

Choosing one perspective permits only one half of the story about

America to be told, and it has caused critical mistakes in two major areas. First, a "single" version of what transpired in America prohibits the opportunity of a different viewpoint to corroborate or dispute the facts as white Americans interpreted them, or to evaluate which events were actually historically significant. As a result American textbooks and scholarly histories currently present an incomplete record of the American experience based on biased observations of the events that transpired. It is imperative to open minds to the major erroneous claims of the mainstream American version. The gross error is that Christopher Columbus "discovered" America.[3]

America was misrepresented as "free" land for the taking. It was not a "Garden of Eden" without an indigenous people, as historians have described this frontier experience while justifying the imperialistic expansionism promoted by Manifest Destiny. This is one point of view of an idealized America that most Americans believe. While scholars of the late twentieth century have produced a growing corpus of work to emphasize the importance of Native men and women as central players in Native history, much more needs to be done to change the public consciousness to include the truth that Native people participated in shaping the history of this country.

The rhetoric of the American myth taught in the classroom, using the slanted textbooks and mainstream optimism implanted in public historical consciousness, created an American selective memory. Furthermore, modern urban growth has enabled a "pervasive influence" to modify our environments and how we perceive regions and places.[4] The majority of Americans seek to fulfill their individual needs while disregarding the views of others, and they are willing to accept textbook history rather than questioning it. More recent history has attempted to correct the old myths of American history. In the case of early history written about Native people, the public consciousness needs to be more informed about the recent scholarship since the late twentieth century putting Native people at center stage of Indian history as equal partners with white historical figures. In other words, this more recent scholarship is still filtering into the public mind; when Indians are the subject of conversations, most people remain most likely to know only the stereotypes about Indians. In this myopic way, perception and interpretation have advanced the public consciousness of history to the disadvantage of indigenous interpretation. This has created a "subaltern" that Gayatri Spivak has already addressed.[5] In the process, public historian David Glassberg noted how Michael Frisch's "shared authority" concept has had "profound implications for how all historians will do their work in the future, and the quality of the relationship that Americans will have with the past."[6] This authority establishes an ownership of history and how it should be interpreted by historians and presented to the public as participating partners. Each side should try to discover the truth rather than relying on what has been written as history, especially about Native people.

To buttress the point about misinformed Indian history, historian Warren Susman observed that Frederick Jackson Turner "took a major American myth and made from it effective history" that denied and suppressed the Medicine Way of Indian history.[7] With his frontier thesis, Turner steered the intellectual consciousness of historians for the next half century and produced a school of like-minded scholars. Turner's view became the driving force that influenced others, such as Charles Beard, Herbert Bolton, and Carl Becker. As a tool of social analysis, Turner's interpretation of historical development led to American understanding of culture, enriched with symbols and a permeating "thickness," according to Clifford Geertz.[8] Geertz suggested that intensive studying of a tribal community would be a proper way to understand the thickness of the Native culture. I hope the Medicine Way can influence public consciousness of history by encouraging those within the western paradigm to rethink such views from the standpoint that this call for change maps out.

The consciousness of western-minded historians at various levels is what is addressed as one of the challenges of the Medicine Way of Native history. The Medicine Way consists of consciousness and subconsciousness combined, whereby Native people include visions, dreams, and prophecies in accounting for their history. Hence the objectives of the present work are twofold: (1) to establish acknowledgment of the Medicine Way of Indian history, and (2) to influence scholars regarding the consciousness of historians at all levels, and public consciousness as well, to balance the understanding of the American Indian past.

The Native view represents an entirely different understanding of Indian-white relations or the American experience, starting with the Great Encounter when the eastern hemisphere met the western hemisphere on October 12, 1492. This Native viewpoint is not found in historical documents produced by non-Indians; it must be searched for and reconstructed from such misleading documents and from other forms of evidence. Primarily the oral tradition accounts for much of the Indian version of history.

The lack of written Indian languages (in forms known to western civilization) offered no challenge to the historical narrative of America as portrayed by Columbus, other explorers, early travelers, and military personnel. In the emotional frenzy of "discovery," "exploration," and settlement of the "frontier," these observers presumed false notions upon landing on the eastern shores. They presumed to have discovered the Americas, claiming the lands as part of their empire and ignoring the rights of the indigenous people. Their collected views became the European reality of America seen through the eyes of a non-Indian ethos; it was an incomplete truth. At best, their versions represented a true reality of America to them.

Such powerful themes as discovery, exploration, and Manifest Destiny have denied the full picture of the American experience. Artists paint the beauty they wish others to see; and like the hand holding the brush, in this case the newly arrived parties propounded a history of optimism, and good over evil, with religious justification codifying all actions. Thus reformative action needs to occur in all venues, including classrooms, textbooks, museums, historical societies, and academic circles.

Entertaining an Indian version of the American experience would present multiple versions from the numerous Indian nations. Yet a categorical "Indian" version of this historical experience does exist, and it needs to be widely acknowledged for a correction of the historical record. To illustrate this point, any two people are unable to recall the same incident in exactly the same way—and the difference is greater if the two observers were on opposite sides during the course of events. The different versions vary further if the two observers are from different cultural backgrounds. Their viewpoints clash. A dualistic historical record results, as when American Indians and whites opposed each other in the struggle for the western hemisphere.

During contact and the establishment of relations between Europeans and Indians, land became the commodity of competition and conflict. As a result of continual friction, the American view of history has been one of military conquest, politics, scientific advancement, and economics, with lesser appreciation for the historical development of society, intellectualism, and cultural interaction. This limitation has validated the narrow view of the American experience through time. Textbooks perpetuate the view, teachers reinforce it, and ethnocentric Americans blindly accept it; or they simply do not care.

As a second area of critical mistakes, mainstream chroniclers had serious misconceptions about Indian people and their participation in the larger picture of United States history. The short-sightedness of the non-Indian chroniclers has caused negative stereotypes and harmful misunderstandings about American Indians. The "wild savage," "drunken Indian," and "dirty redskin" are but a few early stereotypes that written history upheld, causing irreparable and continued negative social and psychological repercussions for Indians. Columbus and others, who had limited knowledge about Indian people, failed to understand the complexities of Indian life, the depths of indigenous philosophies, and cultural differences. The academic discourse on Indians has evolved past this point, and yet much still needs to be done to reach the public consciousness to correct presumptions and misinformation about Native people.

Misnamed as "Indians," Native people became subject to a generic racial view that all Indian people were alike, although belonging to more than five hundred different nations of various cultures, languages, and dialects. Living throughout the western hemisphere, Indians developed multiple philosophies, numerous religious beliefs, and significantly varied economic systems. In fact, each Indian nation had its own history and established relations with each newly encountered European people. In essence, each Indian nation included in its stories the periods of European contacts, which initially were often secondary experiences, until the Europeans and Americans became the main threats. Indian-Indian relations—meaning Iroquois-Huron, Cherokee-Creek, and Ojibwe-Dakota relations, for example—were more important than Indian-white relations because much of the time, the nations were at war with other Indian nations. Obviously this relationship changed as Indians and whites waged wars. The various cultures of the Indian nations differed fundamentally from the Europeans' cultures, thus disallowing a mutual appreciation.

Europeans valued land as property to be owned and used in whatever profitable manner was desired. Land represented potential wealth to be exploited. In contrast, traditional Indian cultures believed that land could not be owned and that it represented a homeland for the tribal community. Logically, one could only put a handful of dirt in one's hand and carry it away; the rest remained. The homeland was the environment with space for humans, animals, plants, and all other things. This was the Circle of Life.

Black Elk described the importance of the circle as a part of nature:

> You have noticed that everything an Indian does is in a circle, and that is because the Power of the World always works in circles, and everything tries to be round. Everything the Power of the World does is done in a circle. The sky is round . . . and so are all the stars. The wind, in its greatest power whirls. Birds make their nests in circles, for theirs is the same religion as ours. The sun comes forth and goes down again in a circle. The moon does the same, and both are round. Even the seasons form a great circle in their changing, and always come back again to where they were. The life of a man is a circle from childhood to childhood and so it is in everything where power moves.[9]

Like the Circle of Life, the Indians' records and the stories they maintained about themselves strive to come full circle. Buttressed with pictographs and drawings on hides, the oral tradition conveyed

Native stories about the hundreds of peoples. Then came the introduction of writings by soldiers, settlers, and officials about Indian-white relations from the perspective in the First Dimension. Next, the Second Dimension of studying the dynamics of Indian-white relations inspired new books and articles, encouraging a deeper understanding about American Indian history but still from the non-Indian point of view. At last the Third Dimension of Native scholars studying their peoples' past, and non-Indians becoming interested in the Native ethos and reality, have provoked a fresh approach in the literature and a different way of looking at American Indian history—the Medicine Way. To enable this awareness, we need to construct a cross-cultural bridge of understanding to permit people to cross back and forth between western-mindedness and the Natural Democracy of indigenous existence.

As I left on the last day of the OAH conference in Louisville in April 1991, I boarded the elevator with my luggage. The elevator stopped at another floor and one of my Indian friends got on with his suitcase to check out. I asked him how the blues had been the other night, and he replied that I had missed some great music. As we got off the elevator, the other Native historian was standing in line to check out of the hotel. We razzed each other one more time, tribe-about-tribe teasing. We said our goodbyes and told each other to take care as we headed back to our respective universities to teach and to try to bring our Indian perspectives to Indian history.

2

Native Ethos of "Seeing" and a Natural Democracy

Standing high on Harney Peak in the Black Hills, Black Elk, Holy-man of the Oglala Sioux, talked about "seeing." Holding his wrinkled brown hands out to the sky, he recalled:

> Then I was standing on the highest mountain of them all, and round about beneath me was the whole hoop of the world. And while I stood there I saw more than I can tell and I understood more than I saw; for I was seeing in a sacred manner the shapes of all things in the spirit, and the shape of all shapes as they must live together like one being. And I saw that the sacred hoop of my people was one of many hoops that made one circle, wide as daylight and as starlight, and in the center grew one mighty flowering tree to shelter all the children of one mother and one father. And I saw that it was holy.[1]

In studying American Indian history, viewing life from a different perspective becomes an enlightening revelation from another reality.[2] Different cultures throughout the world "see" the universe from their own perspective, and this point of diversity can be applied to the understanding of Indian history. American Indians of many different tribal nations—more than 500 in North America alone, at least 60 in Mexico, and some 360 in South America—possess their own worldviews with separate philosophies based on a non-European

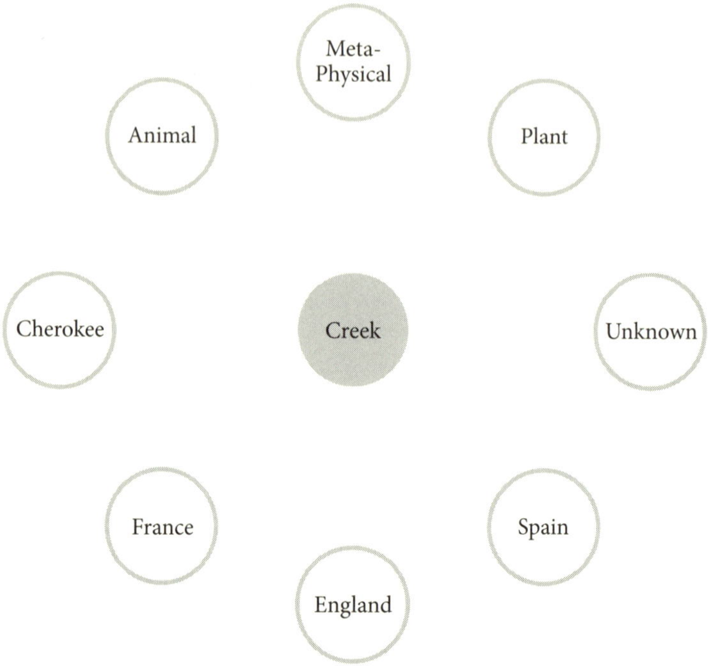

FIGURE 4. A Native community in a Natural Democracy has human and nonhuman relationships with a combined physical and metaphysical reality.

version of history.[3] After more than 500 years of contact between the Indian and white races in North America, opportunity is long overdue for a writing of Indian history that strives to acknowledge and appreciate fully an Indian point of view. Simply put, to understand the complete history of Indian-white relations, both sides of the story need to be heard. As with a coin possessing two sides, both need to be acknowledged, explored, and comprehended.

Atop Harney Peak among the Black Hills on a summer day in 1873 Black Elk described seeing in a manner that he called sacred. In a unique way Black Elk saw things and sensed them at the same time, in a single moment. This is the Native way of seeing all things in relationship to one another. Seeing things and remembering them as experiences, not as events, is central to the Native ethos. Seeing in this way means understanding all things in the Native context of one's people and their natural surroundings.

Thus Native ethos is characterized by a Natural Democracy that acknowledges the presence of all things and sees them as related to one another on the basis of mutual respect (see fig. 4). This network is inclusive and contains all the living and nonliving, from a deer in a forest to a boulder atop a canyon. Both possess energy and power, but one is active and the other is at rest, although the latter can become active energy, if some force were to push the boulder down into the canyon.

Imagine how Native people might see things from their perspective; everything possesses some kind of power. In figure 4 the Creeks respect the power in each relationship—with the Spanish, English, French, other tribes, plants, and animals. For this reason, the Creeks respect the medicine powers of all those with whom they have a relationship.

This discussion centers on the Native peoples of this country and how history as an academic discipline applies to indigenous peoples throughout the western hemisphere from a western point of view. The initial questions that arise are three: What is meant by an Indian perspective? How does an Indian perspective change our understanding of current Indian history? And how might an Indian perspective be constructed for non-Indians to understand? First of all, it has to be accepted that exploring the Indian point of view is necessary. Some scholars, including some Native scholars, may oppose this assertion, arguing that a single Indian perspective does not exist. On this point, of course, they are correct. What is meant here is that a general Native ethos (and thus an Indian perspective) exists, but the specific form the perspective takes varies from tribe to tribe.

As an example, Black Elk was a seer. He was also a visionary, medicine maker, and prophet (and later a Catholic). Born in his Native tradition, Black Elk was observed early to be a person with a special gift. In the early years of his life, ancient voices haunted the Oglala Holyman when he was a boy growing up among his people. He had a vision at the age of nine. Despite translation problems, in his testament to John Neihardt he described this vision, in which he crossed to the spiritual side and encountered the Lakotas' understanding of the six powers of the universe that they called the Six Grandfathers. The voices visited him again and again. The more he listened to them, the more he became confused, and this frightened the youth. At certain times he did not know which reality he lived in—with his family and relatives or with the voices.

Black Elk was not alone. Many other Indians from various tribes are like Black Elk and see as he did. Sweet Medicine of the Cheyenne, the Shawnee Prophet, and Wovoka of the Paiute are among the better known seers, and seers continue to play important roles in Native communities to this day. Stories are told about Indian men and women, boys and girls, who hear voices or talk to animals or spirits. Lakota elder Ed McGaa concluded:

> Each animal has its own power or gift to convey because they were so endowed by *Wakan Tanka*. Does not a mountain lion tell us that we can become independent and walk those lonely chasms of change undauntedly? Doesn't a portrait of the owl, the eagle of the night, tell us not to fear the dark or mysterious places? Surely the beavers convey a serene security and pace brought forth by a steady endeavor if we can be so fortunate to find our own bliss. And yes, we all need endless scenes of the freedom of hawks, eagles, wolves and the great orcas of the seas to forever implant a resolve that we must never lose our connection with the vast soothing solitude of Nature.[4]

Native seers or prophets of the past lived their tribal ways and practiced their people's values. Their Native ethos was not just one way of seeing the physical; they saw also in a metaphysical way. Their way of seeing derived from their spiritual values and distinct tribal ways that continue today.

Theoretically an Indian perspective represents an estimated 4.5 million American Indians in the United States alone, and 566 federally recognized Indian tribes, and even more that are not formally recognized. In essence, the traditional Indian perspective contextualizes the Medicine Way to represent all tribes. This "one" voice represents various tribal traditions stressing a nonlinear view of life; it is an ethos that includes environmentalism framed within a circular philosophy.

With this specific understanding of "an Indian perspective," American Indian history needs to be defined within an indigenous context for a dialogue to begin in analyzing such a Native point of view. As stated, the historical consciousness of both mainstream academia and the public understands American Indian history as the history of Indian-white relations or the history of U.S.-Indian relations based on federal-Indian interactions. However, the *longue durée* history of Indians existed long before relations with the United States and well before the arrival of Christopher Columbus. Scholars of historical acuity and the majority of textbooks have attempted to correct this version of the history of the Americas, although other scholars continue to categorize the history of Indian peoples before Columbus as prehistory, and history on this side of the Atlantic as beginning with the contact between indigenous peoples and Europeans. At risk is the public consciousness of history that typically accepts the old notion of Indians having no history until the arrival of Columbus.

One issue here is to understand the origin of the American Indian perspective. What is its source? Indian history is the genesis of life found in myths and legends and shared stories via the oral tradition. This ethos is the cultural past of Native people and the history of minor and major events, including Indian-white relations and well beyond, to include relations within tribal communities. It is the "shared experience" of a physical and metaphysical reality for Indian people who view life from a categorical Native ethos.

In theory the Indian perspective can be classified into four basic categories. The first is the Indian response to Indian-white relations. The second is an Indian perspective that is a "tribal view" about being Native, external experiences, community, and culture. The third Indian perspective is the voice of the Indian woman. She has been ignored by the mainstream and muffled by American cultural prejudice toward women in general and particularly toward minority women. The fourth view is that of Native speakers who speak only their own Indian language. Isolated by having less opportunity for communication with others, Indian people have been forced to voice their views in English in order to be heard in the mainstream culture. These basic categories are not mutually exclusive and they overlap with each other.

In addition to the four theoretical categories identified here, fundamental concepts need to be recognized as a part of Native reality. These basic concepts are time, space, causality, mass, and place.[5]

Time in the Medicine Way is nonlinear and is measured by cycles of the earth's rotation. Space is broadly explained in inner and outer spaces of the body, which includes nonhuman bodies and those spaces that are deemed sacred. Causality includes human and nonhuman forces, plus divine influences. Mass goes beyond the physical and includes the metaphysical, especially where they overlap, such as in a trickster like Coyote, who is human and spiritual. Place is mental and physical but mostly connects Native people to their home or natural environment.

The incongruence of Native cultures and mainstream culture has created a dichotomy such that Indian people and mainstream Americans "see" things very differently. For example, settlers saw (and Americans continue to see) the land as a commodity that could be farmed, bought, and sold. Indigenous people, at least those who are close to their cultural traditions, see land as the earth that offers resources, knowledge, and home space. The two worldviews remain different, although they share the same continent, and many Indians and whites have intermarried and have shared values in life.

Among Indians an Indian perspective is seemingly incomprehensible since *perspective* is not a word commonly used in Native languages; rather, perspective has to be described. Instead of perspective, "seeing," as in the physical act of seeing, is a more appropriate way to describe the way in which Indians understand their worldview. For example, among the Muscogee Creeks, the word for seeing is *he jus*. Furthermore, some "gifted" Indian individuals, such as Black Elk, have the ability to see into the future, and they might be called prophets or fortune tellers. Other gifted individuals include persons called *key-tha* among the Muscogee Creeks; these individuals have special insight about dreams, visions, and other experiences. *O-walv-a* is the Muscogee word for prophet.

Such seers and visionaries whose biographies are known lived a disciplined life, among them Black Elk of the Oglala Sioux; Lame Deer, of the Sioux; Severt Young Bear, another Lakota; Wovoka, a Paiute; Neolin, a Delaware, and Handsome Lake, a Seneca.[6] Their gifts were not permanent, and they adhered to strict guidelines in order to retain their power of special foresight. They possessed the ability to see, and some even had the ability to see through the eyes of animals in their dreams or visions. This was their metaphysical gift that those elders who were also seers encouraged and helped to develop.

How Indians see is their way of interpretation. More specifically, how they see is how they understand life and the universe.[7] This Native gestalt of combined consciousness and subconsciousness is applied to the fundamental elements of nature and the universe. Seeing is a way that includes reasoning or logic. Severt Young Bear remarked, "If a Lakota sees an eagle circling above him and then going east, he'd say, 'Hey, there's a reason why the eagle circled around me and went east, so I'll follow him.' So this is why traces of the Lakota are found in all the four directions—in Canada, the East, into Mexico and Salt Lake and beyond."[8] Through seeing, Indians come to understand and appreciate the seeing powers of all things in the Natural Democracy, including nonhuman beings.

According to the Native worldview, all that we are is within the Circle of Life, which hosts all things. In this sense all things are related. The Circle of Life is a totality of all things living and nonliving. Based on circular logic according to the rotation of the earth and seasons of the year, seeing is knowing that experiences and events occur in cycles. Circularity is much more complex than we imagine until we begin to realize how many things involve circles and cycles. The migration of animals, rotation of planets around the sun, and the shape of the sun, moon, and the earth are strong reminders of this perfect geometrical shape that is fundamental to all cultures. For various reasons, the numbers 4, 7, and 28 are significant to many tribes. There are four seasons and four directions, while some tribes say there are seven directions (the four cardinal directions, plus up, down, and inside us); there are twenty-eight bone joints in two human hands and feet, twenty-eight ribs of a bison, and twenty-eight days in the lunar month.

Time is also fundamental to existence and is conceptualized differently by Indians and mainstream Americans. The American mainstream thinks in a linear fashion, which is very different from the circular fashion of Native traditionalists. These two models of thinking are in constant conflict due to the different ways they interpret time, mass, space, causality, and place. A person familiar with only one conceptual model naturally assumes that this is the correct way of thought. Linear thought is basically rationalizing how something originates at point A, is affected by some force or influence, and transforms into point B, point C, and so forth. This vast difference between the Euroamerican linear understanding of time and time as understood by Indian people in a traditional sense needs to be addressed at length. To Native people, time is less relevant, and it is the act of doing something that is more important. Stories are told about experiences and deeds that actualize the past into present acceptance. There is little difference between the past and the present, however, when stories are told in the oral tradition.

The written history of American Indians by non-Indians strongly reflects the Euroamerican understanding of time in a linear sequence of events. This is another acute cultural difference between Indians and whites that leads to another important question: What is Indian history? Or, to begin with: What is history? To traditional Indian people, history is a collection of experiences instead of events. As a part of the oral tradition, stories are told about experiences with a deemphasis on events. Relating an experience to another person, for example, is much more vivid and meaningful than trying to describe an event to another person.

Furthermore, history written by professional historians generally involves only empirical evidence called documented facts. How would one document Black Elk's great vision of the Six Grandfathers? Because many American Indians live in a reality of both the physical and metaphysical, nondocumented evidence is also an integral part of their life and past. Other forms of evidence are permissible and are required if the past of Indian reality is to be properly understood. Stories told in the oral tradition are the most common evidence, as are winter counts, which are hide recordings of noteworthy experiences. Cultural items are reminders of the past, for there are stories about them. For example, stories may reveal to whom a bow, a rattle, or an eagle feather belonged and how this person used the item.

At the same time, all evidence is speculative and relies on the evaluation and interpretation of trained historians. Why not, then, train students to understand the Medicine Way of American Indian history based on a Natural Democracy?[9] Why not train them to evaluate evidence required to get at the Indian perspective truly? Historian Wilbur Jacobs points out that other "sources [are] not always used by historians, such as records of Indian speeches and treaties, Indian oral history tapes, the great mass of data compiled by our leading anthropologists and geographers, plus insights from the writings of modern Indians, such as N. Scott Momaday and Vine Deloria."[10]

Written records about Indians began with Spanish exploration and the exploitation of indigenous peoples in the western hemisphere. Following the initial historic contact with non-Indians, the imperial European invasions of the Spanish conquistadors, French soldiers (i.e., the Natchez, Chickasaw, and Fox wars), Russians, and American militiamen and armies left little trace of more than a dozen tribes, which became extinct.[11] Their stories died with them and will never be told. Their pasts can only be speculated about, and gleaned from bits of evidence, and gathered from parts of other peoples' histories. Such imperialism committed genocide in the Americas and erased the histories of some indigenous peoples.

Presently the general story from the point of view of the American Indian is barely mentioned in textbooks and scholarly monographs. What happened on the "other side" of the frontier? How did the Arawaks react when they received Columbus, a strange being, who appeared confused and lost? From American Indians and their diverse cultures much can be learned about life and the history of the Americas. Unfortunately in almost any American history textbook, the first chapter includes Indians in discussion of Christopher Columbus

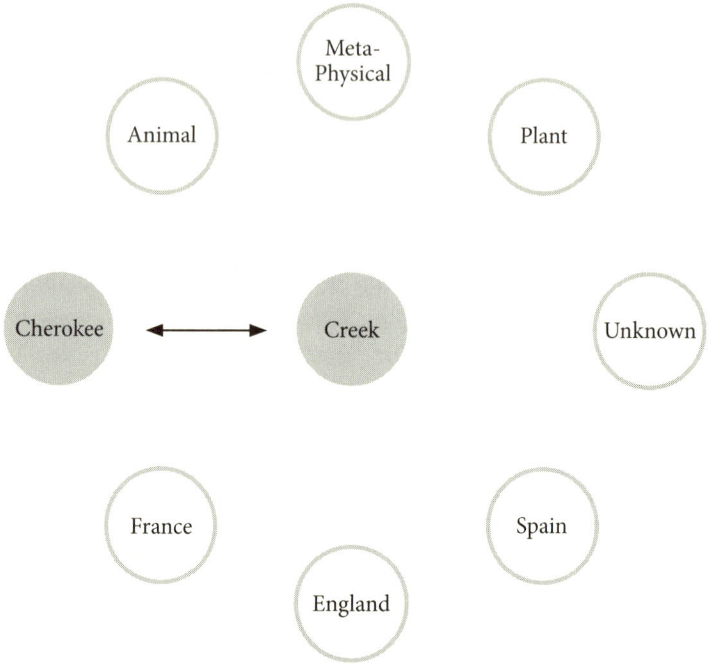

FIGURE 5. A Native community has a reciprocal relationship with another Native community within a Natural Democracy where all relations are recognized, even the unknown.

"discovering" America and usually in a later chapter about the Plains Indian wars in the West. Other than these two instances, many textbook accounts imply that Indians have played virtually no role in the history of the United States, rather than that they actually played a role, even though the indigenous peoples were not totally conquered until 1895, when the last of 1,642 military campaigns against American Indians ceased.[12]

In order to understand properly and attempt to construct an Indian viewpoint of any subject of Indian history, a theorized model needs to be in place. For example, this methodological approach requires starting at the beginning in reconstructing a Native community. Entertaining a historic reality of the community is essential. One must consider all the factors and influences that would have had an effect on a historic Indian community during the time in question. The previous figure depicts the relationship of interaction between the Creeks and Cherokees in a binary equation, Creek-Cherokee, that can be applied to all beings within the Natural Democracy. Thus the Creeks have a constant reciprocal relationship with all things except for the metaphysical, which is explained later. It is important to understand "seeing" and the context of Natural Democracy in order to reconstruct a real Indian past.

To attempt to construct such a model, or to view a tribal community as a case study, or to write a biography of an Indian person, several factors are involved. These are Native thinking or thought, cultural values, communal philosophy, Native reality, oral tradition, Native language, and Native worldview or ethos.

A first step is trying to understand how Native people think. Analyzing indigenous thought involves reconsidering the words of Luther Standing Bear, Charles Eastman, Black Elk, and other Native individuals who have spoken deeply about their experiences and cultural ways. Their Native ethos helped to define their cultures and guided their decision making in daily and historical experiences. Even their ideas and views of the past were defined by their tribal cultures and individual experiences, plus the heritage of their peoples. Tribal values, communalism, environmental determinism, and group identity influenced their Native thinking within a combined physical and metaphysical reality.

Although an American Indian philosophy has been recognized to express Native views about the environment and about the balance of living a good, moral life, Native philosophers have received scant recognition. Sitting Bull, Black Elk, and others are noted indigenous philosophers, and their words have been studied and regularly misused. New Age thinkers are among the few non-Indians who have embraced Native philosophies; and some have appropriated these philosophies in inappropriate ways, essentially claiming ownership of them. But studying Native philosophy is pertinent to understanding the indigenous ethos of a particular community as a collective voice, leading to understanding the viewpoint of an indigenous person.

In addition, understanding Native thought involves knowing Indian cultural values and how they have changed. Indian values are based on an understanding of the Native person positioned within a kinship system and in an order of a Natural Democracy. Such values are the guidelines that place significance on everything that exists, such as physical landscape that includes a rock, or nature in motion, such as the flowing water of a river, or an abstract aberration, such as a vision or a dream. As one Native scholar observed, "another value common to all Native American communities was the importance of wisdom and knowledge and Indian people learned from the herbs and plants and from their life experiences in both physical and metaphysical reality."[13] This Medicine Way stressed doing things in a particular manner to establish order for decreasing the chance of confusion and minimizing the occurrence of problems.

Life's norms among Indians are ritualistic and ceremonial within a natural paradigm. The overwhelming presence of the natural environment influenced Native thought to respect and develop a rationale for understanding the powers of nature. Rather than viewing themselves as above all things, Native people have traditionally viewed themselves as part of the environment, and it was essential to be a member of one's community. In this communal context, people understood that many things were more powerful than a single person. In the natural environment, many dangers posed a threat to the Native people, and they learned to deal with the threats after observing their behavior.

The person or being is but one part of the whole. The emphasis is that the whole community is greater than a single person. As mentioned, there is strength in numbers, and Native people have accepted this notion as a part of their thinking and reality. These ways of seeing the world are common to many Native peoples.

Each Indian nation possesses a reality of dualistic interpretation of the physical and metaphysical spiritual world. Combined, these realities encompass the cultures and peoples of Native America. Their world, in a general "Indian" perspective, entails functioning within both realities, making this way of life difficult for the western mind to comprehend, much less to keep a written record or history of this dual reality. The ability of the Indian mind to include it by instinct enables the tandem of the two realities to exist as one.

Indian people thus experience a different reality from that of the American mainstream or that of other minority groups. Indian people lived and in many cases still live a complicated life of the physical environment and metaphysical "other world"—a kind of dualistic reality where the metaphysical existence had much more to offer than did life on earth. In his power vision during the late 1800s, Black Elk of the Oglala Sioux stated, "I knew the real was yonder and the darkened dream of it was here."[14] What did he mean? That the importance of life, the true reality, was the preferred life in the spiritual world and not the life on earth, where life was a struggle, involving hardship, hunger, losing loved ones, and physical and mental anguish. In order to meet this challenge, Native people found strength in one another as a community.

Oral tradition held the community together and continues to do so. Myths and legends played important roles in the lives of American Indians by providing stability and continuity. The inertia of life itself is grounded in and perpetuated via the myths. In lodges, especially during winter nights, elders shared these accounts with the youth around campfires. The creation of animals, stories of humans, creations of the universe, and even the prophecy of the coming of whites to the Americas were told.[15] Records of the myths and legends represented the traditional oral way of keeping history among the Indian nations until their written languages evolved in the late nineteenth century and twentieth century. Their way relied on the human mind to remember and for everyone to hear and realize the wisdom imparted through the stories. Parts of facts, bits of truth, lessons of morality, and knowledge composed a sociocultural embodiment of the past, providing a Native identity for the people of each tribal nation.

Although individuals have criticized oral tradition as inaccurate, it nevertheless reflected major events as pivotal points in the history of a tribal community. The constant telling of the oral tradition varied to some degree, but common major points reflected basic truths. The refusal of many historians and other scholars to acknowledge the importance of oral tradition rejects the utilization of the main available tool for obtaining an Indian version. Thus historians and the reading public are left with the same one-sided history, unless they can speak the Native language of the tribe in which they are interested.

The expression of a Native perspective is shared through language. Language enables the indigenous voice to be heard, according to various tribal dialects. Based on cultural influences and what was believed to be important, the language denotes what is significant and why an event or being is important. Like a historical opinion, language emits a Native logic that tells us about the Native reality encompassing the language and the Native perspective.

Language and beliefs are the basis of culture for American Indians, and the people express their beliefs via their language, which limits and directs their views, thereby defining and shaping their philosophies. Ancient words had to be modified and new ones invented as contact with other Indian groups, experiences with nature, and later contact with non-Indians enabled the growth and development of indigenous cultures. Language via the oral tradition connected individuals, families, social groups, and communities within the same context of understanding. This way of words within language created a growing dependence on orality.

For American Indians, their oral traditions, tribal values, and Native philosophy help to define their ethos. This Native worldview is complex and informs non-Indians of an extraordinary reality that exists beyond the rationality of the western mind. Within this cultural matrix, the combination of concreteness and abstraction "involves humans and nature and animals all yoked in common to places with great power."[16]

This indigenous ethos or worldview developed in the western hemisphere with an enormous abundance of land and space. Dependence on wild food resources involved continuous interaction with the natural world and its flora and fauna. With a continuous interaction with nature, Native peoples became heavily influenced by nature in their thoughts and in their beliefs. Nature became the source of their philosophies and their views of the world and the universe.

The interaction of Native people with others depicted a Natural Democracy of respected equality. For example, social relations played a major part in Native life in North America, both in personal lives and in the role of life in the community. How one's life fit into the community's was based on social acceptance from other individuals; thus a desire for social acceptance governed people's behavior. This is true of the Creek world shown in the previous figure, but note that the Creek world existed within a larger democracy, as would the Cherokee world, if this tribal community were at the center of the figure. Kinship bonded the people into families, clans or peer groups, and into the general populace, a tribal nation consisting of two or more communities.[17]

A social emphasis on communication is imperative for harmony in the Circle of Life where all things are connected and where Natural Democracy is presupposed. Harmonious socialization required a positive social network within the tribal community. The basic elements—person or people, family and extended family, clan or other society organization, and village or tribe—constituted most of Indian life. The emphasis fell upon bonding social relations with kinship terminology and clan membership. There was strength in numbers: enough hunters for securing food on a hunting expedition, the expected amount of warriors in a war party to attack, a sufficient collection of protectors to defend the people, and a mass of people to perpetuate an identity of "who we are."

It is important to realize that this proposed Native perspective is inclusive. Flora, fauna, and people were equal in this universe, according to the various tribal worldviews. This democratic characteristic influenced the perception of Native peoples to prohibit them from placing themselves above others, or else they would be criticized by their peer group.

Due to the emphasis on social relations, American Indians think in a mode of "relatedness." Indigenous thought involves the inclusion of all factors possible. Native people mentally respond to the precaution of excluding anyone or anything such that this holistic thinking views the "large picture." In this broad perspective, Indians traditionally thought in terms of considering all factors in the large picture, shown in figure 5, thereby emphasizing the relevance of details in a different way. Furthermore, viewing the large picture through time was a part of this way of seeing and thought. For example, if placed in the center of figure 5, the Lakota thought carefully and long about their most difficult decisions because they considered how their decisions would affect the next seven generations of their people and all of their relations.

The relatedness of all things is a holistic approach and a deliberate, slow process for comprehension and problem solving. The logic of this Native thought process is socially inclusive, categorizing all things and beings according to importance and roles. This nonlinear logic is circular by nature and emphasizes continuity. This assumption of continuum describes a conception of time that is forever without a beginning and without an end, like a hoop.

A Natural Democracy of balance is the purpose of life for Native traditionalists. This is harmony. The equation of life includes all things on earth and in the universe. All things move and change in various manifestations of energy, but all the while they are in balance with one another, and hence the big picture needs to be considered when discussing the multiple relationships in an indigenous community. One Osage-Cherokee person remarked that "respect for creation emerges out of our perceived need for maintaining balance in the world around us. Thus Indian spirituality is characteristically oriented toward both the everyday and the ceremonial balancing of the world and our participation in it. When the balance of existence is disturbed, whole communities pay a price that is measured in some lack of communal well-being."[18] Nature with its supreme power responds with droughts, storms, and other harmful acts.

The balance of a community is its well-being, which does not occur all of the time. Rather such balance is temporary and irregular. As Native people strove for balance every day in their community, a Natural Democracy of equal representation imposed itself on the living to permit the understanding of inclusive relationships within the community. Like well-being in a temporary state of existence, such a Natural Democracy of equality was sought by the people until the need for status and rank became an important part of the culture to maintain order.

The worldview envisioned a systematic network in which the environment and universe contained all things and all known people. Relations enhanced by diplomacy, trade, marriage, respect, and other positive efforts in the natural environment in a respectful way entitled an Indian nation to relate to other Indian nations, the flora, fauna, even the foreign European nations, Americans, and the "Creator" or "Master of Breath." All presences were acknowledged in the order of life and the universe.

The collective "all" is within the holistic circle. Many Indian tribal philosophies, like those of the Lakota and Indians of the Great Lakes, are based on the circular concept that all things are related and kin to one another in the form of a circle or hoop. The basic concept is that all should be included and that everyone has a role within the circular order of community. This outlook orients one's life and thinking toward being inclusive, requiring that individuals should not place themselves above others or at the center.

Of the fundamental geometric designs, the circle is the one continuous configuration that has no bends or angles. This configuration suggests continuity and equality since all points of the line of the circle are connected and contained by the outer limit of the circumference. In addition to the ancient ancestors of American Indians, the Egyptians, Mayans, and other ancient civilizations of the world viewed the circle as elemental to their cultures and to life.[19] This basic geometric design is found in many Native cultures throughout North America and the world. For Indian people, it is symbolic and ceremonially integrated into their philosophies and stories. Since so much involves the circle, it has become central to the Indian mind and how Native people view life and time. They are the same.

This practice became a way of understanding and accepting inclusivity in nature. Inclusion of everyone and all things in the Circle of Life and Natural Democracy also means including those that are incongruent; even if they are the enemy and reject this ethos.

Contact with non-Indians altered the development of Native views and heavily influenced change in their cultures. For example, following the invasions of European imperialism of the 1500s and 1600s, European colonialism began to subvert indigenous people. In a devastating way, the foreign colonialism altered the ways of Indians. Europeans forced their religions on Native peoples and attempted to redirect Native ways of thinking by replacing indigenous values with new ones.

Due to the cultural incongruence between Indians and white Americans, "acceptance" has been difficult. In the U.S.-Indian example, in the late 1700s the Delaware, Iroquois, and other Native nations possessed much more powerful armies than did the United States. As the military power shifted from the advantage of the Indian nations to that of the United States after the War of 1812, federal policy decreed that Indians should be assimilated into the dominant culture. Notable progress on the Indians' part in education, learning English, and in instances of success in the business world has not permitted Indians to be comfortably assimilated into the American mainstream.

Assimilation into the American mainstream has been difficult for Indians on their own, due to societal discrimination and retention of tribal ways. However, assimilation has worked best on a voluntary basis when each Indian person acts as an individual in deciding to want to be a part of the American mainstream. This course is much easier when the mainstream welcomes the Indian. When an indigenous person increasingly becomes a part of the mainstream, it is likely that the individual's Native perspective will be lost at the same ratio as the progression of the assimilating process. Hence the high cost of assimilation is the loss of indigenous perspective.

Theoretically the Native perspective could disappear at some linear time in the future. But as long as the rock art records of petroglyphs and pictographs are maintained and stories are passed down to the next generations, the Indian perspective will remain alive. Although such remaining evidence could be misinterpreted, scholars and learned individuals in tribal knowledge, especially Indian people, have the responsibility to interpret correctly the Indian perspective of the past. And they must first be willing, and then be trained, to do so.

American Indians have learned to adapt to situations, and this has actually been a "cultural adaptation." From Native people, we can learn that adapting rather than attempting to force change can be less costly. This knowledge could be of critical importance to the United States and the world, as all of us will be facing extreme environmental problems on a global basis in the near future.

Unfortunately, federal Indian policy and the general treatment of Native people have been Amerocentric and inconsiderate of Indian ways and those of other minorities. This sense of "othering," as described by Edward Said and more specifically in relation to Indians by Robert Berkhofer, has helped to explain the difficulty of the mainstream in accepting Indians.[20] This is always the case when there is a majority and a minority, although on an intellectual level the ideas and perspectives of both should be entertained equally. The mainstream prejudiced view and current textbooks tell us that the minority perspective is not equally recognized by the mainstream. Until that happens, the American Indian perspective and those of other minorities will continue to be heard only through efforts of each group.

To understand Indians is to know the significance of kinship relations in their cultures and communities. American Indians traditionally viewed the Earth Mother and Father Sun in a "maternalistic" and a "paternalistic" manner. In this light, paternalism is a positive sense, revealing that Indian people respected a force stronger than themselves. They fully realize and continue to respect the fact that metaphysical forces at work in the spiritual world can easily affect their lives. The mainstream society does not seem to be aware of this aspect, nor does it fear the danger as economic desire exploits the environment. This paternalistic characteristic resulted in the harming of Indian people particularly after 1824, when the Bureau of Indian Affairs (BIA) became the officially appointed federal guardian of Indian interests. Unfortunately the Indian cultural interpretation of a positive paternalism had become politically interpreted to the advantage of the federal government and Amerocentric people.

From a maternalistic point of view, nature and the earth are one presence that is deeply associated with the role of woman, the female being, in the universe. In this light, all life comes from the Earth Mother. Many tribes have this sense of maternalism in their cultural beliefs. Stories are told of creation, reinforcing the notion that Native people are instruments of the more powerful forces of a paternalistic Creator and maternalistic Earth Mother.

Due to the acceptance of paternalism and maternalism, American Indians depended upon the metaphysical forces and respected the Mother Earth and Sun Father. This philosophical outlook should be noted, as the environment (the mother) and the sun's light (the father) are to be respected, or else the people and all relations will suffer the consequences.

Today's circumstances are difficult in regard to the psychological conditions. As stated earlier, American Indians on an individual basis have to make a choice between remaining within tribal communities or becoming to some degree a part of the American mainstream. To live in both worlds is spiritually challenging, but some have chosen that kind of life and succeeded. It is a balance that we all seek, even in the American mainstream—a balance within family and community, and a balance within one's self. To find one's balance between two cultures is an ongoing task of acceptance of one's life and acceptance by both cultures.

It is community and culture that give a person "identity." Although place is important, the community of one's family and friends is imperative for placing a person within the context of kinship and membership in the larger community. While this is the nature of American Indian identity and balance in a traditional sense, Indian identity is different in the non-Indian world.

Modern Indian identity is the struggle of Native people to realize balance within themselves and to maintain this balance outside the tribal community and in the mainstream. Maintaining healthy identity in a non-Indian mainstream is the supreme test for Indian people in two ways. First, the Native person must maintain a healthy psychological balance. Second, the Native person has to find a personal balance among non-Indians who will accept him or her. In each case, the Native person has to maintain proper perspective so as not to get lost in either culture or caught in between them.

That Native people hold a different perspective is typically ignored by the mainstream. Because it is a different perspective and because it is a minority view, the Native voice goes largely unheard. Yet the Indian voice is clearly heard by Indian people. Native oratory has been a tradition among Indians, and many individuals have become recognized for their speaking skills. Throughout Indian history, many noted leaders—Pontiac, Tecumseh, Sitting Bull, and Ten Bears—also possessed powerful oratory that was remembered and often translated into English. Sometimes such Native leaders also spoke English, and their speeches have been recorded accompanying historical events, especially in the twentieth century. In essence the spoken word lived and found its way into recorded history.

At the turn of the twentieth century a small number of Indians wrote history. Typically they wrote about their life experiences and about their tribes' histories. Dr. Charles Alexander Eastman, a Santee Sioux, wrote nine books about his life and his boarding school experiences as he became a part of the white society. William Warren wrote about the history of his Ojibwe people. Other Indian individuals wrote as well, but the Native perspective was lost in the wave of Frederick Jackson Turner's frontier history that became popular during the years of American Progressivism.

As more Indian children attended boarding schools, many of them kidnapped against their will, the opportunity increased for written Indian perspectives. The impact of World War II and the federal relocation program of moving Indians to cities during the 1950s and 1960s increased the potential for an Indian perspective in academia. By the mid-1960s the Vietnam crisis and societal strife in the United States provided ripe timing for minority groups and women to express their frustrations. Protests and political marches became common. The New Left, underground protest groups, Vietnam protests, the Civil Rights Movement, and the National Association for the Advancement of Colored People took action during the 1960s.

John Kennedy's presidency in the early 1960s alerted society to new ideas and embarked on a "New Frontier" for reform. When Kennedy was gunned down in Dallas on November 22, 1963, Lyndon Johnson inherited the roiling problems of American society. As the scholar Harold Isaacs described these years of strife, "In other mostly non-white groups—the Mexican-Americans and other Spanish-speaking groups, the American Indians, the Chinese-Americans and Japanese-Americans—something of the black pattern began to be reproduced, with radical fringe groups appearing and reflecting—and momentarily speaking for—the much more widely felt and deeply laid feelings of whole populations that their status in the society and their image of themselves somehow had to change."[21] In other words, Isaacs considered the protest of African Americans to be a call for change so that civil rights would be properly addressed. As in this case, the Native voice needs to be addressed throughout all academia.

Since the early 1970s the Indian perspective has become increasingly political in nature and less traditional. Its focus is based largely on Indian-white relations, and it is more individualistic due to dynamic leaders such as Dennis Banks, Winona LaDuke, and Russell Means. In this sharper political atmosphere, the traditional Indian voice became less important as young Native leaders spoke out about the past mistreatment of Native people. In this way, a second Native perspective was heard that challenged the traditional one for national attention. With the passing years both Native views would voice the same concerns of challenging the U.S. government to address past government relations with Native people and help Indian people in the twentieth century.

This Indian perspective has struggled for a voice and place in academia. Among Indian people, this Native perspective is known, but in the mainstream this voice becomes lost. With each generation this Native perspective is decreasing as a result of the declining numbers of indigenous communities, as more Native people assimilate into the mainstream, and as the mainstream becomes larger, with other concerns.

However, more outlets for Native scholars are being made available, and they are becoming more effective. Simultaneously, non-native scholars have become increasingly interested in what Native people think, and they are willing to entertain the American Indian perspective. Like cycles of the past, this interest could wane, yet the

Native voice deserves a place in the public mind and in academia. And the Indian perspective needs to be understood in its fullest scope. Like the early prophecy of the coming of whites, Indian prophecy needs to be understood, for it is part of the way of Indian seeing. This seeing is the Indian point of view that relies on prophecy as well as present seeing, for both are one in the Indian mind. To see in this way is to see the past, present, and future as one, much as Black Elk did many years ago, standing in the rain at Harney Peak before he began to walk down.

On this same path, my son Keytha and I made a pilgrimage to the top of Harney Peak, a three-mile trek, on an unpredicted rainy afternoon during the first weekend in August 2004. It was one of those climbs when you first look at the top, then look at your watch, and think: it is a very long way up. You think about the possible danger, and about the sore muscles afterward, with no Bengay in the car. Then someone much younger, a nine-year-old, says, "We can make it, Dad!" Youth overcame cautious wisdom, even though side trails halfway up started out with small boxes on poles with pencil and paper to leave your name and phone number—for your next of kin, I presumed.

Finally, at the top a playful sun hiding behind the clouds made a grand entrance as we stood where Black Elk had stood, and we saw what he saw years before on his final ascent of Harney Peak on a different summer's day. Black Elk had wished for rain as he prayed and cried to thank the Thunder Beings one last time. And it rained on us. The Beings responded to his tears with rain. The same vista folded into dark blues and purples before our eyes, as we saw the horizon connected to the sky. Mountains beyond mountains appeared like unreal shadows. My spirit lifted up and wanted to go to the beyond. The dropping sun let us know it was time to start our descent down Harney Peak. For a moment, we could see in the same way that Black Elk described. It had rained, like the last time that Black Elk was there. I could feel where Black Elk had stood on the same rock. All was connected, a hoop that is sacred, as Black Elk said it was.

This was the sacred way of seeing. Everything was connected in a

Natural Democracy. All was in its place and acknowledged to exist. In that moment one could imagine how in his Native ethos Black Elk saw Nature's democracy at work with all things connected. We walked quickly down from Harney Peak that day as it began to get dark, the air fast cooling. It was a long walk, but faster going downhill. Now a strong memory to both of us, it was an experience for me to see many years later what Black Elk may have seen, to stand where he stood and to see.

3

The First Dimension of Indian-White Relations

During the spring of 1984 the *Sapulpa Herald* newspaper reported that a young Euchee Indian with Down syndrome died while trying to visit his mother. He lived near Kellyville, Oklahoma, and his mother lived not too far from him:

> The body of a 28-year-old man was found in woods west of Sapulpa Friday afternoon by two men surveying a piece of property before laying a gas line. Creek County Sheriff Bob Whitworth said the body was identified as that of Richard L. Brown. Brown probably died from exposure, Whitworth said. Brothers John and Branson McElroy found the body laying [*sic*] in an isolated and heavily wooded area approximately 7¼ miles west of Sapulpa and ¼ mile south of Highway 33, at about 12:30 p.m. Friday. Branson McElroy said his brother noticed what appeared to be a bedroll laying [*sic*] in the woods. When the men took a closer look, they discovered it was a body. Branson McElroy said they were walking the property for the first time in more than 13 weeks, which is when they began preparing for the gas line project. Creek County medical examiner, Dr. Philip Washburn, said the body showed no signs of foul play. The body was taken to the state medical examiner's office in Tulsa Friday for further examinations. 'There is no indication of foul play,' Whitworth said. 'We are surmising that he died of exposure.' Brown, whose mother lives in rural Sapulpa, had a Tulsa address, according to Whitworth. His mother lives less than a mile east of

> the location where Brown's fully-clothed body was found. Sgt. Camelia Denton said the mother told the Sheriff's Department she last saw her son about three weeks ago. Authorities did not know if Brown's wife, Sharon, of Tulsa had reported her husband missing. Whitworth said Brown was reported missing May 3, 1984, and was found 10 days later. Joining Whitworth on the investigation were Denton, Capt. John Post, deputies Ron Morris and Rock Pinson and Assistant District Attorney Keith Hamm.[1]

Richard Brown lived in the rural countryside and his mother resided about a mile away. On that afternoon the young Euchee man stepped out of his small house to go to his mother's. The temperature began to drop and was unusual for that time of year. The young Euchee had Down syndrome, but he visited his mother regularly. He walked along Highway 33, which went near her house. This time the biting cold persuaded him to change his mind, and he took a shortcut through the blackjack trees. The blowing wind swirled and soon nothing seemed familiar, as the day became twilight. Becoming frantic, Richard unknowingly began to walk in circles; he became lost. He never arrived. Weeks later when the authorities examined his body, the *Sapulpa Herald* reported that the young man had died of exposure. The Euchees said something different. Tradition says that when you get lost, especially if the area is where you should not be, the little people play tricks on you. The little people make imitative sounds from different directions to confuse you. Next, you might hear someone calling your name. Perhaps you hear a relative calling you. Then you walk toward the voices, not realizing you are walking in circles. Panic sets in, and you are lost. You become more confused, and now you are at the mercy of the little people, who do not like to be seen and are mischievous; but they can be helpful when they wish. People have said that sometimes the small ones even give medicine to Indians, although a person like Richard Brown intruded into their domain. Ironically his body was found less than a hundred yards from the highway.

Little people can be found in the stories of many tribes, and Native people believe in them. Most of the time you can hear them, small voices, but not see them unless they come out of hiding. This part of Native life is integral to the metaphysical side of Indian reality discussed later in chapter 5 on the Third Dimension.

In a similar way, Black Elk heard voices and they taunted him as a young boy. He heard them often and thought he was going insane. Black Elk was afraid to tell anyone for fear of being called crazy. All of us sometimes think we hear the voice of our spouse, mother, father, brother, a friend, or someone close to us. Sometimes we may think we hear the voice of someone who has passed away. In the case of Black Elk, one distinct voice led to several other voices—the Six Grandfathers of nature's forces.

Like Richard Brown, Black Elk had experiences that connected him to the Other Side of life. Interestingly, the Richard Brown story has two different versions: what authorities thought happened and what Euchees believed. These views represent two sets of reality for this tragic event—the white historical reality and the Indian historical reality. Common knowledge demonstrates that at least two points of view can be expressed on an issue if two sides are involved, but in the history of Indian-white relations, mistakenly called "Indian history," only one perspective has been generally accepted—the westernization of history. So why not examine the other side of the issue, the other side of Indian-white relations—the Indian point of view as evoked from an Indian reality? This will be done in a later chapter; the point here is that almost all of Indian history is written from the mainstream ethos. Thus mainstream scholars who are writers of the First Dimension place non-Indian values on Native people and their past. Imagine a map of North America and the expansion of colonists on the eastern seashore spreading westward, from right to left. If imagined as an equation of "Indian-white" history, almost all of Indian history has been written from the right side or white side of this binary relationship. How this has occurred is the point of the present chapter.

The idea of an "us and them" Indian history began with the initial contact between Indians and whites, and it started with the invention of "Indian." When a lost Christopher Columbus landed on the shore of Hispaniola in the West Indies, he saw people. But he saw them through the eyes of a prejudiced European, and also as potential resources for his quest to fulfill his mission for the Spanish monarchy. As we know, Columbus claimed the land for Spain. To the king and queen of Spain, Columbus wrote his observations of the indigenous people of the Americas:

> They all go naked as their mothers bore them, and the women also, although I saw only one very small girl. And all those whom I did see were youths, so that I did not see one who was over thirty years of age; they were very well built, with very handsome bodies and very good faces. Their hair is coarse almost like the hairs of a horse's tail and short; they wear their hair down over their eyebrows, except for a few strands behind, which they wear long and never cut. . . . They do not bear arms or know them, for I showed them swords and they took them by the blade and cut themselves through ignorance. They have no iron. . . . They are all generally tall, good looking and well portioned. . . . They should be good servants and of quick intelligence, since I see that they very soon say all that is said to them, and I believe that they would easily be made Christians, for it appears to me that they had no creed. Our Lord willing, at the time of my departure I will bring back six of them to Your Highness, that they may learn to talk.[2]

Columbus's description of Indians had a devastating effect for Native people. His ethnocentric view informed the world for future generations; American Indians, Columbus argued, were subordinate to whites. Their ways and dress were not like those of Europeans. Uncertain that they would survive in the strange land, some early European colonists initially viewed Indians as friends, allies, mercenaries, slaves, and trading partners. The colonists needed them, but once they were not of use, the polarity between the cultures created a sociocultural chasm between Indians and whites.

Other Europeans even more prejudiced than Columbus viewed

Native people as "savage." The brutish Indian was etched deeply into European and colonial minds. Stripped of human qualities, the pagan red-skinned inhabitants represented the opposite of civilization. They were a part of the land to be conquered. They were not people; they were not human. In the minds of most colonists they were wild savages who possessed no rights to the land. Christian colonists believed it was their divine right to inflict punishment upon the "Indians" and to take the land.

When whites saw Indians, they did not look like whites, and vice versa. The initial distinction of color differences helped to institute racism as a historical dark phase of this country. The human eye sees things in color and understands objects according to the knowledge of each person.

The colonists made various assumptions as they entered new associations with Native peoples. Initially some colonists thought that Indians were much like themselves. Others had a different view. "The first of these beliefs held fast throughout the colonial period and beyond; the second [view] underwent a slow but drastic change in the late seventeenth century and throughout the eighteenth as mainstream Americans shifted their perception of Indian color from innately white to innately dark and eventually to red," wrote historian Alden Vaughan.[3]

Perception of skin differences set the tone for how the colonists viewed Indians, as Vaughn suggested; limited evidence has been left behind of Indian people's first perceptions of the colonists. Indians called the colonists white strangers with long hair on their faces. Early travelers, writers, and explorers described Indians in physical appearance as "olive, tawny, or brown, occasionally russet or yellow, and sometimes a combination of such colors."[4]

In earlier observations of Indians, Europeans expressed a variety of perspectives. In 1578 George Best argued against climate as the cause of human complexion, partly because "under the Equinoctial in *America* the people are not blacke, but white." In 1587 Frenchman René de Laudonnière, commander of an ill-fated Huguenot outpost in Florida, depicted the Indians as olive. However, he explained that "when they are borne they be [sic] not so much of an olive colour and are far whiter. For the chief cause that maketh them to be this colour, proceeds of annointings of oyle . . . and because of the sun which shineth hotte upon their bodies." A Dutch scholar, Jan Huygen van Linschoten, echoed Laudonnière: "When they come first into the world," he wrote in 1598, they "are not so blacke but very white: the blacke yellowish colour is made upon them by a certaine oyntment. . . . Their colour likewise changeth because they goe naked, and with the burning heate of the sunne."[5]

The European othering planted the roots of anti-Indianism that fostered in the East the early American attitude of the ignoble savage. In sharp contrast, some people viewed the noble Indian as a steward of the forest. But in the backcountry of colonial settlements, the changing view of Indians from the "noble" savage to the "wild" savage fostered the idea of "Indian hating" that went westward with pioneer consciousness. As literary critic Roy Harvey Pearce observed, the Indians' rejection of assimilation produced more anti-Indian feeling: "When the cruelty and rigor of events, white impatience and the Indian stubbornness would not allow for such absorption, American thinking changed its emphasis and direction. It was based more and more on the notion that the gap between Indian and white society was too great to be closed."[6]

American thinking postulated that people unlike Euroamericans in appearance existed as savages. If Indians were more like Americans in appearance, then the most degrading term, *savage*, likely would not have been the word used to refer to Indians. The distance from American likeness polarized Indians and whites, making their cultures stand apart even more.

In various eras of world history, nations have defeated other nations, and the triumphing victor has recorded the feats as great. The conquered, if they survive, are left to accept or reject the victor's version. Because the conqueror possesses the power, this one-sided version then becomes the mainstream history. In the western world of whites, the greatest achievements flew "under the banners of civilization."[7] In the western mind, this was a white man's human history, excluding white women, ethnic groups, and the rest of the natural environment. Gary Nash supported this observation in his classic

Red, White and Black: The Peoples of the Early America, when he singled out the "'historical amnesia that has blotted out so much of our past' and left us with a 'white oriented, hero-worshiping history.'"[8]

Ethnohistorians have realized that frontier historians and American historians in general continue to resort to a subtle racist history by excluding the American Indian in writing history. Ethnohistorian Fred Hoxie noted that "modern historians like [Bernard] Bailyn, while rejecting the racism of [Francis] Parkman, still fall back on the view that American history is essentially a story of civilization overcoming primitivism." Hoxie continued this point, stating, "from this point of view, Indian history is significant only when it intersects with the history of European settlement. . . . And Indians themselves are significant primarily as 'obstacles to progress.'"[9] With this denial, historical amnesia allows racism to be dismissed as part of the historic view of early Americans in their contacts with Native people.

The American history of heroes involved "great events." In American history, "great men" made history by forging great events as Americans searched for heroes. Every year the United States celebrates October 12 as Columbus Day, and the majority of the country hails Columbus as an exalted hero without realizing the repercussions of the Indian-white encounter. Historian Lewis Hanke commented that "Columbus started the practice of writing about America, and many followed his example, for the conquest so stimulated their imagination that they came to look upon it as the greatest event since the coming of Christ."[10]

Great men were viewed as conquerors, the victors who wanted their deeds recorded in the annals of history. In every conceivable way—social, legal, cultural, and scientific—America has tried to justify its actions in seizing the western hemisphere from its original inhabitants.[11] "Paradoxically, the Indian, the original settler of the United States, is a marginal figure in American history," stated historian Arthur Gilbert; "he does not seem to fit into the story of this country, and as a result he is treated by historians as an impediment, a stumbling block who occasionally gets in the way of the march to the Pacific—or he is not treated at all."[12]

The impact of scholars writing "about" the indigenous peoples of this continent has been a mono-perspective from the non-Indian point of view. American scholarship carried on from the European tradition, and it monopolized the historical interpretation of the American experience, including Indian history. In fact, Indian history is centuries older than American history.

In analyzing Indian-white history, we must first understand the definition of history and its origin. The word *history* in the English language is derived from a Greek noun meaning learning. The Greek philosopher Aristotle observed that history involved an orderly account of natural phenomena, not specifically a chronology, and this understanding of "natural" history has prevailed in the English language. Through the ages the Latin equivalent, *scientia* ("science") became regularly used to designate "non-chronological systematic accounts of natural phenomena." Chroniclers used the word *history* mostly in reference to chronological accounts of phenomena when regarding human affairs. Since then the definition of history has come to imply "the past of mankind." In comparison, for history the Germans applied the word *Geschichtie*, which is derived from *geschehen*, meaning "to happen." *Geschicte* is "that which has happened."[13] The German approach to understanding history laid the foundation for future professional historians.

In the nineteenth century many historians concerned themselves with writing narrative chronological compilations of fact for illustrating "how things really were," as advocated by Leopold von Ranke in the 1830s. Consequently historians placed a greater emphasis on recording what happened as they understood it rather than on analyzing situations as "unique occurrences and events and as products of particular complex circumstances and contexts."[14] Furthermore, nineteenth-century historians depicted political events as most significant. Such histories centered on nation-states and great men who determined their nations' destinies. Thus in the German "scientific" seminars of the nineteenth century, teachers mandated that students write history "*wie es eigentlich gewesen*—as it had really been."[15]

The German model became the western approach to writing history. Historian Edward Carr noted that for the next three generations

German, French, and British scholars relied entirely on empirical evidence in their conscious approach to history.[16]

America's written history well into the twentieth century has been "hero" history. More specifically, America's history has been one of conquest, expansion, and violence that developed a historical consciousness of conquering the frontier and its inhabitants.[17] Thus those perpetrating such acts of conquest and violence have received a significant amount of attention in the historical record. Following the Louisiana Purchase of 1803 and the subsequent period of expansion, plus the annexation of Texas and other regions in the 1840s, writers and journalists wrote glorified accounts of the development of the American West. Compelling stories set a standard, which typically involved interesting individuals, meaning men. Still considered a young country at the time, America was focused on heroes such as Andrew Jackson, Daniel Boone, and others east of the Mississippi River as the West looked for its own collection of stars and saviors. Writers of history in the nineteenth century—George Bancroft, William Hickling Prescott, John Lothrop Motley, and Francis Parkman—"painted in dramatic colors" and "carved their characters to an impressive size." As they wrote, other heroes arose in the likes of Jedediah Smith, Jim Bridger, and Kit Carson, heroes "whose qualities are the qualities of an age."[18] Writer Charles Averil introduced Kit Carson to easterners as a hero in nearly twenty-five novels about the frontiersman, although Carson himself could not read them because he was illiterate. The "wannabe" hero George Armstrong Custer craved attention at the risk of losing his life and the lives of the men under his command, and indeed Custer has received an exorbitant amount of attention in the historical record.

In America's continuing quest to find heroes as models for paintings in the halls of state capitols and for busts and statues placed in state or national parks, the deeds of white men (and not women) were to the fore, with commemoration usually recognizing violence. Women and people of color have received considerably less attention from historians as makers of history (with the notable exception of Sacajawea, of whom there are more statues than of any other woman in the United States). Victors and conquerors won approval in the public eye as people identified with the struggle of the sung hero. This egotistical epidemic to claim history was a borrowed European tradition, dating back to the Greeks and Romans, who stressed great leaders as part of their treasured heritage.

The late nineteenth century proved to be fertile ground for historical scholarship and the shaping of modern academia with advancements in science. The study of the history of the American experience received a tremendous boost due to the scientific movement.

Scholars had previously accepted the European germ theory whereby European colonial values and ideals were imported to America and accounted for United States history.[19] Its history was part of the glorification of the British Empire. Easily enough, America was presumed to be an extension of Europe. However, this approach began to be challenged by the late 1800s. During this period of industrialization, the United States entertained new areas of development in terms of modernization, defining a national character, and advancing fresh ideas about the past. The frontier had ended when the steady advancement of settlers reached California and the Oregon country. Geographically the regions of the United States were completed.

On July 12, 1893, a young history professor named Frederick Jackson Turner presented an essay titled "The Significance of the Frontier in American History." Turner's presentation of his frontier thesis at the American Historical Association during the Chicago World's Fair doomed the American Indian from a historiographical perspective and perpetuated a denial of Native people as being relevant in history. The meeting changed the course of American historiography and introduced a new "frontier school" that influenced new historians to exclude Indians and other minorities and to minimize women as part of the American experience. In the process the Turner thesis excluded Indians almost completely from the explanation of the development of the American West. In his famed essay Turner mentioned or referred to Indians in but a dozen instances, while giving the vivid impression that they did not merit sustained consideration. He put the white rancher, white miner, white railroad builder, and white pioneer at the forefront of reshaping and settling the country and ignored the contributions of Native people, other people of color, and women. The ethnocentric-minded Turner simply dismissed Indians.

To Turner, Indians existed as part of the frontier to be conquered in the West; he naturally identified cowboys, pioneers, and other white men as the good guys. In the East, Indians had been part of the fur trade economy of a newly developing United States, but Indians' roles decreased with westward expansion. As the West fell before the plow and railroads, so should the Indians who stood in the way, according to this view. They were savages, not people.

As a result of Turner's essay and the extent to which it was embraced by the scholars of the time, "selective" history began to emerge, steeped in myth and legend. As the United States tried to earn its recognition among world powers with the dawn of the twentieth century, America hunted for heroes and distorted facts to paint broad strokes of optimism, rugged individualism, freedom, and Christianity with hands outstretched to convert. An idealized melting pot was imagined for all. Progressive leaders like President Theodore Roosevelt stressed hero history, which promoted the vision of the white man winning the West and doing so as an individual—a cowboy, frontiersman, soldier, pioneer, or businessman. In the late nineteenth century Roosevelt had done more than just deemphasize Indians. He had denounced them, stating: "I don't go so far as to think that the only good Indians are the dead Indians, but I believe nine out of ten are, and I shouldn't like to inquire too closely into the case of the tenth. The most vicious cowboy has more principle than the average Indian."[20]

"Frontier history" proliferated from the compelling influence of Turner's thesis. In the eyes of many, the frontier—and the individualism and innovation that the frontier required—broadly defined the American character. By the mid-nineteenth century scientific thought prevailed, precipitating white American belief of superiority over Native people. In the late 1800s the destroyed South and financially rebuilding North were recovering from the cost of the Civil War, thus creating a need for a new focus, and the West provided a plethora of opportunities for adventure and growth, according to Turnerian thinking that heavily influenced the next generation of historians.[21]

Even pseudoscholars took up the pen and wrote what they wanted, with little regard for actual fact. They imagined a historical reality inclined to selectivity and subjectivity. Scholarly history had hardly begun, thus allowing concurrent historians to exercise liberty to write what they pleased instead of seeking the truth through analyzing the facts. Anthropologist William Hampton Adams observed: "What the historian is doing, when he fancies [that by writing] he is merely cognizing past events as they actually happened, is in reality organizing his present consciousness."[22] American historians of that time, influenced by Turner, attempted to define a history that would be comforting and not disturbing to the conscience of the public. Adams continued to observe that in the Turnerian vision of America, "what we call history is in reality only an image or hypothetical conception of the actual past."[23] This distortion of the facts became acceptable due to an insecure America wanting justification for its acts of violence and the unruly nature of its citizens in their own efforts to become civilized and bring order to their lives.

On the other hand, Native peoples already had order in their so-called savage lives, and they professed their views about this order of life within their Natural Democracy. Phenomena, places, and experiences influenced Indians' accounting of history. Individuals and deeds had their place in the oral tradition describing the past, but individuals and heroic events received much lower priority than in the Euroamerican historical tradition.

On the actual frontier in America, Indians and whites lived side by side, and they regularly fought against each other. On the western frontier the most frequent references to the defeat of the "red man" involve the Plains Indian wars. Although Indians and whites both lived on the frontier, whites believed that the land was theirs for the taking. Indians believed that they were there to take care of the land and that no one owned it. To them it was actually "earth" that held meaning, philosophy, and knowledge.

In real life Indians and whites were also often friends and helped one another in times of emergency. Harsh rural life was an equalizer, cutting across language barriers, cultural bias, and racial prejudice. However, the study of racial scientific discoveries would not allow local viewpoints an equal place beside the history profession in an increasingly ethnocentric America and its historical consciousness. This state of mind, also influenced by Turner, underwent tremendous changes while the nation's growth developed toward a modern industrialized civilization.

In the early twentieth century the French Annales School focused on social history rather than politics. At the same time other European scholars concentrated their studies on nationalism and the nation-state. From this European understanding of history, American historians of the twentieth century portrayed the history of Indians from the viewpoint of tribes as quasi nation-states and Native leadership as involving one principal individual as the leader of his people. It bears repeating that Native communities, not nation-states, represented the most essential unit of social organization. Unfortunately postmodern scholars have continued to describe Indians as members of tribes in a nation-state context, and in this rationale, American Indian history is the history of Indian-white nations' relations. Many Indians also consider Indian tribes to be nations, but the point here is that *community* is the best word to demonstrate Native historical reality using the Medicine Way.

In the larger context of historiography, Turnerian historians dominated the approach to interpreting and writing history in the United States during the early decades of the twentieth century. The end of World War II brought many changes, both confirming American values and generating challenges to them by young Americans in the 1960s. Protests over civil rights and the Vietnam War inspired a historiographic shift and the rise of ethnic histories and women's studies.

In 1971 historian Robert Berkhofer Jr. called for a "new Indian history" that would shift the focus away from "White-Indian relations." Berkhofer insisted that historians and other scholars should focus their efforts on "the remarkable persistence of cultural and personality traits and ethnic identity in Indian societies in the face of white conquest and efforts at elimination or assimilation."[24] As historians heeded Berkhofer's warning, they were forced to grapple with how this new approach might be constructed. Growing pains for a new kind of Indian history occurred, as some scholars felt compelled to search harder to understand Indian people and their past. This compulsion was heightened by the high-profile activities of the American Indian Movement (AIM). During the early 1970s AIM organized the "Trail of Broken Treaties" march to Washington, took over the BIA building, and seized Wounded Knee, South Dakota. These events attracted historians and other scholars to write about Indians, beginning with Stan Steiner's timely work *The New Indians*, published in 1968, the founding year of the American Indian Movement.

In the quest to write a better Indian history, historian James Axtell challenged historians to use their "imagination" in reconstructing the Indian past. This human trait, according to Axtell, represented a critical tool for envisioning Indian history and piecing together a more realistic version.[25] Naturally Axtell was advising non-Indian historians, who have written the majority of articles and books about American Indian-white relations. He observed further that in general the history of America is a "shared discovery" that includes Native people being a part of the first contact experience as the "other." Historians have the responsibility to "translate" their vision and understanding of the past for readers. This task is not easy, according to Axtell, who believed that the historians' first goal should be to tell their own story by including Native viewpoints in such a way that readers would virtually "experience the past rather than simply hear about it." The historian's second task was to "find a way to translate the foreign idiom of the past into that of his own time, without breaking faith with the past."[26]

As historians continued to write about American Indians, many found examining government documents to be the easier route, as had the empiricists of the past. This implies a continued focus on Indian-white relations, but the usage of government documents resulted in a steady production of Indian policy studies, including some of my own work. Colonial historian Gary Nash once warned that "instead of additional studies organized around questions of White-Indian policy," new examinations were needed about "internal change in Indian communities during three centuries of contacts with Europeans."[27] Berkhofer's and Nash's observations in the 1970s represented notions that Indians already knew about, but it took mainstream scholars to articulate this new approach to thwart the tide of "cowboy and Indian" or "us and them" history; in other words, to hear the other side of the story. This call for change has been an uphill climb to put Indians at center stage as equal actors in shaping history. At the same time, the rise of new western history in the mid-1980s included Native people, other people of color, and women as vital parts in rewriting the West. This occurred about the same time as the challenge to write a more accurate Indian history. Despite the fact that some historians attempted to follow Berkhofer's and Nash's lead, meaningful change has been difficult and slow, because the western historical consciousness is so ingrained and because the American public has been slow to embrace new ideas about American Indians that challenge long-standing narratives. Simultaneously western writers who have steadily poured out popular literature have captured a large readership.

Lakota statesman Luther Standing Bear reminds us that "the white man does not understand the Indian for the reason that he does not understand America. . . . The roots of his tree have not yet grasped the rock and the soil. . . . The man from Europe is still a foreigner and an alien. And he still hates the man who questioned his path across the continent."[28] Thus the insecure white Americans had to find their own balance in life and justify a history of violence as the accepted record of the past. To continue this point, mainstream Americans are still in the process of learning about themselves and their relationships with the earth, and this is pertinent to learning about each other. Indians view the land as earth, and whites see the earth as land.

But on the frontier in the West, Indians and whites clashed for control of land, and America's history is one of countless episodes of violence and conflict, as is pointed out in Ned Blackhawk's *Violence over the Land: Indians and Empires in the Early American West*.[29] Ethnohistorian John Ewers responded to this point by suggesting: "I think it is much more meaningful to consider the history of the Indians in the American West in terms of Indian-white confrontation than to treat this subject as a background study of one of the present-day minority groups in our country. . . . Nor do I see the role of the historian of Indian-white relations to be that of being kind to either party in this historic confrontation. But I do think he should study this very complex theme in both breadth and depth, consulting and weighing all the sources he can find, so that he can be fair to both sides."[30] Fair and equal treatment of Indians has remained elusive in the writing of Indian-white relations, simply because the same mainstream attitude produced documents that favored prejudiced American actions. Trying to produce a more just historical interpretation is indeed an uphill effort.

Due to historians' portrayal of the frontier, the American public as a whole has been seduced into believing fabricated myths that have become accepted as truth. However, reformers like Helen Hunt Jackson, with her classic *Century of Dishonor*, have influenced some people to take special interest in American Indians. According to Native scholar Jack Forbes, historians observed that they had "created a one-sided frontier, an Anglo-American frontier that did not adequately conceptualize the Indian frontier against which it abutted."[31]

A lot of Indian history involves the West, although many historians of eastern woodland Indians, like Laurence Hauptman, have demonstrated that much of Indian history has occurred east of the Mississippi River.[32] In essence the frontier was conquered by whites without looking back at the destruction that they committed. In Hauptman's view, the uncivilized lay before the frontier, and this masked all of the criminal action committed by the so-called civilized white race following frontier settlement. The right of might ruled on the frontier in the East and the West.

The frontier, whether west or east of the Mississippi, involved inevitable conflict between Indian and white, allowing the victor to write the history from the First Dimension, according to the discourse of this book. As relations between Indians and whites soured, whites looked for a rationale to defeat the Indian race and to justify this action. American attitudes developed a one-dimensional consciousness of Indian people as less than human. They became opponents in the competition for land, and concepts of "Manifest Destiny," with slogans of "rain follows the plow," "Oregon or Bust," and "Go West, Young Man!" became a part of the American psyche, according to Reginald Horsman.[33] And Anglo-Americans took the land in large chunks through treaty negotiations, war, land runs, and swindling. This version of "frontier history" represents the First Dimension of the binary paradigm. "The Indians who appear in it are cardboard figures set up to be knocked down," stated ethnohistorian Francis Jennings, adding, "It cannot be anything else so long as the frontier is conceived as a line of separation constantly being pushed 'back.'"[34] Again, the line marking the frontier in a linear sense from right (East) to left (West) distinguished what land and space had been taken or conquered as a part of the western movement.

The one-sided historical paradigm in America obviously disregards an Indian version of history, and it ignores the historical interpretations of other minorities. Women's history has been similarly disregarded by mainstream historians, although women's studies as a discipline has made much progress in countering this denial. The 1970s witnessed the emerging of ethnic studies and the writing of minorities' histories. The reason for this bias is the malpractice of mainstream historians and mainstream chauvinism.[35] For example, while explaining the development of modern America, historians like Merle Curti in his *Growth of American Thought* have left Indians, other people of color, and women out of their historical narratives.[36]

Such one-sided histories facilitated the acceptance of racism among non-Indians as well as Indian people. Racism is a product of the perception and thinking of human beings embedded in culture. Our cultural values influence how we perceive our surroundings and other people. Naturally we—including white Americans, Indians, and other groups—form opinions according to the information we have, but this is unfortunately sorted in our minds according to basic colors and cultural differences without allowing our prejudiced consciousness to entertain fairly the differences between ourselves and other people.

White Americans are generally able to see the racism that has been compartmentalized in our history, such as slavery and Jim Crow. They are less likely, however, to understand the way in which racism has been incorporated into federal policies like land allotment, boarding schools, or the Indian New Deal. The history of federal-Indian relations is direct in trying to destroy Native people with racial tones in government reports, yet federal-Indian policy has also favored Native people in trying to assist them to improve their livelihood. Since history has often been written to record good deeds over bad people, the victors writing the history deny racism in their accounts. Victors do not want to be remembered as racists and murderers; they desire to be acclaimed heroes who won. In *Race and Manifest Destiny*, Reginald Horsman explains: "Internally it was made quite clear that the American republic was an Anglo-Saxon republic; other white races would be absorbed within the existing racial mass while nonwhite races would be rigorously excluded from any equal participation as citizens."[37]

But what about those who did not win? Indians have been victims of the American experience, but they survived. An important point here is to realize that a lot can be learned from victimization and survival. Like the mirror effect as applied by Edward Said in his study of Orientalism, whereby viewers learn more about themselves and their culture, studying a victim's story reveals much about both the colonizer and the suppressed indigenous people.[38] Finally, in addition to studying the conquering of the land and people, why it was done is a valid question to explore in writing about Indians in the First Dimension. We need to move beyond this point in order to understand the Medicine Way.[39]

The irony of Indian victimization is that Indians are still here. The astonishing reality is their sheer survival after losing perhaps as many as 18 million people in North America.[40] The emphasis is the same even if smaller estimated numbers are plugged into this example. In the United States, the fact is that the original estimated population was reduced to fewer than 238,000 Indians by 1900, according to the U.S. Census Bureau.

Difference usually results in disagreements and violence. As settlers pushed westward, regular contact with Indians occurred on the frontier. The white desire for land forced displacement of Indian tribes, and wars resulted. "Frontier violence" occurred in every sector of the country when white Americans met Indians. Physical violence became part of the way of life on the frontier of settlement. In the path of "Manifest Destiny" stood the Indian, a barrier to be conquered with the environment.[41] In his introduction to *Facing West: The Metaphysics of Indian-Hating and Empire Building*, Richard Drinnon writes that in the American subliminal mind are "the roots in there intertwined with more general repressive attitudes towards nature and the body, and with concomitant association of dark skin *color* with filth, death, and radical evil generally. Out of this psychosexual complex arose the generic *native*, that despised, earthy, animalic, suppressed 'shadow self' projected by the Western mind."[42] In total the United States government authorized more than sixteen hundred wars, skirmishes, and battles against Indian people.

The academic view of the West has resulted in history positioning Indian people as the enemy in a kind of "soldier and Indian" history, while newer scholarship has portrayed Indians as victims. Yet there is a dearth of scholarship addressing the violence against Indians. The work of historian Karl Jacoby can be seen as an exception. In his words, paradoxically, anti-Indian violence has "all too often been considered mere prologue—segregated from the rest of American history as 'prehistory' and 'ethnohistory'—or collapsed into a single, amorphous story of conflict."[43]

Frontier violence was part of the American experience, thus it is a common theme in American Indian history and American history. This theme connected the equation of Indian-white relations, in which one side affected the other. And we can learn about both sides by examining the dynamics of frontier violence in the Indian-white equation. Unfortunately such violence has been misrepresented as the brawn and physical force decreed by God to conquer the West, as Frederick Jackson Turner promotes in his thesis. This American strength has been admired and written about, especially by progressive historians and historians of foreign policy. The desire for American strength has become an admired quality in the public consciousness despite late twentieth-century scholarship that began to examine the full picture of how the United States rose to prominence as the world's leading industrial power.[44]

American history textbooks continue to inform elementary school children that defeating the Indians and settling the land was necessary, and that brute physical force was a necessary way of life. However, the same textbooks fail to tell us that American Indians remained victims of continued frontier violence even into the twentieth century.

From the Indian perspective, what can we learn about the Indian experiences of such violence and near genocide? We can learn about survival. The victim does not have to be presumed vanquished, as portrayed by James Earle Fraser's "End of the Trail." Fraser's sculpture depicted a defeated warrior holding his spear while sitting on his horse. In the case of the victimized American Indian, Native identity remained intact. Normally we assume that the strong is the victor, the one who conquered. In actuality we can learn more from the victim: how did the American Indians survive? Tremendous resilience and determination are required to go on. We know this from examples around the world: the Jewish people surviving the holocaust, African Americans surviving slavery, the various ethnic groups surviving Russian communism. In the Southeast of the United States during the 1830s and 1840s, the Five Civilized Tribes (the Cherokees, Creeks, Seminoles, Choctaws, and Chickasaws), survived the Trail of Tears when the federal Indian policy of removal under President Andrew Jackson forced the march of these nations to present-day Oklahoma. About one-fourth to one-third of their populations died on the Trail of Tears.

As of 2010 there are a total of 326 reserved Indian lands, including reservations, rancherias, pueblos, and villages. Thirty-four tribally controlled community colleges exist as of 2010 throughout Indian Country. Yet in spite of these lessons of survival and little known steps of progress, in the American mind the American Indian remains the Hollywood-portrayed "savage," "drunken Indian," or "heathen," in line with at least thirty-four pejorative stereotypes I have personally counted.

The public consciousness of the majority of the American population has stigmatized American Indians to be portrayed as relics of the past. Stereotypes from the past five hundred and more years have been aided by the power of television and radio. People's addiction to the movie industry and misguided literature have embedded a mental image of the Indian into the minds of most Americans.[45]

The image of American Indians via the stereotypes has been a destructive one created from history written by the conquerors and the dominant society. Both have viewed history through Amerocentric eyes, disregarding the positive qualities of American Indians, other minorities, and women in contributing to the development of this country. This troubled phenomenon developed even in Mexico and South America, as the Native people were viewed in the same manner as North American Indians.[46]

As important as the impact of the negative image on the influenced ignorance of mainstream Americans has been the impact of the negative image on Indian people themselves. Indian people have been so saturated with negative stereotypes and savage imagery that they began to feel unworthy and insecure; they began to doubt themselves, their culture, and their identity. Most in the dominant society know little about American Indians, and the information they do possess is often erroneous. Furthermore, society's judgmental impulse exemplifies a lack of sensitivity and minimal understanding about Indian behavioral patterns.

Indian history in its current state is not acceptable. Although important progress has been made in representing Native people, there is an obvious need for revision and rethinking of American Indian history after so much damage has been done through discrediting and misrepresenting it. This point was recognized years earlier when noted historian C. Vann Woodward deplored the parochialism of some American historians in these words: "The fault of Americans lies largely in their habit of looking within for the significance of historical experience and assessing it narrowly according to preconceptions and legends of democracy, equality, and frontier-flavored determinants of exceptionalism." This subliminal myopia also explains why Americans have been so slow "to understand the significance of the influence they have exerted beyond their borders."[47]

In addition to well-known historians dismissing American Indians from American history, scholars who write about Indians have not received the recognition that they deserve for writing about so-called marginal people. Historian James Merrell stated: "The writings of James Axtell, J. Frederick Fausz, Francis Jennings, James Ronda, Neal Salisbury and Wilcomb Washburn (to name only a few of the leading authorities on Indians)—are for the most part ignored by the larger community of scholars studying early America."[48] And these are white historians being ignored by other white historians.

Wilcomb Washburn was among the earliest modern scholars to utilize interdisciplinary sources in search of a revised account of the American Indian past. In agreement with Washburn's approach, Wilbur Jacobs advocated an analysis of "the Indian point of view. In fact, I am suggesting that we revise certain of our traditional ideas about the frontier in American history with a hope of seeking a balance. . . . My purpose here is to refute that [frontier emphasis] assumption; indeed, the Turnerian theme of progress and development as an explanation of frontier advance is largely an interpretation of Euro-American white history of political party changes and the evolution of sectional characteristics and national ideals."[49]

Clearly the confrontational "cowboy and Indian" or "us and them" history about the American experience continues to be written by military historians writing about Indians and biographers who leave out Indians even when they were involved, such as fighting for the colonists in the American Revolution and fighting for the United States in World Wars I and II. Filled with romanticism, seeking the maintenance of superior status, and desiring to prove that America is free to all willing to "pull themselves up by their bootstraps," some scholars and writers continue to write in this selective manner. Perhaps this is due to the relatively small number of Indians—less than 1 percent of the American population—but historians generally do not consider the Indian presence, especially in the twentieth century. As their works continue to be published by mainstream presses and their textbooks are perpetuated, this racist history continues. Not everyone wears cowboy boots, although many western Indians do. But the point is that Indians are outside the mainstream interpretation of history. Other peoples outside the mainstream in America are urging that their views of history need to be written and accepted by other scholars, writers, and the general public.

In revising the record of Indian-white relations, much progress has been made in scholarship in American Indian history since the 1970s, but there is much more to do. The call for a new Indian history has placed Indians in clearer focus alongside whites as makers of history. This was the state of Indian historiography at the close of the twentieth century. The effort for Indians to be put on center stage of Indian history and U.S. history is being made, but needs to be completed.[50]

The damage launched by Columbus and Turner has advanced a biased history, and the challenge has been issued as a call to turn the tide. The worst sin of scholars is not necessarily to distort history and distort the descriptions of Indian people; rather it is to deny their existence and their place in history as a part of America. This is historical cleansing by denial, if ethnocentric people write the textbooks. The other side of history needs to be told and considered as part of the truth.

As in the story about the young Euchee who met his fate while traveling during winter to see his mother, there are two versions of this reality. One is described by non-Indians reporting on the event. The other is just as valid and needs to be considered, and it is more believable in the First Dimension of Native reality, if one looks from left to right at the Indian-white equation. This event is told from an Indian point of view, and it involves other external forces that need to be accounted for to understand the other side of the story. We should question what we read and seek a different perspective, especially when history is written by a people about another people and their experiences.

Many times I have driven the same road that the Euchee Richard Brown walked along. This road is north of Sapulpa, past the city limits and past the turnpike entrance to Oklahoma City. Still going north, up and down the hills, the area becomes open and devoid of houses. There are no people nearby, only nature and what is meant to be. This is where it happened. The man's death seems meaningless, but it contains an important lesson for the living. There is more. Perhaps during a coming twilight in winter's stead, the voice in the cold is more discernible. Perhaps we hear the same voices that called to the

Euchee, saying it was alright to come home to the Other Side. In this way reality is more than we think it is. Native reality is both the physical and the metaphysical. We need to know more about the Native reality and these two worlds. This crux is the threshold where we can learn more about the spiritual side of life. There is a spiritual part in all people. This Other Side is where Black Elk visited and many others like him who were gifted to see and hear the voices of the others.

4

The Second Dimension of Interacting Indian-White Relations

More than two hundred years ago two brothers stood at a place near what is presently Battle Ground, Indiana. Along the Wabash River, lined by towering oaks, maples, tulip trees, hackberries, sycamores, and elms, they discussed their troubled fate. Their decision became their stand against the encroaching white settlers. The younger brother Tenskwatawa, the Shawnee Prophet, stood nearby. Here, at what the Indians called Prophetstown, Tecumseh, the older of the two brothers, said:

> It is true I am Shawnee. My forefathers were warriors. Their son is a warrior. From them I only take my existence; from my tribe I take nothing. I am the maker of my own fortune; and oh! That I could make that of my red people, and of my country, as great as the conceptions of my mind, when I think of the Spirit that rules the universe. I would not then come to Governor [William Henry] Harrison, to ask him to tear the treaty, and to obliterate the landmark; but I would say to him, Sir, you have liberty to return to your own country. The being within, communing with past ages, tells me, that once, nor until lately, there was no white man on this continent. That it then all belonged to red men, children of the same parents, placed on it by the Great Spirit that made them, to keep it, to traverse it, to enjoy its productions, and to fill it with the same race. Once a happy race. Since made miserable by the white people, who are never content, but

always encroaching. The way, and the only way to check and stop this evil, is, for all the red men to unite in claiming a common and equal right in the land, as it was at first, and should be yet; for it never was divided, but belongs to all, for the use of each. That no party has a right to sell, even to each other, much less to strangers; those who want all, and will not do with less. The white people have no right to take the land from the Indians, because they had it first; it is theirs. They may sell, but all must join."[1]

Indians and non-Indians see things differently, thus creating a binary model for a proposed Indian-white equation.[2] This difference helped to provoke one of the greatest battles in American Indian history—the Battle of Tippecanoe, also called the Battle of Prophetstown. On November 7, 1811, power met power; the Medicine Way of Indians was pitted against the white desire for land. Along the Wabash River following a steamy green humid summer stood the many lodges of the Shawnees and their allied nations among the tall oaks and maples and heavy underbrush. Fall gave way as winter approached, with sturdy oaks dropping their acorns; leaves of yellow, light red, deep red, and orange covered the ground. The serene place encountered death as night ended and blood permeated the sandy brown earth. The predawn mist gripped the landscape in a steady cold a little above freezing. The two opposing sides of conflicting beliefs and distinct worldviews clashed on the battlefield. The end of the story is well known. William Henry Harrison marched his soldiers toward Prophetstown when Tecumseh was away recruiting more warriors. As Harrison camped nearby, eager warriors attacked prematurely. In a little over two hours Harrison defeated the Shawnee Prophet and the warriors. The warriors retreated to the Prophetstown but could not hold it, and Harrison ordered his men to burn it to the ground.

Present scholarship on Indian history tends to focus on the interaction between Indians and whites. Unfortunately almost all of these relations have been in war, but there were interludes of trade, conversion to Christianity, boarding school experiences, fighting side by side in World Wars I and II, and intermarriages in which Indians and white Americans shared common ground in the Second Dimension of the Indian-white paradigm. These interactions typify the interchanges between Indians and the white mainstream—the hyphen or "shared experience" of Indian-white relations history. This shared experience presents a new reality of the Indian consciousness and subconsciousness and the white man's consciousness. In theory they are equal partners in making history together, although their versions differ.

Insightful scholarship entertaining the dynamics of two cultures interacting in the Second Dimension includes Francis Jennings, *The Invasion of America: Indians, Colonialism, and the Cant of Conquest* (1975); James Axtell, *The Invasion Within: The Contest of Cultures in Colonial North America* (1981); Richard White, *Roots of Dependency: Subsistence, Environment, and Social Change among the Choctaws, Pawnees and Navajos* (1983); and J. Leitch Wright Jr., *Creeks and Seminoles: The Destruction and Regeneration of the Muscolgulge People* (1986). Other significant works include James Merrell, *The Indian's New World: Catawbas and Their Neighbors from European Contact through the Era of Removal* (1989); David Rich Lewis, *Neither Dog Nor Wolf* (1994); and Daniel Usner, *Indians, Settlers and Slaves in a Frontier Exchange Economy: The Lower Mississippi Valley before 1783* (1992).

More recent contributions include Daniel Richter, *Facing East from Indian Country: A Native History of Early America* (2001); Gary Anderson, *The Conquest of Texas: Ethnic Cleansing in the Promised Land, 1820–1875* (2005); and Ned Blackhawk, *Violence over the Land: Indians and Empires in the Early American West* (2006). In the context of this discourse, they are in the Second Dimension (Indian-white interaction) of the Natural Democracy.

Ask any Native person who is close to tribal traditions and that person will confirm that there is a difference of perspective between Indians and whites. Several obvious reasons account for this polarization of opposite perspectives, yet almost all the written history about American Indians has been produced by mainstream academics who see things in a different way than do traditional Indians.

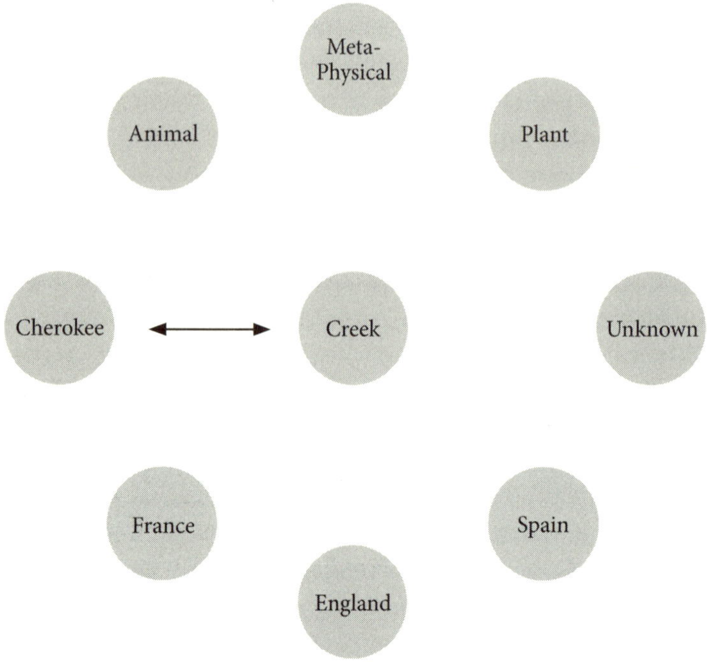

FIGURE 6. Each community has a Natural Democracy matrix like the Creeks in this model. For example, the Cherokees would have the same theoretical sociocultural relations as the Creeks.

Language differences (including between Native groups), cultural value differences, different relationships with the same environment, and the different ways in which Indians and whites approach metaphysics basically account for the juxtaposition of the two perspectives. This "us versus them" or "one against the other" situation is complicated by the fact that many Indian people are mixed-bloods. Even some full-bloods who have been assimilated and separated from their traditions view their surroundings in a manner that is more closely aligned with a mainstream American perspective. It is imperative to consider that there are fundamental differences between Indian and white perspectives and there are various worldviews—

from a Mohawk perspective, Navajo perspective, Lakota perspective, and so forth.

However, returning to the traditional perspective, in figure 6 the focal community is Creek and the binary involves the Cherokee. To avoid belaboring the discussion of Indian-white relations, the following analysis addresses this Indian-Indian binary model. It should be noted that the model can be applied to other communities and in considering animals and plants as communities as well.

In the following discussion the binary paradigm is addressed using three examples: (1) Indian-Indian or tribe-tribe, (2) Creek-Animal, and (3) Creek-Plant.

In the Creek-Cherokee binary we have the same theoretical "one to one" within a Natural Democracy of other communities as in the Indian-white relationship. Tribal communities, however, differ in identity, just as European nations do. In theory the same binary could be used for England-Spain or England-France or Spain-France—all mentioned here since they also had binary relationships with some of the tribal communities in Indian Country.

The Creek-Cherokee binary has had a history much longer than that of Indian-white relations. At some point in the early 1700s the Cherokee moved into the present-day western North Carolina region, encroaching on territory used by the Muscogee Creeks. This competition for the region represented the northernmost area claimed by the Creeks. The Cherokees and Creeks vied for the same hunting domain, and increased migration enabled the Cherokees to establish a new homeland. The relationship remained contentious with the exception of sporadic lulls of peace and temporary alliances. In the early 1750s the Cherokees and Creeks went to war, and these hostilities occurred irregularly, culminating in 1755 with the Cherokee victory at Taliwa. This setback forced the Creeks to leave the Tennessee River valley. In 1792 and 1793 these former enemies allied to attack Buchanan's Station near Nashville and Cavitt's station near Knoxville.

Finally in the Creek War of 1813–14 with the United States, part of the War of 1812, the two tribal nations clashed again. The Creek War became much more complicated when factionalism divided the Upper and Lower Creeks, the latter being known as the red town communities, which represented only about one third of the entire Muscogee Creek people. The Lower Creeks built their towns along the Chattahoochee River. At their zenith of military strength they may have possessed as many as four thousand Red Stick warriors.

Settler encroachment compelled the Red Sticks to defend their homelands and provoked the United States to send Andrew Jackson to head a militia to march against the Indians. Indian agent Benjamin Hawkins, who had lived among the Indians, skillfully recruited Upper Creeks to join. Seeing their chance for opportunity against their nemesis, two hundred Cherokees joined Jackson's war effort to defeat the Creeks in a final battle at Horseshoe Bend on March 27, 1814. Afterward the Cherokee-Creek relationship became less adversarial as both now contended for their homelands, turning their attention toward the Creek-white and Cherokee-white relationships, which were characterized by war and removal.

Different tribal communities have their own specific needs, not reflected in the Indian-white paradigm, where different tribal communities saw themselves in the same Indian-versus-white relationship. Yet it is also the case that members of different tribes have shared the same belief—for example, the Shawnees, Potawatomis, Ojibwes, and others with the Shawnee Prophet at the Wabash. A similar shared experience of belief was experienced by the Cheyennes and Lakotas at the Sun Dance prior to the Lakota-Cheyenne victory at the Rosebud Battle against George Crook and George Armstrong Custer's defeat at the Little Bighorn. Logic in the Medicine Way would suggest that the different tribes experienced the same spiritual energy. In certain places some people see things that most other people would say were unreal. Perhaps the spirits at the Little Bighorn battle site still linger even after much time has passed. In the eyes of Native people these are distinct places to be respected for their power, and sometimes they are sacred places. Sacred places for Indians have their own reality; they are often empowered with a spiritual presence and energy that can be good, bad, or both.

Generally Indians accept such places and visual occurrences. But they try to understand them, for everything extraordinary possess-

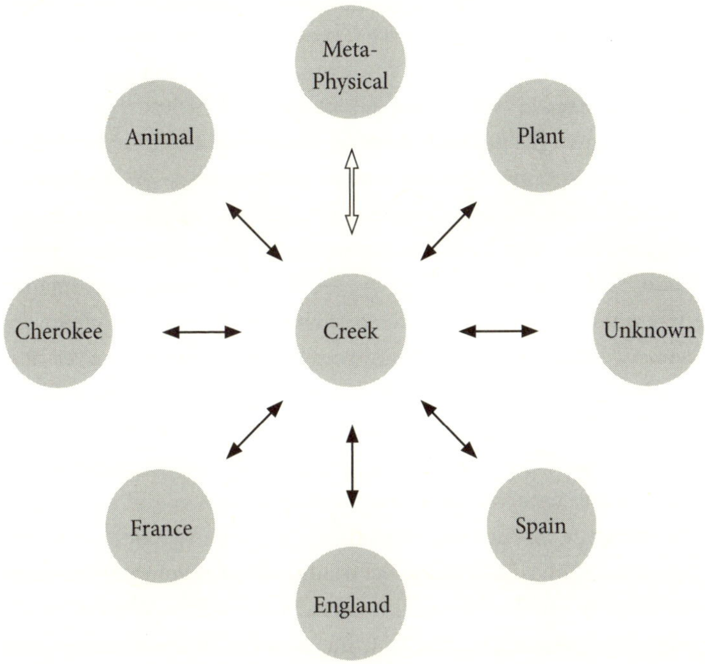

FIGURE 7. The Creek community has reciprocal relationships with other communities, including nonhuman communities, except for the metaphysical, where the Creek community does not have a regular relationship on a daily basis. The metaphysical contacts the Creek community when it wants to.

es meaning. Mysterious phenomena yield stories that are repeated for generations. This is part of the oral tradition among Native peoples, the telling of accounts of the past that still live on; such stories persist to have a life force of their own. This way of telling stories and correlating similar information is how the Indian mind functions and is absorbed into the indigenous consciousness.[3]

As noted, the Cherokee or any other tribal community could be the center community like the Creeks in the figure. In the same way the Cherokees would view the Cherokee-Creek binary as more relevant than Cherokee-white relationship until the latter became more threatening in the 1820s, thereby lessening the importance of the Cherokee-Creek binary.

It is necessary to note that in the binaries depicted in figures 6 and 7 the relationship is not always human to human. For example, the sacred is found in plants and animals as well, which makes the relationships with the flora and fauna equally valid in the totality called Natural Democracy. Like the Indian-white equation, the Creek-Animal relationship held special meaning and still does.

For clarification we should examine the Creek community. The infrastructure of Creek society consisted of people and their extended families. The third sociocultural unit was a clan system of various totems, each totem representing a separate clan. Thus there were bear people, wolf people, wind people, and so forth. The rest of the infrastructure consisted of communities that made up the tribe or nation.

The same Creek-Animal equal meaning can be applied to the Creek-Plant equation. This relationship of human and nonhuman communities, as illustrated in figure 7, had its place in the Natural Democracy. The Creeks depended on the plant community to supply food, to cure the ill, and for other critical tasks that the Creeks recognized and respected.

In their natural environment the Creeks formed relationships with all entities. They studied each one and learned about its characteristics and strengths. For example, a medicine maker might visit a riverbank in search of red root to prepare for the Green Corn ceremony. The plant is of particular importance for the purification of men and women for the annual Green Corn dances in midsummer. The medicine maker and helper(s) went along the bank, reaching down to harvest the red root. Yet the Creek–red root relationship was not a one-way affair. The red root was first located and then dug up later, at the right time prior to ceremonial preparation, to be at its highest power. Sometimes the red root communicated back to the medicine maker through a dream or vision, or it simply would not be there to be found. Or it might offer too much power or too little. Sometimes the medicine maker would pray, sing, or talk to the herb on a spiritual level, asking it to participate in the purification ritual.

It is important to realize that all of this discourse begins with the theoretical binary of Indian-white, with the history discipline and the rest of the academy being on the right side of the equation. The white perspective is well recognized in the First Dimension, with book after book written about the Muscogee Creeks and other tribes as well as voluminous amounts of articles. The white perspective operates from an advantage in addressing the shared experience or "common ground" in the Second Dimension of Indian-white interactions. The western mind has developed empirically, based on the experiments of science, to exclude nonphysical reality. The five senses of the human body have acted as a determinant in the mind of mainstream Americans to limit the existence of all nonphysical things and abstract elements. To believe in dreams, visions, aberrations, and hauntings is too much for the western scientific mind to accept as reality. In this light, science historian Thomas Kuhn suggests that the prevailing paradigm be shifted to make room for the revelation and acceptance of new knowledge, in this case the Medicine Way.[4] While some people accept such nonphysical existence, the majority of Americans are skeptical of Indian beliefs about the supernatural and about metaphysical reality.

To help refocus the western mindset, recall that we have seen three approaches to studying American Indians: conducting Indian studies from an external point of view, analyzing the dynamics or exchange of Indian-white relations, and investigating the Indian point of view. Most of the publications in the literature derive from the first approach or First Dimension. In the last dozen years scholars have been working on the second approach or Second Dimension with the application of ethnohistory. Several have now attempted to produce studies in the Third Dimension.

This discussion of common ground in the Second Dimension addresses the idea of whites being the primary historical actors and Indians, too, being central on the stage of history. This generation of historians and the next one will continue to write "about" American Indians as long as they see Indians in a non-Indian reality. Basically historians who are linear in their logic regard Indian history and Indian-white relations as one kind of reality. They have been trained this way in the western paradigm. James Axtell explained that "historians . . . tend to work with the flow of time, 'downstream' from the past toward the present."[5] Furthermore, mainstream historians tend to write about human-action events as the basis of history, while disregarding nonhuman-oriented subjects, such as environmental history. Historian Morton White added that "historians write histories of nations, civilizations, scientific societies, philosophical movements, revolutions, economies, religions . . . they do not usually write histories of planets, animals, stars, rocks, or galaxies . . . so we know that they are primarily concerned with the social behavior of human beings."[6] As a result this genre of history is limited by the exclusion of the natural environment from the defining and shaping of history, while presuming that history is limited to human history of great deeds and great men.

Before American Indian history can be taken seriously as a respected area of the historical profession, scholars and academia must accept that Indians have viable cultures and Indian history. Acceptance in the history academy is necessary to prevent academic racism. Too often, historians place greater emphasis on white history and less on the histories of people of color. This discourse for explaining the Medicine Way has been intentionally designed with the introduction of the Indian-white binary for mainstream academics to realize how minorities' histories have been marginalized. Such marginalization of Indian history is due to cultural differences. Studying culture is key to learning more about Indian history. Anthropologist Edward Burnett promoted the idea of culture as the main force in developing the field of cultural anthropology, and this cultural emphasis has helped for understanding Native historical reality.[7]

Cultural and racial differences should not be denied as relevant for suggesting what is significant history for modern historians to study. Cultures and races that differ from the mainstream have caused marginalization of American Indian history, making it acceptable only as Indian-white history.

The record of Indian-white relations has been a contest of clashing cultures with different worldviews and ideologies.[8] It is in this common ground or shared experience that Indians and whites meet, enabling the dynamics to occur with the purpose of studying the interaction between the two sides. Throughout the centuries of contact between Indians and whites, beginning with imperialistic Europeans, in particular the British, then the Americans, Native people and non-natives have interacted on battlegrounds and competed for home space. The two opposing groups have met on these grounds of contention over military engagement, religious beliefs, and logic systems. The British-Indian and U.S.-Indian binaries are examples for examination in the Second Dimension.

James Axtell elaborated that "a second approach to the history of Indian-white relations does attempt to view the colonial contest from an Indian perspective. Sporadically since the nineteenth century and increasingly since the militancy of the 1960s, historians and publicists of Indian descent have claimed that Native oral traditions, and insights born of their cultural and racial heritage, allow them to write the history of American colonialism from a perspective to which non-Indian scholars are not and cannot be privy.[9] In practice, however, an 'Indian' perspective often consists of the familiar Eurocentric position turned on its head, in which the English are villains and the Indians are heroes."[10] Using Axtell's argument, the victims become the underdog champion. Unfortunately this scenario of "us versus them" has carried over to the classroom. Axtell suggests that the Indian-white binary is more complicated, and my call for change attempts to demonstrate an analysis of understanding the "shared experience" instead of arguing which side was right.

The teaching of the history of Indians in classrooms and the training of graduate students in Indian history has resulted in a colonized acceptance of American Indian history, even by some Indian people themselves. This mishap occurred in academia and in schools because textbooks were written by the colonizers; almost no Native professors were teaching in graduate programs in history until the 1960s, and only in the 1970s did a few American Indian professors begin to write, such as Alfonso Ortiz, Vine Deloria Jr., Elizabeth Cook-Lynn, and Jack Forbes, the only one among these four noted scholars who was trained in history.

In fact, Forbes observed that "all scholars should welcome with open arms the appearance of writers of non-European descent and should especially encourage the latter to help break through the bonds of conceptual colonialism. What is needed, then, is a thorough going and radical revisionism developed collaboratively in a multicultural spirit."[11] Such a revision is struggling in coming, and how soon it will be accomplished is another issue entirely.

Three things have not helped. First, the history discipline has not fully accepted American Indian history as a field or as a curriculum in mainstream academic departments at colleges and universities. Second, the current historical approach toward studying American Indian history has proved too limited when researching and analyzing archival documents from a non-Indian point of view. Third, other academic disciplines have not made sufficient collaborative efforts to help the history discipline. For example, anthropologists were the first scholars to study American Indian history seriously from a cultural approach, but the majority of them asked non-historical questions.[12]

Among professional historians the study of American Indian history was not taken seriously by significant numbers until the 1930s. The historiography began when Grant Foreman published on the Five Civilized Tribes (Cherokee, Creek, Chickasaw, Choctaw, and Seminole) in 1934. About the same time, Angie Debo wrote her doctoral dissertation on the Choctaw and published it as *The Rise and Fall of the Choctaw Republic*, which won the American Historical Association's fourth John H. Dunning book award in 1935. Both authors wrote from an outsider's perspective using historical documents in the First Dimension, as described here, although they were very familiar with Indians and had many Native friends.

The limitations of conventional history as a discipline in understanding Native people has properly caused consternation. This concern leads to a timely question: how can we write better Indian-white history of the shared experience in the Second Dimension? Ethnohistory has provided a more promising approach to understanding Indian-white relations. According to Axtell, as "a hybrid approach fathered by anthropologists who needed to document the history of Native groups seeking redress from the Indian Claims Commission after 1946, ethnohistory tries to surmount the problem of one-sided English sources by bringing ethnological sensitivity to the use of traditional written sources and by employing other material familiar to anthropologists but less so to historians."[13]

The interest in American Indians continued, bringing together anthropologists, historians, and other scholars who were seriously studying indigenous people. The journal *Ethnohistory*, founded in 1954, has published more Indian articles than have similar journals of interest in other disciplines.[14] This collaborative effort of anthropologists and historians led by the former tried to piece together the Indian past in a cultural matrix, while curious historians realized that another version of history in the American experience seemed to be missing. William Sturtevant was one of the early anthropologists in the ethnohistory movement. He contended that "historians, archaeologists, and some ethnologists share an interest in diachronic, historical explanations, while other ethnologists and (descriptive) linguists favor synchronic, structural explanations. These are two different but complementary ways of understanding any cultural or social phenomenon." He concluded: "It is possible to concentrate on one type, ignoring the other nearly completely, without affecting the validity of that explanation; but more complete understanding results from the use of both synchronic and diachronic explanations."[15]

While anthropologists took American Indians more seriously and studied their cultural development, historians continued to typecast Indian people and froze them in old stereotypes.[16]

It has been difficult for all academic disciplines to study Indians as central actors with the mainstream. Yet the Indian perspective has managed to elude scholars who are now studying the common ground of Indian-white relations.[17] This paradigm shift to study the common ground is most evident in the first decade of the twenty-first century.

In short, American Indian history must move from being primarily a narrative of Indian-white relations to become the story of Indians that is Indian-Indian relations, Indian-white relations, Indian-Mexican relations, and Indian-African American and Indian-animal/plant relations in communities or regions in the United States (or North America) over time.[18] As clear as the demand for a new Indian history, a new focus is needed to meet that demand of exploring the complexity of the Second Dimension of the common ground and the Third Dimension of Native ethos and reality.

The same common ground in the Second Dimension can be referred to as a shared experience of two different mindsets. Scholars who write history must translate their version into an "achieved awareness," and this narrative needs to be presented in a convincing manner to the reader of popular history. This is an increasing challenge if the mainstream society grows farther from this common ground or shared historical experience and opts to focus on self-interest.[19] This paradigm shift would also suggest transcultural acceptance of the popular historical consciousness to include shared experience, such as the Battle of Tippecanoe or Little Bighorn. For example, popular readers would put themselves in the position of a Native participant, like the Shawnee Prophet who could not stop his warriors from attacking too soon or Sitting Bull perhaps beginning to panic when Custer began to attack. Hence this dialectic of action and reaction becomes a viable learning method for popular history readers to consider a different point of view. In the Medicine Way the popular history reader would understand the cultural consciousness of the Shawnee Prophet and Sitting Bull as they acted and made decisions in these two epic events.

In light of this discourse, it is pertinent to keep in mind that cultural differences enable people to see other perspectives and their own surroundings more clearly. It may even be said that individuals of the same culture perceive everything differently, according to their personal points of view. However, persons of the same culture will likely perceive an idea, point of discussion, or solution to a problem in a generally similar way.[20] In observing American Indians researching at the National Archives, a mainstream scholar disclosed that "when the American Indian scholars come to the National Archives and read the histories from those sources, their interpretation of the action of the Bureau of Indian Affairs, for instance, is quite different from mine. Sometimes the interpretation is parallel, but sometimes it is exactly opposite from mine."[21]

This observation would seem logical following the premise that has been established, but it also notes two polarized perceptions.

Why they are opposite is clear, but how they came about invites discussion about their origins. Since they are opposing points of view and both are products of their cultures, then they would have to be exemplary of their cultures. The point here, however, is that the continuous interaction of Indians in the Second Dimension has caused many Native people to think from the mainstream perspective. For example, traditional full-bloods of a tribe who have become educated in a mainstream school may have developed different ways of reasoning. Or a mixed-blood who is from both tribal and mainstream backgrounds may have a combination of these polarized perceptions.[22] In this case, one subverts the other, and often the mixed-blood chooses to be Indian.

How humans perceive is through physical sight, but images are interpreted through the lenses of cultural knowledge and social ethics. Yet we depend overly on our physical gift of sight and do not pay as much attention to the feedback of our other senses, both physical and innate. Thus sight is the immediate preceptor for opinion, which influences our perspective. I maintain that perception is not perspective but helps to determine it.

Sight also reveals to our minds the color, shape, quality, and unusualness of a subject. Because human minds are products of culture, we quickly categorize the observed subject into our memory bank of knowledge and all too often formulate biased opinions from limited information. In ethnocentric cultures, judgments are quickly formed, since people naturally learn by comparisons. All of us as human beings compare objects and people to what we know, and we compare other cultures to our own.[23]

The hyphenated area or common ground is one of imbalance. It is mostly a story of conflict and destruction from wars. One side tries to outmaneuver and usurp the other. This Second Dimension of strife should seek a balance that has been irregularly witnessed in the long history of Indian-white relations. A peace treaty, or even an agreement on the part of both sides to withdraw for the time being, can hold this balance.

The imbalance is the natural dichotomy of peace-war in times of war, left-right during confusion, good-evil when an ill deed is done, right-wrong when euphoria distorts reality, and other examples in the universe. How we understand it is of the utmost importance to seeking the balance. Unfortunately this is not easy. It is a continuous task, and past failures have yielded a long record of destruction, including occasions of conflict within a person who is half Indian and half white—a tormented soul searching for identity.

Philosophical differences between American Indian intellectualism and mainstream intellectualism help to explain the binary. Yet the difference is not strictly between Indian intellectualism and mainstream intellectualism but between mainstream intellectualism and the different tribal intellectualisms. This may seem obvious, but often stereotypes negate the differences among the various tribal nations and their cultures, promoting a generic "Indianness."

The abstraction of Nativism versus the concreteness of mainstream academics causes immediate differences of opinion. For example, a noticeable characteristic of tribal elders (traditionalists) involves the tendency to generalize rather than to supply a direct answer. They communicate in an abstract manner to promote solidarity to keep families and the community bonded.[24] This is an Indian characteristic of generality that contrasts with the mainstream's detail-oriented mind. Yet the abstract tendency allows compromise and promotes openness and inclusivity in the family and the community. The results yield an "us and us" paradigm for understanding the Indian-Indian shared experience and common ground within a family or community.

Unlocking the knowledge of culture is the key to understanding the Indian dynamics of this contesting binary relationship called the Second Dimension.[25] Learning the ways of Native people requires patience and understanding matters as they do. A means to understanding the common ground is identifying the themes that are involved. For example, acculturation is one such theme in the "us and them" accounts.[26] Another theme is power that both Indians and whites use, but their understanding of it is different. Political power is typically viewed in mainstream politics as one person being influential. In the Indian world, political power means to help tribal members in the community.

In imagining the past, historians should examine events in their fullest context, with all conceivable evidence taken into consideration. This applies particularly to real American Indian history due to its complex reality and indigenous ethos.[27] Present scholarship has challenged those writing Indian history to consider other forms of evidence and the various methods other disciplines have used to collect and understand this evidence.

More important, careful analysis of such evidence requires careful consideration for its historical value. "What did this evidence mean to the people in their historic reality?" would be a proper question.[28] We need to ask the right questions, but we need to ask these questions from a different mindset, as demonstrated earlier in the case of Sitting Bull at the Little Bighorn and the Shawnee Prophet at the Battle of Prophetstown.

The record of history needs to be revised by the best scholarly approaches of the history profession. From time to time, the history discipline needs to be challenged by new approaches of analysis.[29] By reexamining Indian-white relations for how their history has been written, both sides of this historical relationship can be equally studied and reweighed.

This could very well mean changing the general understanding of history as a discipline, or at least the categories of history.[30] Comparative history offers a means for a methodology and a beginning for discussion.[31] This implication requires accepting more than one version or interpretation of the same event.[32] By studying the cross-cultural experience of two groups, careful consideration is given to both groups of people and their cultures.

In postmodern American society, Indians of traditional thought are functioning outside their cultural worlds for a large percentage of their lives. As a result, they are very likely products of two educational systems and two cultures. Initially, this is a difficult process for the traditional person striving to learn in the non-Indian educational system. But once this is done, the Native person can draw upon traditional knowledge and mainstream knowledge to put forth a modern Indian intellectualism.

Indian intellectualism is needed to contribute answers to difficult questions. It is possible that many answers can come from tribal cultures and can be applied to mainstream problems. This is a good reason for mainstream academia to be completely open to the study of American Indians.[33]

This raison d'être requires thinking outside the box and calling on one's imagination to be resourceful in rethinking Indian history. It also involves mainstream academia and the history discipline in seriously considering the Medicine Way of American Indian history. Academics need to study the Second Dimension equally in considering both actors, Indian and white, in the shared experience that is their common ground.

In the Battle of Tippecanoe and others, like the Little Bighorn, there were two sides involved. For each issue or incident of history where two or more sides are involved, there is more than one perspective, but does the mainstream listen to the other voice? For only one view of history to be accepted is a false understanding of history, and it lacks objectivity for the full consideration of what happened at the Battle of the Little Bighorn or any other event in American Indian history. This is a problem. For American Indian history to be truly understood, the Indian view of history needs to be studied from the Indian mind.

At of the site of the Battle of Tippecanoe is a park that commemorates the fight involving the whites and Indians. The green grass has grown over to camouflage the past, but the openness of the field hints of the major event near the river, where the lodges of Indians stood along the river's bank for more than a mile. On the other side of the open field, now a farmer's land, is the Prophet's Rock where Tenskwatawa went to pray, asking for power and guidance to help his brother Tecumseh in their endeavor to defeat the whites. I gazed upon this site one Saturday afternoon in November 2007, almost two hundred years after Tippecanoe. Studying the sandy earth covered with autumn's leaves, I thought of the coolness of that fateful morning and the cold mist hanging in the air when the Shawnees and other tribes met defeat. During winter's approach was not a good time to fight a war, as scores of warriors had traveled far to join the gathering army of many nations. No doubt the minds of the warriors were heavy with thoughts of their families far away, for these men had traveled to this place where the Tippecanoe and Wabash rivers meet to defeat the whites once and for all and to save their homelands. Part of me is Shawnee by blood, and I have relatives who fought on this battlefield. The Indians were shocked that the soldiers' bullets did not turn into sand, falling harmlessly to the ground, and their own blood now stained the ground, the earth. What alarmed them was that the whites' medicine was more powerful than the Prophet's. That day was not the day to fight. According to Native logic, not until the right time, when the Medicine Way of the Indian proved to be greater than the white men's bullets, could victory have been won. By nature's dichotomy, on that day two sides of different beliefs clashed and one side won over the other, but the conflict continued in other ways.

5

The Third Dimension of Physical and Metaphysical Reality

> My Brothers! The white people got some of our chiefs to sign a paper to give our lands to them but our chiefs did not do as we told them to do; they done wrong; we must do right. The agent tells us we must go away from the lands we live on—our homes, and the graves of our Fathers, and go over the big river [the Mississippi] among the bad Indians. When the agent tells me to go from my home, I hate him, because I love my home, and will not go from it.
>
> My Brothers! When the Great Spirit tells me to go with the white man, I go: but he tells me not to go. The white man says I shall go, and he will send people to make me go; but I have a rifle, and I have some powder and some lead. I say, we must not leave our homes and lands. If any of our people want to go west, we won't let them; and I tell them they are our enemies, and we will treat them so, for the Great Spirit will protect us.[1]

Indian agent Wiley Thompson took charge. On October 21, 1834, Thompson called the Seminole leaders to meet with him at the Seminole Agency at Fort King in Florida for the distribution of their annuity payment. With the annuity money the Seminoles bought powder and lead balls. Thompson called the Seminoles together to talk about removal. He tried to persuade them that the Creeks wanted them to live among them in the West as one people, as they used to be. Thompson found this a hard argument to make to the Seminoles, especially to Osceola. Outspoken and a proven warrior many times over, Osceola bristled at Thompson and other whites who wanted to remove his people from their Florida homeland. Osceola's reputation in war and medicine was well known. His credentials in medicine derived from the teaching of his elder friend Abeca, a renowned medicine maker who was also known as Sam Jones.[2]

This fateful meeting began at 11:00 a.m., as the bright yellow sun approached midday. Leaves of the oak trees had already fallen, marking the cycle of the seasons. Thompson reminded the Seminoles of their previous signing of the Treaty of Fort Gibson on March 28, 1833. A Seminole delegation of several leaders had been transported to visit a potential new homeland in Indian Territory, located west of the Mississippi River. American officials persuaded the delegation to sign a removal treaty. Thompson asked the Seminoles at Fort King several questions and pressed for their responses to support removal. He asked if they would accept the invitation of the Creeks in the West to live next to them in Indian Territory. The agent asked if they wanted cattle or money upon their arrival in the West. He wanted to know if the Seminoles would go by boat or travel over land. Last, Thompson wanted to know if they wanted their next annuity in money or in goods.

The Seminoles withdrew to talk among themselves and wished to meet with Thompson later, possibly the next day. As they discussed the situation, Osceola grew furious at the idea of giving up their homeland and being moved to some strange land in the West. In this moment of anger, he rallied the support of his fellow Seminoles with his speech above. Osceola shared the personal experience of rejecting the ways of the whites although he was part white.

In 1804 a young Muscogee woman gave birth to a bright young child. The child, who would one day be known as Osceola, was born in a cabin along the Chattahoochee River near present-day Tuskegee, Alabama.[3] Osceola was born in a red *tvlvn* (town) called Tallahassee, which supplied Red Stick warriors to fight and defend other *tvlvns*, while white *tvlvns* provided peace leaders and studied the ways of nature; the two categories of communities are described more fully later in this chapter. Young Osceola learned early in life to respect the Chattahoochee and all other waters as water represented one of the four elemental powers of the Muscogee-Seminole universe. In this way of the Muscogee people, Osceola learned the ancient ways. His elders told him creation stories, where they came from, and how the clans were formed. The oral tradition was central to all aspects of his education and obtaining knowledge of the past.

Osceola's town or *tvlvn* was across the river from the *tvlvn* "where the Panther people live," called *gatsa aboketa* in the Muscogee language, and the Panther Clan was renowned for their medicine making.[4] Young Osceola would learn much about the Medicine Way from the Panthers. He learned why medicine was important and why it should be respected.

In the Third Dimension of Indian-white relations, Osceola is on the left side of the equation with the other Seminoles who opposed removal and disagreed with agent Wiley Thompson. Osceola and others viewed the situation from a Native ethos. This way of seeing combined the physical and the metaphysical, as Osceola said the Great Spirit would help them.

A fundamental component of the clan system was that individuals in a given clan learned all they could about the strengths of their totem animal and endeavored to emulate these strengths. Among Osceola's people, individuals obtained their clan totem from their mother. Osceola's mother was of the Bird Clan, the second most important clan next to the Wind.[5] The Bird people were the overseers of the laws. They first made laws for their people and the community placed them in charge of enforcing these. The Birds were the first animals that the people saw when the Wind blew the mist away in the Muscogee origin story, which gave them the ability to see.

The Medicine Way includes all life, and it is imperative to attempt to understand this process of seeing. To begin with, the Third Dimension is characterized by the type of "seeing" described in chapter 2. For example, Black Elk's experience in which he heard voices and saw his Great Vision exemplifies this type of Native seeing. This reality involves most Native people who are close to their traditions, although we must take into consideration the role of John Neihardt, who wrote down Black Elk's vision, and the time and distance of recalling childhood experiences. Like most oral history interviews, Neihardt's transcription of Black Elk's words and the translation from Lakota into English provide ample opportunity for mistakes, misinterpretation, and embellishment. Despite these caveats, Black Elk's words as related by Neihardt are integral to helping us understand what Black Elk saw as important. Thus they help us begin to appreciate the fullness of the Third Dimension. To try to comprehend the Third Dimension all at once would only cause confusion; it is advisable to digest these words carefully in order to understand the process of seeing in this manner.

Writing from an American Indian perspective requires attempting to think in a way an Indian person might think. For this mental transition to occur, one must understand the sequence of the relationships of each person to each entity in this unique universe. This is the true reality of traditionally oriented Indian people.[6]

The universe rests in a delicate balance, always vulnerable to periodic changes.[7] As a part of the totality, called *Ibofanga* in the Muscogee Creek-Seminole language, Native beliefs resonate with nature for they are a part of the universe. Native beliefs hold that the universe is in balance, but Indian people believe also that all humans should try to be in balance within themselves and with the universe. As an example, a balanced life begins within each person. Every normal person knows right from wrong, good from evil, and light from dark. Nature's dichotomies offer other examples of opposites, and the struggle for balance is initially waged inside all of us.

Outside ourselves balance occurs within families, although it is possible at some points that this social unit may be in disagreement with its clan or society. In addition, personal balance in accord with family and clan or society may be in disharmony with the community. This can be resolved, if the right actions are taken. All social units must strive to work together. Personal and external balance is ideal when the momentum of this energy from all groups exists in perfect harmony and all is good.

From a cultural perspective, American Indians believe that there is a reason for the existence of all things. Furthermore, all things are related, and how these relationships form and develop involves a dedicated quest for harmony. But consider that in the United States and throughout Indian-white history, Indian people have been forced by mainstream influences and focused government programs to live and function in a non-Indian reality.[8] On a daily basis they live and work in the mainstream culture that has become second nature to them; it is almost predominant for many Indians. In essence they live in two different realities—one Indian and the other mainstream American. Yet most Americans do not realize this dual reality exists for Indian people. It bears repeating that all of this pertains to Indian people who are close to their Native traditions and values. Admittedly large numbers of Indian people have found the mainstream reality to be comfortable, and they are alienated from their tribal reality, since many have become urbanized and others are mixed-bloods who prefer the mainstream way. With due respect to the dangers of overgeneralizing, the point is that some American Indians no longer live in an Indian reality, while others may live in dual realities—Indian and white.[9]

Theoretically all societies must deal with change as a part of reality. For example, major change occurs when a community is moved to another location, as was the case for many southeastern groups during Andrew Jackson's Indian removal policy in the 1830s and 1840s. When faced with demographic and environmental change, people must maintain their beliefs through a set of values and preordained norms. Transporting these sets of values and cultural norms reestablishes communities as they strive to harmonize a balance with other communities that are different in values and norms.[10]

Cultures change normally through the social mobility of humans. Hence mobility acts as a catalyst for change over time, as Indians have adopted the horse, gun, bingo dauber, and other items from the white mainstream. The Indians' adaptability is a survival method for making their lives easier and making their economies more successful.

For the past twenty-five years or so, the history discipline has begun to listen to Indian people talking about their Native reality of the physical and metaphysical. This is progress, but the history discipline on the whole does not include this combined reality of the Indian world. Yet some historians who are not Indian have entertained the possibility of such an existence, like Calvin Martin and others mentioned in chapter 1. In this way, these few open-minded historians have begun to believe as Indians do. However, historians need not necessarily believe in the Medicine Way; they only need to understand it. At the same time it is fair to say that not all Native scholars write from the indigenous paradigm. This is the first required step toward understanding the left side of the Indian-white binary.

Reality to American Indians is an inclusive sense of one's natural environment and life experiences, as described in chapter 2.[11] Communalism is a sine qua non in Indian reality, as is the recognition of sociocultural relationships with all things. It is a holistic reality, and this is how Indian people understand their past. Thus an Indian Indian history of the Third Dimension is actually the First Dimension from their viewpoint. This reality contains episodes of ceremonies, positive or negative experiences, and memories shared via the oral tradition. Their history is their past reality, and the oral tradition allows the people to relive experiences so that in a sense these episodes are part of the present. This conception makes history, reality, and time all part of one another.

While the existence of the Third Dimension may appear philosophical to non-Indians, it is very real to Native peoples. Generally Indian people are practical in meeting the daily needs of life throughout their histories.[12] However, their practicality involves much more than the physical existence of all things. Common sense guides Indian thinking and actions, but this logic considers both physical and metaphysical concerns. The Native mind draws from both the conscious and subconscious in considering responses to issues of concern and for interpreting things that need to be explained.

Textbooks inform us that the history of the American experience began more than five hundred years ago when three tiny ships lost their way and ended up in this part of the world. Historians have recorded this affair as the "discovery" of the western hemisphere, disregarding the presence of some 15 to 20 million or more Native people in North America and South America. The journal of Christopher Columbus included descriptions of Native people who would later be called "Indians," then "American Indians" in the late 1800s.

Additional documents would be recorded of negotiations, laws, and general relations between these American Indians and Euroamericans. Writing Native history must involve archival research in order to consider seriously the depth of the Indian-white binary. By studying communities and their evolution, scholars can ascertain the developments, transitions, and catalysts that led to changes in American Indian history.[13] It is this "relationship" of the equation of Indian-European, or Indian-white relations, that now constitutes most of the historical literature written about American Indians, as emphasized in the last chapter. The remainder of the literature attempts to describe the life and history of American Indian groups. Academic historians are trained by graduate programs to research and examine the documents. But if the documents were produced by non-Indians years ago, they are also observations of only one side of the equation.

Unfortunately the early scholarship of Indian history produced descriptive narratives of American Indians that cast an image of the noble savage or wild savage, stereotypes perpetuated and amplified by the media and movie industry in more than four thousand movies. These stereotypes about American Indians, based on a dearth of truth and limited knowledge, have tainted the minds of most Americans and the rest of the world even as the United States celebrated in 1992 the European "founding" of the Americas.

Since the mid-1970s historical scholarship has been striving to unlock the inside story of Indian history from Native viewpoints. Scholars are starting to examine the Third Dimension and even more the Second Dimension, using mostly ethnohistorical methods to analyze and write Indian history.[14] In processing the idea of the Third Dimension, it is essential to realize that nature's laws and powers are forces greater than human forces. In our human environment, economic, religious, technological, institutional, ideological, and military forces have altered history.[15] The same can be said for Native history in the physical reality that exists. Upon realization of the great powers of the universe beyond the control of humans, Native people have

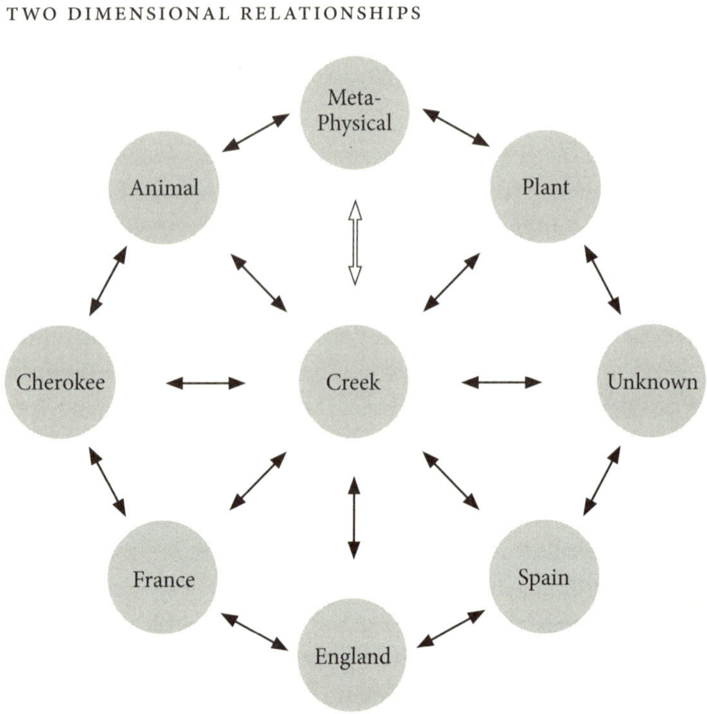

FIGURE 8. The Creek community and the other communities all have reciprocal relationships, except for the nonreciprocal relationship with metaphysical community.

integrated this understanding into their cultures. Attempts to translate this understanding have caused misinterpretation by non-Indians, who struggle with the significant amount of symbolism in the cultures of American Indians, such as the circle for the Circle of Life and the number four for the elemental powers of the earth, fire, water, and wind.[16]

Among the three dimensions introduced here, it is the Third Dimension (that is, the First Dimension to Native people) that is the most difficult to study. It is challenging to research, yet it reveals the inner gestalt of indigenous communities where abstract beings in the form of spirits and medicine power blend together with daily life.

The Third Dimension includes Indians as members of a group, community, or nation, and this is so complex that most in the mainstream fail to recognize even the limited perceptions of it that do pertain (see figure 8). Mainstream Americans are surrounded by nonhuman life and physical entities that have meaning to Indians and with which Native people try to communicate. How can this be true? Consider that in the mainstream, many people who have dogs, cats, and other animals will admit that they talk to their pets. The animals respond in their own ways, thereby establishing a reciprocal relationship as illustrated in the figure.

This left side of Indian-white history deals with the combined reality of social and cultural relations intertwined in a totality. Native people respond and think according to external forces beyond this physical reality that the mainstream believes is the world. It is from this combined physical and metaphysical reality that distinct tribal histories have evolved. Indians live in this sociocultural dual reality of relations, so how do we study this dimension that involves spiritualism?

Believing is essential for the existence of spirituality. Among the Athapaskan Indians, *nakhani* is a belief in the presence of many dangers in the woods. Hunters experienced *nakhani* as they traveled through the woods and had to deal with this unknown possibility from the metaphysical that was beyond their control.[17] In a similar way, rural Germans believe in spirits inhabiting the Black Forest, sailors accept mysterious ways of the seas, and many non-Indian cultures believe in at least some aspects of the metaphysical. In this view the greatest unknowns exist deep within the forest and in the crevices of our minds. In Native reality there is a place in the totality for the unknown as people seek more information for understanding these dark places. Among Indians we go to the elders, who are like libraries filled with knowledge or stories of experiences that help us to comprehend the dark unknown so that we will not be afraid of such things.

In regard to the Third Dimension, life becomes spiritual in a way that outsiders might call religious. This metaphysical influence affects the attitudes of an individual and an entire community, much like Christians believing in the Holy Ghost and like many people seeing the Virgin Mary in different parts of the world. But if the metaphysical experience is negative, then naturally individuals or communities seek release from that which holds power over them.[18]

In the quest of the hunter and the hunted, a person develops a relationship with the hunted animals.[19] This is the Medicine Way that has developed a set of clan totems and how Native people value plants and animals. For example, the Muscogee Creeks and Seminoles of the Southeast shared a common culture and core of values as the means for constituting their societies. Steeped in centuries of tradition, they transported this culture and set of values with them along the infamous Trail of Tears to Indian Territory (now Oklahoma) during the 1830s and 1840s. This ability to transport their infrastructure is called "moving fire," when a ceremonial ground is moved from an old ground to a new site. Fortunately the Creeks and Seminoles experienced a similar new homeland of green flora and humid summers with a similar climate. "Place" is important because the physical environment plays a large role in shaping culture and influencing human behavior. Hence the physical reality remained virtually the same, thus enabling the continuity of the metaphysical reality that they had known.

The old ways of medicine making usually depended on elders who wrote down formulas or drew pictures to pass vital information down to the next generation. This medicine knowledge represented a means of preservation, as others were taught about plants, herbs, and curing. Some medicine makers among the Cherokee adopted Sequoyah's written syllabary to use as a tool for their own means.

In the Cherokee cosmology there are seven levels above the horizon and another world below the surface. In the world below, springs of water and rivers are entrances to communities of other beings in physical and mythical form. Meanwhile the upper world, called *Galunlati* for "above everything," is referred to as the "seventh height." The above is the sacred visible day or night sky made of stone. Traditional Cherokees believe in great heavenly powers and a world of animals with special qualities, after which they named clans. The ancestors of the animals had considerable powers, and there were those who lived on the earth and those who lived above with the Thunder powers.[20]

In writing about the Cherokees James Mooney noted that "Cherokee myths may be roughly classified as sacred myths, animal stories, local legends, and historical traditions. To the first class belong the genesis stories, dealing with the creation of the world, the nature of heavenly bodies and elemental forces, the origin of life and death, the spirit world and the invisible beings, the ancient monsters, and the hero-gods."[21]

The ideology of the Tewa pueblo of New Mexico stressed the importance of maintaining balance and harmony within as well as between the two worlds of the natural and supernatural.[22] To live traditionally meant keeping the two realities in perspective, so as not to become overwhelmed by one or the other. This meant walking the good road of life and keeping everything in an indigenous context as the main purpose in life. Daily rituals, cultural norms, and ceremonies provided a sense of order and illustrated how things were done and why. The Medicine Way held answers to questions and concerns that one might have.

Within this sphere of Native reality is the space or homeland of the community.[23] That homeland means "space" is relevant to an Indian understanding of indigenous life in a traditional sense, and this is possibly common to other indigenous peoples in their perceptions of space and homeland.[24] Within indigenous space, the physical and metaphysical exist jointly, and space and place become the same as people adapt to the natural environment within the Natural Democracy diaspora. It may help to borrow from Henri Lefebvre's *The Production of Space*, in which he theorizes that geographic space is not inactive but is trialectical, involving one's understanding of mental space, social space, and physical space such as the environment.[25]

Multiple approaches can be applied while recognizing the need to draw from other disciplines to research data for documenting this "Native existence." By using anthropology, sociology, literature, linguistics, and other scholarly approaches we can begin to understand this Native side of Indian history. Naturally the Indian side of history is more complicated than the mainstream view of history because of the combined physical and metaphysical. The evidence for the Indian reality is less tangible, since the metaphysical dimension is difficult to document with physical evidence. One would have to have faith as well to believe such evidence. For example, Christians are led to believe in the Holy Ghost of Jesus who spoke to Mary, according to the Bible. Hence, why should the White Buffalo not be able to talk to two starving Lakota warriors hunting to feed their people? Why can we not accept an animal or plant talking to a Native person? How societies recall such critical experiences, according to Paul Connerton in *How Societies Remember*, is a cultural experience of social group participation and practices that "silt" into a human consciousness.[26]

One theory of animism suggests there are divisions in the Native world. One half concerns itself with after death, when the souls of each being continue a spiritual existence into the next life that includes animals. The second half consists of spiritual existences of the souls in a present reality of powerful deities of various ranks.[27] For example, Richard Brown heard the voices of the little people, and Black Elk heard the voices of the grandfathers.

In the Native languages, "the Iroquoiah *orenda*, the Central Algonquian *manitou* and the Siouan *wakanda*" are words that convey the spiritual presence of the metaphysical world in Indian life.[28] This spiritual presence resides inside and outside the minds of Native people. Indigenous people are cognizant of such presence, yet spirits can present themselves anytime and anywhere.

As shown in figure 9 a community like the Creeks desired to be in constant communication with the metaphysical, but the spiritual world was irregularly connected to the Creek community. The binary system of a community having reciprocal relationships with every community, like the animal community and the plant community, does not exist with the metaphysical. Similarly, those people who see the Virgin Mary can only see this phenomenon when it wants to be seen.

In Native life, tribes have worked out systematic interpretations of their worlds. This threshold is where nature and Native societies

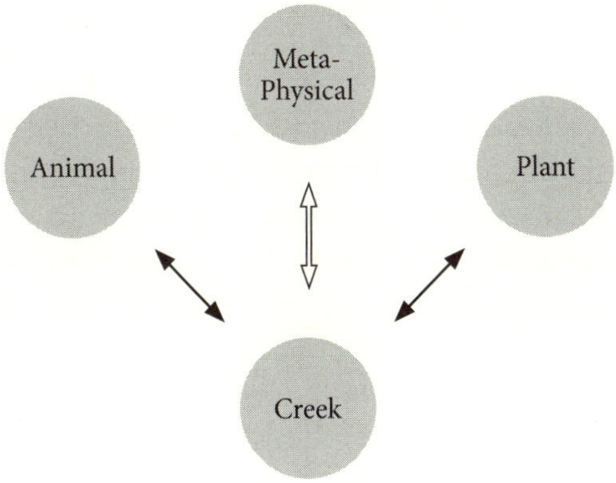

FIGURE 9. The Creek community does not have reciprocal relations with the metaphysical community but has reciprocal relations with the animal and plant communities.

intersect and interpretation gives a sense of order to understanding life as the indigenous know it. This Native intellect continues to teach each new generation as long as the community believes it and accepts that it is their own ethos of the natural world.[29]

The traditional reality includes the lives of plants and animals and the existence of spirits and little people. Little people exist in the worldview of the Muscogee Creeks, Seminoles, Cherokees, Choctaws, and many other tribes.[30] They are analogous to the gremlins of servicemen during World War II and the leprechauns of the Irish. Mysterious in nature, they are magical, they are keepers of medicinal knowledge, and sometimes they are tricksters. Little people are feared, for sometimes they have seduced children into following them to play. The children were often returned to their parents as the little people showed them the way home, but the children were different after their visit in the metaphysical world. The same can be said about Richard Brown and his death. He was received by the little people. As a boy, Osceola knew about the little people and their powers and that he should respect them. He wanted them as allies who would not harm him.

The Crows believe in little people, and their oral tradition includes a story of the "Lost Boy and the Little People." On a certain hill in their homeland stands "the Medicine-rock of the Crows, sacred as the home of the Little-people, the Dwarfs, who made the stone arrow-points."[31] Over the years the little people raised the child into a tall young warrior who, using sacred arrow points, hunted elk for them to eat. The little people gave him super strength so that he would not tire in bringing home the elk he killed as he disappeared into the rock to join his little people parents. Finally, it was time for the young warrior to return to his original people.

The Lost Boy, now a young warrior, joined his real parents and the rest of the band. He told his story: "I have been living with the Little-people in the Rock. I do not know when I went there to live with them. Until four suns ago I believed that the Little-man and the Little-woman were my father and mother. They have told me that they found me on the mountain and carried me into the Rock where they live. The War-eagle had told them I would come to the mountain, so that the Little-people had been expecting me to come and live with them. Their language is Absanakee. They were kind, and I grew up happy and contented."[32]

The Seneca tell a story about a time when their people were starving, and this incident involved little people. The Seneca hunted along a long trail and found a place where deer came to a salt lick. The Seneca hunters waited in the trees, and they killed many deer. They killed so many that they had to throw away the meat in order to save the skins for leather. The story goes on: "There was more meat than the wolves could eat, but the hunters shot many deer every day, until no more came. The hunters went on carrying great rolls of deerskin, which were very heavy, and said: 'Our wigwams will see us no more. We shall starve, and the deerskins will never be used.' They sat by a great rock. One of the hunters hit the rock with a stick, and a little man appeared. The little one said: 'You are starving because you killed and did not eat. You fed the wolves; now the wolves will feed on you. We have driven the deer to another forest, where they may live and be found by other hunters. You were selfish. You wanted all the deerskins in the forest. You were not wise.'"[33]

In Osceola's Seminole world, the real and surreal were the same. Medicine power was a part of daily life. He learned from Abeca, a Seminole medicine maker, how to use it and how to respect it as well. In this existence the differences between humans and animals become blurred. Both humans and animals have spirits, therefore the people have developed respect for the animals and the natural environment.[34]

Among the northern Athapaskans, the people believe in a multiple world of spirits that influence people's lives on a daily basis. Such influence affects the people's future, and spirits are everywhere. A spiritual relationship among animals and the Athapaskans includes fire, wind, and rivers. A so-called land of spirits or land of the dead is believed to exist as the next life, where both human and nonhuman spirits dwell, with the latter being more numerous.

Within such an order of life, Native people made inclusive adjustments when new entities and other people became a part of their world. The complex spiritual order of humans and animals was flexible due to continual adaptation in Indian-Indian relations before Columbus. As Native America absorbed early European explorers, travelers, and traders, their ideas and objects became a part of the Third Dimension. But this Indianization of absorbing settlers began to reinvent itself as more whites landed on the eastern shores; instead, the reverse occurred, as Indians became more like the strangers via assimilation.

In trying to understand and re-create historic reality we are required to think in that historic reality as much as possible. Hence empirical evidence must include other forms of historical evidence. Moreover, we should think about history as Native peoples would have interpreted their experiences and what was happening in their lifetimes.[35]

In thinking about Indian history in the Medicine Way, understanding relationships within the Indian world becomes imperative. This task is where history as a linear discipline falls short. Other academic disciplines such as social anthropology become essential for constructing the historical memory of Indian metaphysical relationships with nonhuman entities. By this method, the indigenous past and present can be understood in a realistic sense.[36] Learning about community and society is essential for understanding Indian people. Paul Connerton's work on collective memory and identifying with common clothing, mannerisms, and social practices is helpful to illustrate this point. The Medicine Way of American Indian history identifies certain elements about American Indian life and describes a special approach in conceptualizing Indian history. A reconceptualization of American Indian history from a cross-disciplinary methodology and an uncustomary theoretical analysis needs to be risked. This kind of indigenous logic becomes natural and has slowly manifested itself against the conservatism of the history discipline, which relies on interpreting written documents.

However, historians are more visionary than we would probably like to be considered. We see and store mental images of objects, documents, and the works of other scholars in our subconscious. As interpreters of the past, we take clues from written documents and other visual materials to paint a picture in our subconscious as we translate this into the linear form of the written word. We would improve our portrayal of Indian history if we could convince our readers to actualize the past. In considering a trading interaction between an Indian and a Virginia colonist, for example, one should ask a series of questions: What kind of clothes did they wear? What was the value of money then? What was the trade vocabulary they used for bartering? This would be an anticipated step toward reaching the threshold of the Third Dimension's indigenous context. The next step would be to accept axiomatically the spiritual realm of being Indian.

Generally non-Indians have the extra challenge of understanding the historic realities of Indian groups as they differ from tribe to tribe. The primary objective was to adapt new cultural items but to retain one's primal identity. Added to this complication is the "altering state" of Indian reality during the imposed course of "assimilation" into the white mainstream. For instance, Indian reality shifted somewhat as Indian children attended missionary and government boarding schools or as Native people were Christianized. In both cases the space defining one's identity absorbed a limited amount of external influence from boarding school teachers and missionaries.

What constitutes an Indian reality is the ethos of each tribe or Native community and what the people believe is important. For example, at the Battle of the Little Bighorn, no soldiers survived at Custer's last stand. Many readers of this history therefore assume that in this engagement of Lakotas and Cheyennes against whites, no soldiers survived. However, the Lakota leader Sitting Bull instructed his warriors to allow Captain Frederick Benteen's and Major Marcus Reno's men to live, because all life was precious, even the lives of the enemy. Though in war lives are taken as a standard, the door was left open for the soldiers to understand the Native viewpoint. Hence in the larger picture from Sitting Bull's perspective, a greater experience of Indian-white relations was occurring, in which Indians and whites were learning to live together on the plains from then on.

Respect and responsibility are imperative values in Indian society. Examining tribal values and environmental conditions can help us to understand Indian history and the Native viewpoint in the Third Dimension paradigm. This approach means focusing on indigenous reality while relaxing empiricist tendencies. This reality must be analyzed and defined according to careful understanding of a people, their language, and their culture during a particular period. As scholars try to be objective in accounting for all the factors influencing the shaping of history, they nonetheless are subject to their biased conscious or subconscious interpretation of history.[37] To compensate for this possible imbalance, we need to research and consider the various perspectives of the individuals involved. Thus challenging inherent biases through carefully researching and considering various perspectives is a critical component of the scholarly historical endeavor.

Understanding the social structure of Native groups reveals the relevance of connectedness. For example, genealogically studying the relatives of a person tells us if this person had a brother or a cousin who went into battle with a well-known leader. Do we know the brothers of the renowned Sitting Bull or his first cousins? Kinship matters. Furthermore, knowing the members of the household of Sitting Bull or Tecumseh or any other notable Indian person may be more pertinent than we may realize as we begin to imagine and reconstruct a tribal community using Medicine Way pedagogy. Writing Indian history involves knowing the family tree of individuals as much as possible.[38] Being Indian is being connected to community, and how one is related to whom is part of contextualizing Native history.

Within the family system of relationships are varying degrees of power, including medicine power and political power. Medicine power consists of knowledge of herbal cures and of metaphysical forces. Political power involves the persuasion of relations, especially elders. Clan mothers and grandfathers wield a considerable amount of influence within an indigenous community; thus young aspiring Native leaders must work hard to gain the elders' support. The actions of elders influence both a community's actions and its internal interactions. An understanding of these systems of political support and kinship offers insight into the central role of persuasion and the power it has in historical events.[39]

Among eastern woodland Indians, one's clan defined one's role in the community. Ethnologist John Swanton listed among the Muscogee Creeks a clan system consisting of Wind, Deer, Tiger (Panther), Bear, Bird, Raccoon, Alligator, and *aktayatco* (possibly water moccasin) clans, according to totem groupings. The Creek clans were also divided up into two moieties or divisions: red towns and white towns (*tvlvns*).[40] The system of clans varies in each *tvlvn*. Historic tvlvns among the Creeks and Seminoles, such as Okmulgee, Coweta, or Tulsa in Oklahoma, consisted of several clans, designating the importance to the people of their animal and plant kin.

Anthropologist George Murdock studied 250 societies in his noted book *Social Structure*. Murdock defined a clan as being based on four conditions: a clan "must be based explicitly on a unilinear rule of descent which unites its central core of members. A group must have residential unity. . . . [And] the group must exhibit actual social integration. . . . There must be a positive group sentiment, and in particular the in-marrying spouses must be recognized as an integral part of the membership."[41]

In a society where Native leaders and individuals belong to clans, kinship relations are extremely important. These relationships enter into the logic of each person in the community. Kinship has been vastly underused by historians as a category of analysis and as a means to gather the rationale for Indian actions.[42] This means that historians and other scholars can learn from disciplines such as social anthropology, the branch of anthropology that best understands kinship from a western point of view.[43]

By using ethnographic information, one can explore clan relationships in Native communities. The clan kinship system is at the heart of Native identity and is the structure around which traditional systems of government and leadership function.[44] Clan totems have a spiritual presence connecting individuals to the metaphysical. Thus, spirituality is the elemental quality that bonds the infrastructure together.

Among the Muscogee Creeks there are four external elements—fire (*tot kv*), water (*ue wv*), earth (*ekv nv*), and wind (*ho tv le*). These external elements interact, determining all life (*hesaketv*) within all (*om vl kv*) the totality (*Ibofanga*), meaning including all of the known and unknown entities, according to the Muscogee Creeks and Seminoles. The way in which the external elements have been arranged by *Hesaketvmese* (Master of Breath) is through medicine (*heleswv*)—the Medicine Way. Part of the way is communicating with Hesaketvmese by calling or praying or singing to the four directions north (*kv svp po fv*), east (*hv sos sv*), south (*le kot ho fv*), and west (*hv sak lat kv*).

According to the Cherokees, east is red, and this direction symbolizes strength and war. North is colored blue with defeat and unhappiness. West is black, and it symbolizes death. South is white, and it represents peace, gentleness, and sacred power. The Thunder powers (twin brothers) helped in healing and driving back the Black Man of the west who presided over the land of the dead. The Blue Man of the north was involved "with Frost, Cold, and the 'cold-blooded' animals, such as snakes, fishes, and turtles, while the peaceful white Man of the south had primary associations with Old White One, the ancient healing power and warmth of the sacred fire."[45] These elements defined the physical context of the Cherokees' natural surroundings and acknowledged the powers of earthly and supernatural beings.

Among the Cherokees, dreams and visions communicate negative and positive powers. Dreams are insightful signs, indicating parts of the Cherokee ethos of the earth and universe. Medicine makers are called upon to interpret the signs as new knowledge or that which had been forgotten. Sometimes months or years of dreaming have occurred to reveal insightful information or knowledge.[46] The Cherokee world is intricately conceptualized and stored in the mythology of the people.[47]

Cherokee cosmology is based on the relations of power present in all things. To the Cherokees all things are real, with no distinction between surreal and real.[48] This understanding of the world avoids the confusion between myth and reality such that there is just one reality.

It is imperative to keep in mind that this Medicine Way of life is in constant association with the natural environment. Long ago the natural environment was so immense that the Muscogees were in awe of the plethora of flora and fauna. Being intimidated and overwhelmed by the environment, the people observed and learned from the natural surroundings of plant and animal life. The plant and animal worlds provided food and shelter, compelling the people to respect and depend on their natural environment. The Muscogee Creeks and Seminoles then acknowledged a relationship with each other, just as they formed alliances with the plant and animal worlds. Other Indian nations like the Cherokees, Choctaws, Euchees, Shawnees, and Chickasaws would be included in their universe of sociocultural relations. This was their historical or physical reality in the traditional sense, but this was only part of the physical-metaphysical tandem.[49]

This model of the Muscogee Creeks and Seminoles of Oklahoma is proposed to be common to many Indian nations of North America, but with due respect to the fact that it is not appropriate for all Native groups. This internal-external model helps to demonstrate the Third Dimension of American Indian history, purporting to provide an indigenous perspective, the left side of the Indian-white historical equation.

In researching the Third Dimension of the indigenous consciousness and subconsciousness, a scholar must employ cross-cultural analysis. In using this joint method, the usual objective is to study the interaction of two cultures acting on the same issue or involved in the same historical event. However, the scholar must push onward and use the cross-cultural analysis to compare the internal communal life and societal infrastructure. This recommended approach is viable since many scholars learn about other cultures by comparing the other culture with their own.

In the end, examining the Third Dimension allows new theories and methodologies that make sense to Indian people and that must therefore be applied in order to restore a balance to the equation of the history of Indian-white relations, where two different cultures and two dissimilar mindsets intersect. This left side of Indian-white relations may seem radical to some mainstream scholars, unworkable to skeptics, or inappropriate to mainstream historians and scholars of the dominant academy, but new ways have to be tested to obtain a fuller understanding of the complexity of American Indian life and historic reality. This approach promises to reconstruct American Indian history properly and for it to be written in a comprehensible manner for both non-Indians and Indian people to understand. At the same time, in this generation of scholarship and perhaps in the future, this type of theoretical approach promises to deconstruct previous notions and former understandings of American Indian history as observational history from an external perspective.

History from an external perspective is not acceptable to Indian people. It is the history of non-Indians writing about themselves regarding Indian-white relations, and it is about how mainstream scholars see history. For Indian people, history (and even the word *history* is subject to much discussion) is a continuum of life consisting of sociocultural relations within a universal system of flora, fauna, human and physical elements, and metaphysical beings or spirits.

What is insightful about events and experiences in the Medicine Way is that they reveal knowledge about the truth and the reality of the community. At the same time, cultural traditions and values have defined and shaped this indigenous genre of interpretation and the perspective of the people in the community. In brief, the history is a collective experience recorded in many stories of each Native group.

The more complex physical-metaphysical experiences call for greater interpretations by those able to do this. The "meanings" of extraordinary experiences are interpreted by knowledgeable and gifted individuals in a community, such as prophets, seers, and fortunetellers, or *o wa letv*, as the Seminoles and Creeks call such persons. For example, Black Elk was sick as a young boy due to his Great Vision, and he had visited the metaphysical world. Whirlwind Chaser, a powerful medicine person, cured Black Elk to bring him back to the present work, and he told Black Elk's father, "Your boy there is sitting in a sacred manner. I do not know what it is [yet], but there is something special for him to do, for just as I came in I could see a power like a light all through his body."[50]

The proper vehicle for conveying this type of history is through oral tradition. Story is powerful among Indians. It is empowered by the people who give it life and a spirit as it is told by each generation, and the breath produced for each word is energized with a spirit that creates visions and paints events in the minds of the listeners.

Among the Muscogee Creeks and Seminoles, the clan animals are highly regarded for their medicine power and supernatural abilities. The late Willie Lena, a medicine maker, said his father, a medicine person, understood the power of the metaphysical reality that is so much a part of his people. Individuals like the Lenas and Whirlwind Chaser are gatekeepers to the metaphysics of the Third Dimension. They are the ones to whom people go for help when medicine power is against them and for cures due to illnesses. Their vast earth knowledge has helped their people for centuries.

In the Muscogee Creek–Seminole world many animals and plants are part of the Third Dimension. For Native people there are similar animals, plants, and spiritual beings. All are created by the Great Creator, who knows the purpose for each being; Native people try to understand this purpose. Within each being there is a spirit and a power that must be understood in Native people's quest for knowledge. For each being there is a part of the holistic balance of the world and the universe, and this is the Third Dimension of Indians. For

Indian people, however, logically this would be the First Dimension, since this is the traditional reality in which they live.

Indian history can no longer rest as a white interpretation. All scholars writing Indian history now need to be incorporating the Third Dimension into their writings. Calvin Martin concluded: "We should quit deluding ourselves about the significance and explanatory value of such history, for it is essentially White history: White reality, White thoughtworld."[51]

Martin concluded further:

> White history (excuse the oversimplification)—i.e. retrospective White reality, retrospective White thoughtworld, or even the straightforward repetition of reality as perceived and rendered by White observers over the centuries—must be measured against an Indian history (another forgivable generalization)—an Indian reality, and Indian thoughtworld, as these may be reconstructed using ethnographic analogy. Historians are now in a position to rewrite virtually the entire pageant of Indian-White relations from the perspective of another, equally valid, equally serious reality—an American Indian reality—using the ethnohistorical approach. . . . One begins by cultivating an appreciation for the metaphysics of the Native American lifeway.[52]

Furthermore, according to Martin, "to ignore the Indian thoughtworld is to continue writing about ourselves to ourselves. Indian-White history thus becomes White history because it expresses our or our forebears' perception of reality."[53] Calvin Martin's experience of the Third Dimension and his understanding of it has advanced the understanding of Native people. I hope more historians and scholars will do the same.

As American Indians increasingly assimilate into mainstream America, the Third Dimension becomes less like its traditional past as it is reinvented with each generation. This is natural change and enables Native people to carry their new traditions forward as they continue to borrow culture from other peoples. The Third Dimension alters with the generations of Native people as they change their lifestyles, perspectives, beliefs, and values. But to understand the Indian past, the Third Dimension holds the dual realities of the physical and metaphysical in balance. Though it bears repeating that each Native community has its own worldview of the Third Dimension, recognizing that an indigenous paradigm exists is a necessary introduction to the Medicine Way of Indian history.

In the bright late morning that day in 1835 Osceola drew strength from his Bird Clan and the metaphysical knowledge of his people's traditions. At the site where Fort King once stood among the tall oak trees and shrubs one can sense the presence of Seminole life and their beliefs. The sandy colored earth is the same ground where Osceola stood and fought. As I stood on a spring day in May on the ground where Fort King once was, I felt that Seminole part of my heritage connect to the earth. My beliefs in the supernatural are the same as Osceola's. My people's original ceremonial ground is located about four miles northeast of old Fort King. The metaphysical side of life in the Third Dimension remains as a strength to be called upon. As a Seminole, Osceola called upon this medicine in war on a regular basis to empower and protect himself and others in battle.

6

A Cross-Cultural Bridge of Understanding

> Many days later, the Twins heard a voice from the ground. It was from the little man with the red head. "Do not scorn me because I am so small," he said. "I can and want to help you. Put your hands down on the ground and spit into them four times. Now close your fists, saving the spit until you come to the Big Water. There you can wash off the spit." The Twins did exactly as they were told, and after thanking the little man with the red head, they again began their travel. Soon the canyon walls that smashed together loomed ahead of them. . . . They were making no forward progress, so they sang songs taught them by their mother and Spider Woman. They prayed over and over again. When they opened their eyes, a beautiful Rainbow appeared, creating a large bridge for them to cross over the Grand Canyon of the Colorado River. . . . The Twins walked down to the beach to the edge of the water and washed the spit off their hands, singing and praying at the same time. Behold! The Rainbow appeared again! A long Rainbow Bridge stretched before them from the beach to the Turquoise House. Onto the Rainbow Bridge the Twins raced happily, to find their two fathers, the Sun-God and the Water-God, who welcomed them in the Turquoise House at the end of the Rainbow Bridge.[1]

The story comes from the Navajo, who have a legend that describes Rainbow Bridge in Navajoland, where Utah meets Arizona. The story begins a very long time ago when the goddess called First Woman and the Sun-God had a child after his golden rays shone on her. Then the Sun-God traveled to the West. One day not long afterward, as First Woman slept, drops of rain fell on her from the Water-God high above and she had a second child. The child searched but could not find his father. The blessed children were called the Twins, and they looked for their fathers together. A Great Giant threatened First Woman, and she hid the Twins until they grew up. At this point she sent them westward to find their fathers. Along the way the Twins met Spider Woman, who told them about dangers ahead and what to do. She instructed them to pray, sing, and be sincere. The Twins found their fathers at the Turquoise House, waiting for them on the other side of the Rainbow Bridge.

Imagine the bridge and how useful it was to help the Twins to find their dads waiting for them at the Turquoise House. As they crossed the bridge, they found comfort and home.

Far off the highway in extreme northern Arizona stands the Rainbow Bridge, just inside Utah. This bridge of sandstone spans 275 feet, tunneled out by a branch of the Colorado River over millennia. The top of the archway stands at a height of 290 feet, almost as high as the Statute of Liberty. At the top the bridge is 42 feet thick and 33 feet wide.

For hundreds of years Rainbow Bridge remained a secret among the ancestral Pueblo people who lived nearby and later the Paiutes and Navajos. Only local Native people knew of it, since it was in a remote area. In 1909 the rest of the world learned about the mysterious bridge in the desert Southwest. Theodore Roosevelt made the pilgrimage to visit the natural wonder in 1913: "Next morning early we started our toilsome return trip. The pony trail led under the arch. Along this the Ute drove our pack-mules, and as I followed him I noticed that the Navajo rode around outside. His creed bade him never pass under an arch. This great natural bridge, so recently 'discovered' by white men, has for ages been known to the Indians."[2]

Roosevelt's description is more of an experience than an event. He stood before the great rock arch viewing it, and he passed beneath it. As he noted, the Navajo guide respected the sacred bridge and avoided riding directly underneath it. Roosevelt was in Indian Country, surrounded by nature's setting of canyon and rocks and water. He made no attempt to cross nature's bridge, which was not of course constructed as a crossing. Many people likewise choose not to cross cultural bridges.

Metaphorically the Indian-white binary acts as a bridge, if one can understand how it works. In light of this dialogue, I propose regarding the binary as a cross-cultural bridge of understanding. Like all real bridges, it needs to be maintained and refined so that it can be used. Bridges have purposes, and the intention of this one is to reach the Third Dimension of Native reality and ethos.

One's belief system is important, but it can also obstruct the mind of mainstream scholars grappling with ethnocentrism. Among the basic differences between Indians and mainstream Americans are religious beliefs, although Native people have been more accepting of Christianity than whites have been of Native belief systems. Why?

Wooden Leg, a warrior among the Northern Cheyenne, described the influence of Christianity and its impact on him personally:

> I was baptized by the priest at the Tongue River mission when I was almost fifty years old. My wife and our two daughters were baptized too. I think the white people pray to the same Great Medicine we do in our old Cheyenne way. I do not go often to the church, but I go sometimes. I think the white church people are good, but I do not believe all of the stories they tell about what happened a long time ago. The way they tell us, all of the good people in the old times were white people. I am glad to have the white man churches among us, but I feel more satisfied when I make prayers in the way I was taught to make them. My heart is much more contented when I sit alone with my medicine pipe and talk with the Great Medicine about whatever may be troubling me.[3]

Among Indians a Medicine Way of life consists of both realism and surrealism. The combination presents problems for mainstream skeptics. The exclusive nature of the mainstream ethos goes against the Indian logic of inclusivity, which involves and incorporates other cultural ways and ideas. Homi Bhabha, in *The Location of Culture*, has described the liminal space of hybridity where Native people are willing to risk their sacred beliefs to include Christianity.[4] While most Christians refuse to see Native beliefs as equal to Christianity, some have accepted the Medicine Way, like Daniel Boone, who became a Shawnee and learned to live and think like them.

The struggle continues between the old Medicine Way of Indians and conversion to Christianity. In the late nineteenth century and early decades of the twentieth century, missionaries introduced at least twenty-two major Christian denominations to Indians. The conversion experience of many Native people initially presented a challenge for the individual and to the tribal community because there were many who still believed in the old ways. On an individual basis, people have decided to believe in one way or the other and even to believe in both the Medicine Way and Christianity. Wooden Leg, for example, subscribed to both. In this bicultural situation, to understand Wooden Leg's inclusion of Christianity with his traditional belief system requires transdisciplinary analysis of history, anthropology, and religious studies.

Wooden Leg's willingness to convert to Christianity while still retaining some doubts is the experience of many Native people. The strongest area of belief is what guides one's life. To take on another person's belief system is to be open-minded, as in mainstream academics being open to the Medicine Way of Indian history. Such a paradigm shift to accept an indigenous paradigm does not disempower mainstream expertise, as Michel Foucault might argue in his power/knowledge discourse. Foucault's concept of self-empowerment through building structures and exercising authority over others who have no institutional structure presents an adversarial situation. His model for power derives from discourse—and thus the authority to determine and control discourse. Rather, the Medicine Way is its own interpretation of power that goes beyond human self-produced authority, for its structure is the natural order of the environment. From the perspective of non-Indians, bicultural Indians with two religions may seem to have complicated their lives, and mainstream observers often think the Native religion should be renounced. This is not always so with Native people, who can practice two religions simultaneously. To Native people who are bireligious, this is not a dilemma. It is a problem only for outsiders since Christian beliefs call for only one way to worship.

While some Natives have adopted Christianity alongside their Native religion, they may also interpret Christianity in their own way, or they may view the two religions as the same. By a similar route, to help historians and other mainstream Americans to understand the Third Dimension, historians and other mainstream Americans seeking to understand the Third Dimension should become indigenously inclusive in their thinking and utilize the analytical tools of other academic disciplines. Transdisciplinary methodology is the combination of two or more academic disciplines for usage in analyzing research data to produce a new concept. The example of holding two sets of religious beliefs demonstrates the combination of history and anthropology to produce ethnohistory, which has been used by many scholars who study indigenous peoples. In addition, religious studies and environmental history are applicable to produce an analysis of Native spirituality and sacred sites, which serve as germane parts of Indian reality.

Anthropologist Rene Gadacz noted that "some scholars emphasize that ethnohistory is not a discipline but a method and technique. Others suggest that ethnohistory is indeed a discipline—one wherein various explanatory approaches and methods of 'scientific analysis' are more or less applicable. In fact, the scientific approach looked at this way seems to provide for a sort of methodological 'carte blanche.'"[5] Most important, ethnohistory is an approach to studying Native people in a broader way with a multilayered interpretation of research data, which is mandatory in realizing the Indian paradigm and its longevity.

As early as 1909 anthropologists used the term *ethnohistorical* in reference to written documents to supplement archaeological data in reconstructing a prehistoric culture.[6] This may have been the birth of the concept of ethnohistory, although it took more than two decades for it to emerge as a means of writing about Indian culture and history. Ethnohistory is the best research tool thus far to understand the Medicine Way of the Third Dimension.

Anthropologist William Fenton noted that "ethnohistory seems to be an approach and not a discipline—a way of getting at certain problems in culture history . . . that gives unity to the history of an American Indian tribe."[7] According to James Axtell, "a consensual definition of ethnohistory might be the use of historical methods and materials to gain knowledge of the nature and causes of change in a culture defined by ethnological concepts and categories."[8] Ethnohistorical evidence can be overlooked, yet it has much to offer in studying Native peoples due to its dual approaches.[9]

In order to analyze and write American Indian history from an "inside to outside" perspective, a cross-cultural analytical approach is suggested as the best means. Certainly a transdisciplinary methodology needs to be employed in order to present a fuller picture of Indian reality. Academics need to reconstruct a Native reality for a tribal community or reconstruct the life of an Indian person in that individual's reality. Understanding the sociocultural infrastructure and obtaining the essential methodological tools are imperative to reconstructing Native historical communities and recovering the indigenous ethos of the past.

Writing American Indian history for non-Indians also requires new definitions for "history" and the process of historicism.[10] The current mainstream definition of history applies to history written "about" Native peoples, whereas American Indian history from a Native point of view necessitates a definition of its own. Such a definition should be in the context of the indigenous ethos. However, in order to approach this subject with success, the complexity of the history of Indian-white relations needs to be addressed again briefly for a basis of dialogue to avoid misinterpretation and presumption. It is best at this point to discuss Indian history in the context of the Second Dimension of Indian-white relations.[11]

In the history discipline, events are the actions of human beings, individually, in groups, or in masses. Anthropology, on the other hand, focuses primarily on culture, with particular emphasis on its development over time. History involves researching documents and interpreting them with analysis. Anthropologists visit communities and study them for several months or years to collect data and analyze their field notes.

Whether or not scholars possess the ability to gain expertise in more than one discipline, however, is the burden of the scholar who wants a fuller understanding of American Indian history. In short, conventional methods of the history discipline alone are inadequate in constructing the Medicine Way of Indian history. For now the focus is on addressing the engagement of Indian-white relations as a model. With this approach in mind, the Indian-white model can be altered to Indian-Hispanic relations, Indian-African American relations, or Indian-Indian relations, such as Crow-Lakota or any tribe-tribe relations.

It would seem only logical to comprehend the culture of a people more fully before writing a history about them. In analyzing the Battle of the Little Bighorn of 1876, for example, it would seem prudent to take time to comprehend Lakota-U.S. military relations from both points of view, as well as their cultural foundations. In other similar situations the same need beckons new methods of analysis. The Little Bighorn event was both a victory and a massacre, depending on one's point of view. That landmark event has garnered much attention, compelling scholars from various disciplines to study this battle. In the end anyone interested in the event would likely read the literature produced by scholars from various disciplines. Because both Indians and whites participated as central actors in this historical event, it is pertinent to understand all of the cultures involved for cross-cultural comparison and analysis.

As the Cheyennes were also involved, the situation became more complex with the addition of Cheyenne-U.S. military relations. Yet what about Cheyenne-Lakota relations, as both groups were on the same side against Custer and the Seventh Cavalry? The same analogy can be made for Wooden Leg and other Native people who converted to Christianity, and some added a third religion, like the Native American Church with its usage of peyote.

In examining multiple relationships in a historical incident, the historian should be considering broader analytical approaches: "Lucien Febvre and Marc Bloch sought to create a historical discipline that would bring together geography, economics, sociology, psychology, anthropology, philology, and any other relevant human or natural science in order to produce a total picture of past societies, a picture that would relate all the forces at work into an interacting hierarchy."[12] This multidisciplinary approach would seem plausible for Indian history with an emphasis on studying relationships. By not taking into account the full picture, the neglectful scholar has implemented a biased history. Jack Forbes noted that "it would seem that American historians discriminate against the native American, the Indian, by failing to escape from their European past and what some people might call their 'conqueror-consciousness.' They have largely failed to realize that a history of America, properly so-called, is a history of America from America's beginnings, not from the beginnings of the European conquest."[13]

In response to the past historiography of the white conqueror writing American Indian history in the early decades of the twentieth century from this monolithic perspective, Robert Berkhofer issued a new challenge to future scholars. "Even the meaning of the phrase 'American Indian history' shows the dilemmas of cross-cultural interpretation," observed Berkhofer, and "the words *American*, *Indian*, and *history* are all non-Indian in origin, and so the conceptions behind those words that designate the very subject matter of what we seek to understand are grounded in mainstream American thinking and its larger context in Western civilization. Each of the words has its own history and a cultural context that is basic to its conceptualization and understanding."[14]

American Indian biographies have become more popular since the 1970s. In addition, examining Indian history from the "inside," like an autobiography, has become a means for obtaining insightful knowledge about Native communities. Local knowledge and social history within the community help to reconstruct the infrastructure of the tribal community. How this knowledge is perceived by outsiders, especially those of the mainstream, is critical.[15] This statement does not mean one has to be an Indian in order to conduct such research analysis—it means one has to be much more familiar with the culture of the people.

First, it would be useful to address the dynamics of Indian-white relations; that is, of interactions between the two sides of the Indian-white equation. Indian-white history is a field of two diverse cultural sides that are moving closer to each other. The initial inertia that separated the Indian world and the white world were hemispheric in nature, as their cultures evolved and developed in different halves of the world. One developed into a linear-minded consciousness and the other developed into a circular-minded consciousness. Their respective worldviews and senses of logic were based on differing values and separate cultural norms that influenced their basic perceptions of reality.[16]

As two different worlds moved onto a colliding path, the result has been disruptive for both but more damaging for American Indians. It is this intersection where the two cultures meet that sets the critical stage for viewing one culture against the other. This transcultural experience and transcultural investigation has to be kept in perspective so that the linear scholar does not misinterpret the circular reality of Indian people. Imagine a bridge, "Indian-white." The mainstream scholar stands at the right side of it but finds it difficult to begin crossing. At first, like the Twins, the scholar does not see the bridge. By being open to the metaphysical, the Twins see the bridge, enabling them to cross the river. The mainstream scholar can do the same and, by knowing how to get there, can cross over and back.

Studying the engagement of two diverse cultures implies that equal attention should be given to both in this bicultural experience. The bicultural analysis of Indian-white relations becomes more convoluted when more than one tribe is involved.[17] In essence learned scholars must unpack some of their academic training and retool themselves to become more effective in properly studying Indian history. Besides the obvious disciplines that are closely related to history, such as anthropology and archeology, historians can expect to receive assistance from the work of "technologists, physicists, geologists, microbiologists, and scores of other people of any trade or profession who are willing to wield a trowel and push a wheelbarrow."[18] They use different research data and different approaches, which together offer a full picture of Native history.

The complexity of Indian-white relations does indeed require a trans-disciplinary approach and cross-cultural analysis, and this same application can be applied to Indian-African American relations, Indian-Mexican relations, and so forth. The problem consists of realizing how and why American Indians are complex through an analysis of the infrastructures of their societies. This is an important first step of realization with regard to the cultural bridge of understanding and the Third Dimension. Furthermore, it is imperative to understand that an Indian community or tribe had relationships with other tribes.[19]

In this light, the door to the Third Dimension of the Native perspective is at hand. This transition to understanding the Native ethos is the threshold of reconceptualizing history from a categorical Indian perspective.[20]

But what has been learned about the Second Dimension of Indian-white history, before moving to the Third Dimension? Naturally, the dynamics of Indian-white relations involve two incongruent cultures and two separate mindsets facing common issues. How they respond in general and respond to each other in particular indicates the functions of two very different systems of logic.[21] These two logics are based on the premises of separate identities embedded in their cultures.[22]

Perhaps it is wise to raise a note of caution before moving on. Hypothesizing first, a new approach is necessary in the study of American Indian history in order to realize the full picture. A helpful comment comes from anthropologist Ralph Linton, who noted the significance of understanding cultural change. In his classic *The Tree of Culture*, Linton advocates "an attempt to synthesize the experience, the reading and thinking of a lifetime into one volume which traces the evolution of culture from its multiple beginnings at the sub-human level through its divergent lines of development."[23] This observation suggests that knowing the whole cultural development of a Native people is relevant to understanding their entire history.

The next step is attempting to understand the cultural practices of the people by studying a smaller piece of the big picture. Asking the right questions about relationships is essential. To reconceptualize American Indian history, professional historians need to deconstruct some of the previous notions about history. This is a personal decision for each scholar.[24] In sum, it requires admitting that change is needed in the way we think about history and then attempting to create a new pedagogy.

One cannot build a proper bridge while using only a hammer, a single tool. Multiple tools are needed. Social history plays an important role in understanding the dynamics of Lakota and Cheyenne interactions with the Seventh Cavalry. American Indian social history, through its attempt to portray daily life, has helped in the investigation of Indian historical behavior and decision making. For example, early works of social history that sought to portray the daily life of the Lakota include Royal B. Hassrick, *The Sioux: Life and Customs of a Warrior Society* (1964), and John C. Ewers, *Indian Life on the Upper Missouri* (1968). In addition, changes in Indian social life are addressed for several groups in Duane Champagne, *American Indian Societies: Strategies and Conditions of Political and Cultural Survival* (1989).

In other fields such as sociology, religious studies, and education, ethnography has been useful to help depict indigenous ways of life. By understanding the life ways of people, their thinking, ethos, and decision making can be understood. This puts Native history into a better context for understanding the full extent of indigenous communities.

In the course of studying the interaction of two peoples such as at the Little Bighorn or Tecumseh's campaign against William Henry Harrison, a comprehensive picture of the history, culture, and social relations is needed for those on both sides of the engagements. How is this achieved? James Olson has noted that "the interdisciplinary approach can be most effective through the realization by the individual worker that other disciplines can contribute to his own understanding. With this realization must come the ability and willingness, not so much to adopt the methodology of other disciplines as to make effective use of their fruits. This imposes on each of us a two-fold obligation: (1) we must try to understand what the practitioners of other disciplines are saying; and (2) we must try, in our own writing, to be intelligible to the uninitiated or the partly initiated."[25] In order to understand the way in which Indians experienced their interactions with other groups, the complex nature of the indigenous community challenges academic disciplines such as social anthropology to be more innovative in studying American Indian history.[26]

Disciplines within the academy have aligned themselves according to various interests. Bruce Trigger pointed out that "anthropology has developed as the study of the continent's native peoples. Its traditional four branches were concerned with their indigenous cultures, prehistory, physical characteristics, and languages."[27] Trigger's observation also suggests that the historian might learn as much about the culture of the people as possible in order to understand their actions in historical events. Since the 1970s historians and anthropologists have come closer together in focusing on cultural history. This shared approach is noted in the success of the American Society for Ethnohistory and the production of insightful works about Native communities.[28]

Studying Native cultures is a key to the bridge of understanding. Anthropologist Edward Tylor noted in 1968 that "at the heart of anthropology lies man and something more. That which is more is usually known as culture. It is the concept that enables us to bridge such diverse fields as human paleontology, medical anthropology, linguistics, archeology, and the study of society, to mention only a few."[29]

The whole picture of a subject in American Indian history needs to be examined in a cultural context. In support of this notion Tylor noted that "Culture or Civilization, taken in its wide ethnographic sense, is that complex whole which includes knowledge, belief, art, morals, law, custom, and any other capabilities and habits acquired by man as a member of society."[30] How historians define culture is essential and can be limiting in analysis. Utilizing Tylor's understanding of culture would bring historians to the threshold of the cultural bridge of understanding and to being able to comprehend the three dimensions of the Medicine Way.

Cultural anthropology has made significant efforts to understand Indian people. For example, anthropologists study change in society.[31] In addition to cultural anthropologists, social anthropologists have been and continue to be useful in studying American Indians. In fact, they are a sine qua non in order to understand the Medicine Way of Native history.

Ethnography deals with the cultures of nonliterate peoples without a written language.[32] By striving to understand their cultures in a historical context, the first step is made to unlocking the historic reality of the people. Ethnography tells us about inside of communities and how they function. This leads to studying Indian history from the inside. In doing so, theory and method are also important.[33]

The emphasis on culture has supported the development of ethnohistory as a necessary field for understanding indigenous peoples. Additionally, ethnography becomes part of the ethnohistory movement to study Native people in a chronological context. Robert Lowie noted that "ethnography is the science which deals with the 'cultures' of human groups. By culture we understand the sum total of what an individual acquires from his society—those beliefs, customs, artistic norms, food-habits, and crafts which come to him not by his own creative activity but as a legacy from the past, conveyed by formal or informal education."[34] The purpose here is not to study cultural anthropology but to study Indian history as a point of introduction to the Medicine Way of physical and metaphysical reality.[35]

Social interaction is an area to explore in order to cross the cultural bridge of understanding. By examining the society of a particular community, other important elements of Indian life become apparent. More specifically, reconstructing the infrastructure of Indian society is vital for understanding Indian-white interactions. Within the community, village, or band, important social or kindred units exist, such as family, clan, age-group society or military society, moiety, and religious society. These units are placed in a specific order for the community to function, thus the logic of a Native leader derives from all these relationships as well as relationships with the world's nonhuman entities. Disciplines like anthropology and sociology have been helpful in producing studies on the American Indian family unit.[36] Through the use of such studies the historian has the potential to empower the past and resuscitate it. But it must be revived the way the Indians lived it in order to realize how Native people made decisions using knowledge of the earth and what they valued as a people.

Following the deconstruction of previous historical approaches and prevailing ideas about American Indian history, reconstruction then follows. Some might call this a new construction of Indian history, which would involve theory and expanding the concept of socialization to include nonhumans. As an example, historical theorist Alun Munslow observed that "constructionism refers to the 'social theory' schools that appeal to general laws in historical explanation, as exemplified, for example, in the French Annalistes' attempt at all-encompassing total explanations, and other sociologically inspired case-study and biographical work of historians."[37] Although historians might find such social theory cumbersome, understanding the social fabric of Indian communities and thus understanding how Native people functioned is necessary for the construction of the cultural bridge of understanding.

It has become obvious that new theories are required to produce a more comprehensive understanding of American Indian history.[38] New mainstream scholars must first propose models of historical traditional indigenous communities and then examine the forces or causes that have produced change over time.

For those writing American Indian history, the suggestion of theorizing a model is a radical proposition when considered against the conventional approach of archival documented-based research. The works of Pekka Hämäläinen and Juliana Barr are examples of productive efforts at theorizing such a model.[39] Theory represents a new means to entertain seriously the realism of the Indian past.[40] As the attempts to re-create an Indian realism of the past are pursued, Indian people will become increasingly involved. Bruce Trigger noted that "it is also essential that Native people should receive professional training and employment as historians and archeologists. . . .

They will bring important new perspectives as well as a deeper sense of relevance to the study of Indian history."[41] Since Trigger made this statement, growing numbers of Native scholars are writing about their tribal communities from the inside out.[42]

Due to the social nature of Indians, places of hospitality, meetings, and sacredness are important for understanding the practice of oral tradition in which stories and conversations connect people to the natural surroundings. Such communication is integral to the whole scheme of life. Native people are part of place and place is part of them, as in the illustration of the Turquoise House representing a place of power that draws the sons to meet their fathers. The people's environmental surroundings help to identify them. With this in mind, environmental studies become important in understanding Indian peoples and their numerous cultures. Undoubtedly the environment has significantly affected American Indians due to their role in a Natural Democracy that acknowledges all things as a part of their communities.

Related to environment is the geography of natural surroundings. The study of landscape has been germane to the development of Native philosophies. Since the late twentieth century the academic discipline of geography has turned attention to studying the geographic influence on Native peoples, especially because of rapid destruction of the rain forest in South America. The newly emerging field of ethnogeography has been established as geography and ethnography are collaborating in the production of new scholarship in the study of indigenous peoples. Insights from geography are helpful for understanding the significance of homeland, space, earth, human community, and the natural elements as well as the abstract elements, such as spirituality and the afterworld, as both natural and abstract elements have a place in the indigenous understanding of geography. All this is within the totality of the Natural Democracy.

Philosophy is another academic discipline in which practitioners are examining the ideologies and principles held by Indian peoples with regard to the earth and the environment. Like geography and environmental studies, however, philosophy is an isolated discipline. It is limited in its analysis and therefore has to rely on a cross-disciplinary approach in order to study the American Indian as a whole being of many relationships with other beings and with place. If one understands a people's religion and philosophy, their actions in history can be significantly better understood.

In addition, the study of languages has become increasingly relevant to preserving as well as reconstructing American Indian cultures. Language is the vehicle for communicating information and knowledge from a cultural basis. But historians have been resistant to studying Indian languages, although they feel free to write the history of American Indians. A helpful question here is: how can a historian write French history without studying French? In recent years some schools have begun offering courses in Native languages, among them the University of Nebraska, University of Michigan, and University of Oklahoma.

Modern scholarship about American Indians has become an effort of learning the language of the Indian group being studied. While older scholars, with a few notable exceptions, failed to learn to speak Indian languages, younger scholars are realizing the importance of learning an Indian language in combination with learning the methodology of another academic discipline in order to reconstruct the Indian past. This effort is applauded because learning the language of the people means learning how they think and use words to express themselves in a cultural and communal context. As of 2010 an estimated 150 Native languages existed in the United States and Canada, and roughly 600 to 700 in Central and South America.

Another means of examining Native history is by studying Indian movement patterns and the reasons for migrations. Closely related to such demographic analysis is examining the Native economies of Indian groups. The key to these methodologies is to look at movement patterns and economic resources from an Indian point of view, meaning from the tribal standpoint, as it varied with the environment.

One of the observations frequently made about Indians is that some were nomadic while others were sedentary, and still others were seminomadic. Indians depended on their natural environments. Their movements were shaped by their survival needs. As a result

Native peoples carefully observed the cycles of the seasons and the changing of the weather. As generations of people studied the seasons and weather patterns, they began to think in cycles, and their philosophies developed similarly.

The sizes of villages and communities depended on their ability to support their economies. Native communities defended their hunting grounds and their croplands. The communities engaged in wars for their territories. And all along, they depended upon nature. The populations of the communities changed due to various factors both within and beyond their control. The power of nature, in effect, controlled their lives. Theirs were Native economies of dependency.

Demographic studies have enlightened us with new ideas about reconstructing Indian societies of the past and their realities.[43] The works of anthropologist Henry Dobyns and sociologist Russell Thornton have helped tremendously in understanding the structure of Native communities.[44] Similarly, quantitative history has helped to further our understanding of Native history, although the debate over quantitative history versus qualitative history continues, as scholars argue over the most useful approach and the most valid methodology for properly interpreting history.[45] Both approaches are valuable in examining the Third Dimension of Native communities. For example, quantitative history and social anthropology, when combined, would help explain the rationale for Native groups migrating during particular seasons. As a suggestion, Tecumseh's warriors were torn between fighting and returning to their homes, especially those who had traveled far to reach Prophetstown, for logically they wanted to be with their families as the early part of November signified winter approaching.

Communities were made up of tribal members of various types. Full-bloods, mixed-bloods, and captives of other tribes and races constituted the tribal communities. With increasing contact with whites, indigenous communities changed in their cultural matrix. While their belief systems remained intact, the infrastructure began to alter. This shift from traditionalism to quasi-traditionalism was necessary for survival. In other words, tribal communities found themselves reinventing their sociocultural infrastructures. Nature still affected the Native communities as new generations learned to survive amid environmental changes, especially during droughts, storms, or prolonged winters.

External forces like federal policies and programs caused Native communities to react and unite themselves against foreign influences. At some pivotal point the continuous outside influences impacted the infrastructure of Native communities. They were placed on reservations by the late 1800s, and white contact led to the Indian land allotments and dispossession of Native lands. Throughout the twentieth century white contact brought new technologies, which eventually caused considerable change for American Indians. Modern America made many Indian people into urban Indians, who then wondered about their identities and the preservation of their cultures.

As previously mentioned, American Indian Studies has developed as a field since the late 1960s. While it has been slow to gain recognition as an area of scholarship, American Indian Studies has nevertheless survived and is thriving as more programs and departments are established on a permanent basis. The approach of American Indian Studies is holistic in examining all of Indian life, which includes history, culture, language, politics, economy, environment, and religion. As a field and quest, American Indian Studies relies on traditional disciplines such as history, anthropology, and others as a means of collecting secondary literature for information. However, the analysis is within a larger context beyond the data of one discipline. American Indian Studies is currently based on Indian-white relations. It has, however, ventured in limited ways toward Indian-Indian or inter-tribal studies and tribal case studies. Yet the study of Indian-white relations still accounts for the majority of books and articles written. Nonetheless, the politics and federal law of Indian-white relations have dominated American Indian Studies since the inception of the field in the late 1960s. In fact, it is difficult to do American Indian Studies without including federal-Indian law. American Indian or Native studies, due to their holistic approach, can contribute to our understanding of the Third Dimension, such as in understanding the Navajo worldview of the Turquoise House after crossing the Rainbow Bridge.

In conclusion, historians and other scholars will need to be imaginative in rethinking future work in American Indian history. This effort involves taking on another academic discipline or even two in addition to one's original academic training. This is essential due to the complexity of Indian history as exemplified by individuals like Wooden Leg, who converted to Christianity, becoming bicultural and functioning within two belief systems. Such action on his part compounds his identity and makes his value system twofold. Transdisciplinary analysis can trace his transitions as his life changed. New scholars entering the field should be required to train in at least three methodological areas or disciplines in order to study their chosen subject in American Indian history. This is essential for the Indian version of Indian history to be accepted by mainstream America.

Nonacceptance by the majority of Americans was due to their neglect and nonpursuit of deeper knowledge about Native people. Presumptions of knowledge from a western-oriented perspective disallowed consideration of other approaches like the Medicine Way of Indian history. The major battle in this effort to revise history through Indian eyes is convincing scholars of the necessity as well as the opportunity of entertaining the Indian point of view. This revision is most difficult for academics who want to see only their own version of American Indian history; they see no need for pedagogical revision. At this point, however, I hope they are beginning to see a cultural bridge of understanding waiting for them to cross.

Building any bridge is no small task. It takes effort and much time. In the case of Rainbow Bridge, as in the journey of the Twins, it takes a collaborative effort even to get there. In the post–World War II years one had to float down the Colorado River for several days and then hike an arduous seven miles up a canyon to reach the beautiful rock arch. Today the place is still remote, but one can now get most of the way there in two or three hours on Lake Powell in a jet boat, followed by a hike of about a mile to see nature's wonder. The trip is worth it. As the Twins found by crossing the bridge, the experience is rewarding as connections between all things are made for the first time and thereafter sustained.

7

Oral Tradition and Language

Originally from the Southeast, the Muscogee Creeks tell a creation story of the people coming out of or emerging from Mother Earth (*Ekv nv*). According to the story, the Muscogee Creeks were within the earth or underground in the dark and cold. They wandered blindly, hearing only their own voices. They were lost and confused because they had no light, for it had not yet been created. They were cold, for the sacred fire had not yet been given to them. The Muscogee people huddled together for warmth and to console one another as the darkness imprisoned them under the earth. At some point without knowledge of time, the opportunity of human creation by emerging into the natural environment occurred. The Muscogee people felt a sudden draft of air. Surrounded by darkness, without the gift of sight, they used their sense of touch to wander in the direction from which the air was coming. As they emerged from a cave or hole in the ground, they stepped into the darkness and felt the earth of their mother. Still unable to see, as more Muscogees emerged from the ground, they frantically asked their leaders what was happening?

A veil of mist blinded them, then *ho tv le* (*ho doe le*)—the Wind—came and swept the mist away, so that the people could see for the first time. The first people to see became known as the Wind clan. As the rest of the people saw the creation of animals and plants, they took the names of the animals upon realizing the strengths and powers of these strange beings. The people became the Bear, Tiger (Panther), Alligator, and Deer clans and so forth. The Muscogees learned that all living things that breathed the air called *ho tv le* were a part of Mother Earth and that a Great Power called *Hesaketvmese* breathed *ho tv le* into all that lived. *Hesaketvmese* was the "Master of Breath."[1]

For traditional Indians, history as collective experiences exists as a natural combination of oral traditions and community history. In the Medicine Way, oral traditions and community histories accomplish much more than just accounting for the past as a record of history. Rather than merely as an interpretation of the past, like academic history, indigenous societies accept the history of their people in a much larger way that includes accounts of interaction with the natural environment. History and oral accounts help to explain the heritages of all peoples and their identities. Yet Indian history is the inclusion of all things and it is expressed via oral traditions and seen as collective experiences of the community. Elders' memories store the oral accounts as they are the keepers of this knowledge.

Within the indigenous world of Natural Democracy, oral tradition has been and continues to be a life force that holds a community together. In addition, oral tradition, belief in the Medicine Way of metaphysics, and the spirituality of humanization bond tribal communities internally (see figure 8).

The Medicine Way of indigenous history rests on the other side of the cross-cultural bridge in the Third Dimension. This realm is Native life full of stories, some good ones and others not so good, but they are indigenous oriented, according to the people living in the natural environment. Some stories are so humorous that they provoke big belly laughs, causing streams of joy to roll down a person's cheeks. Humor is a vital part of being Indian, especially since there has been so much pain and suffering throughout Native history.

The oral tradition has its place even in academic history, but I hope its status improves and that it is taken more seriously. The Native usage of oral traditions is part of how academic historians should interpret the Indian past. Why do professional historians consider oral traditions and oral history to be outside academic history? Why is American Indian history less recognized by mainstream historians? Some major colleges and universities still do not have an Indian historian in their history departments.[2]

Part of the problem is that oral tradition is not respected by the majority of mainstream academics, who emphasize the significance of empirical data. Furthermore, academic historians have argued that oral history and academic history are far apart and that the former is not an accurate source for research. Oral historian Donald Ritchie noted that history "researchers scrutinize even more intensely" oral history interviews, and "they seek verification [of the interview material] in other sources."[3]

Oral history consists of stories about experiences, like threads that knit communities together in the larger tapestry of Natural Democracy. Story and storytelling are the basis of oral tradition, providing context, identity, membership, and security to Native people. Stories remind people who they are, and each story is within a larger context of the heritage of the people. Fred McTaggart, who studied the stories of the Mesquakie Indians of Iowa, discovered oral tradition to be more than just stories: "I expected to find a few narrative fragments of a dying culture; I found instead a living oral tradition that was functional in many important ways. Through the stories, people can relive important moments of the past; they can justify and explain social and religious beliefs; they can discover what it means to be a Mesquakie."[4] Oral tradition covered the full scope of the Mesquakies' lives and it represented who they were.

McTaggart found the stories to have a deep meaning. He learned that "through stories, children learn about the plants and animals around them; they learn how to find their way through the woods, how to fast and have visions, how to understand the possible and the impossible, the real and the fantastic. Through a story, a child learns the oldest and the most beautiful words of a slowly evolving language; he or she can learn the history of the language as the stories of a shared history are told. And children learn discipline—the discipline of listening to a story and the discipline of living out a story."[5]

The stories are generational, thus allowing the elders of the community to communicate and share knowledge with the youth. Language is like a vessel that carries the essence of the story from listener to listener. Information and knowledge are combined as a teaching tool to the young, and language usage is reinforced at the same time. There is a distinct difference between a story told in the Native language and the same one told in English, even by the same speaker. People think in particular languages and even dream in different languages that they speak fluently.

Stories include legends and myths in the oral tradition. Mythology has played a part in many civilizations, including those of the early Greeks, medieval English, and ancient Irish. "Mythology maintains that all of creation existed first as thought, which was then uttered as speech, by which powers the primal beings took shape (or were given space in which to function)," according to Calvin Martin. He continued that "these primal beings, including animal beings, among them the notorious trickster—transformer, created in turn by manual artifice—again, so the stories say."[6]

Furthermore, "beliefs and attitudes, war practices, the complexities of interpersonal relations, and, of course, shamanism, are also illuminated in the stories."[7] Stories function with social responsibilities that link the past to the present and to the future so that time becomes cyclical.[8] History and myth are "close kin inasmuch as both explain how things got to be the way they are by telling some sort of story."[9] This may seem like a careless proposition, but much of American history is based on myth. Yet myth may very well be considered history without evidence since stories play a crucial part in being indigenous.[10] Where evidence is missing, myth often fills the void to provide needed answers to questions or to make a point demonstrating wisdom.

For Indians, historical experiences are the past, existing in the forms of oral traditions that may also be called oral history. Myths, legends, tales, stories, and songs are all part of the oral traditions of most Indian communities. These oral accounts provide a verbal record of the community with a particular purpose.[11]

In an academic sense, tribal history is sociocultural history in the Medicine Way and involves the Natural Democracy of all things associated with a Native community, including the natural environment. In addition, Native oral history is filled with countless stories of inter-tribal relations, thus showing the complexity of one tribe's history.

The practice of oral tradition accounts for the same historical events as do written documents, although by depending on the memories of individuals and reliving the experiences. In some ways oral history has greater appeal than written history because there is likely more than one account of the same story. The Indians' own accounts of history were based primarily on oral traditions. Memories today of past incidents include the emotions and intensity exhibited. For example, the tension involved in treaty making is demonstrated through the story told about Osceola rejecting the Fort Gibson Treaty by stabbing it with a knife. Under war conditions, Native groups used mannerisms, rhetoric, and a vernacular that sociolinguist John Gumperz has called "speech communities." Speech communities use sociocultural registers like leadership, anger, enemies, and killings in a discourse that invents a war oral tradition.[12] An entire group becomes a speech community when war talk becomes a language, according to Asif Agha in his work on sociolinguistics. He contends that language focuses on social relations that involve identity, gender relations, kinship, and status in communities that include everyone.[13]

Elders shared their knowledge via the oral tradition, passing down historical accounts of the people from one generation to the next. Whether myth, legend, tale, or song, the oral tradition was a means of sharing knowledge, and as noted, it served several purposes. Oral accounts contained parables and lessons, and the young people learned from them; morals of stories told by their elders enlightened them on virtues, values, and the importance of respecting taboos. Stories and tales served in other ways as well. Although they were entertaining, frightening stories disciplined the young when they misbehaved. At the philosophical level the oral tradition explained the origins of the people and the creation of the universe, and it prophesied the future.[14]

Specifically, oral tradition helped to define values, norms, and ethics, while assisting to provide an identity for the community.[15] The American history of heroes involved "great events." In American history, "great men" made history by forging great events as Americans search for heroes. But even when oral history includes a historical experience, there are usually lessons of morality or ethical reminders involved. In this manner oral traditions help to shape the behaviors of indigenous societies in much the same way as social anthropologist Paul Connerton described in *How Societies Remember*.[16]

For Indian people, reality is different, and it is the focus of the Medicine Way based on various tribal worldviews that support the notion of an indigenous paradigm.[17] Oral traditions in Indian history function in the dual reality of the physical and metaphysical. At the same time, the Native worldview is actually a collective ethos of many tribal views. Each tribal community has a view of Natural Democracy consisting of their relationships with their environment, including other peoples, the flora and fauna, and the supernatural. Viewing the world from one's Native relationships with these elements is the Third Dimension.

Oral traditions help to represent the Third Dimension, or the actual tribal view from within an Indian community. This viewpoint or internal perspective is from the inside looking out, but the lack of written documents has been the source of criticism against oral tradition.

Due to the ethos of oral traditions, the subjects are numerous and often include creation myths, trickster stories, moralistic parables, hero accounts, tragedies, myths about deaths, and prophecies. These oral accounts have in common a nontangible quality and speak to the truth that the indigenous communities believe. Whether the oral traditions are right or wrong according to factual information is not the point. Rather the community has accepted the truth as told through oral accounts, and this illustrates the Medicine Way.

Functioning without tangible evidence and relying on their oral traditions, Native communities were comfortable with nontangibles, which often had meaningful influences on their lives. Because of indigenous beliefs in spiritual deities and because of the lack of a written indigenous language (the use of pictographs, hide drawings, and wampum belts notwithstanding), Native communities placed great importance on the spoken word.

The spoken word embodied power and life, exuding a spirit of presence as a life force. In this sense the spoken word captured a moment's energy or spiritual presence, and the moment was born again when the same words were used again in the next telling of the story. People remembered the words, certain phrases, or how they were used in the context of their language so that they were essential parts of the oral accounts, as important as the subject of the story. "A word has power in and of itself," wrote Pulitzer Prize winner N. Scott Momaday in contemplating his own people, the Kiowas. "A word," Momaday says, "comes from nothing into sound and meaning; it gives origin to all things."[18] The spoken word was a tradition of telling stories, and story held the Kiowas and other Indian nations together.

"In the older days, children weren't separate from the community. They heard these stories because they were in the house when stories were told," said Native writer Elizabeth Woody. She continued, "What they absorbed at that time was only limited to what their experience was. As they got older, they remembered a story, and it hit them differently, or they heard it again, and it seemed totally different. It's the same with books."[19]

Oral history involves oral tradition and brings the past into the present, beginning with the interviewing process. To obtain an oral history a scholar interviews individuals and records their experiences. Oral tradition is the process of telling the listener(s) about stories, myths, legends, and prophecies. In a classroom one teacher instructed his undergraduate students to conduct an oral history project involving stories. In reflecting on the results of the assignment, the teacher concluded that "it also made them more conscious about the world around them, even that the places of their everyday life had been at various times, at the center of events of historical significance. . . . These experiences of the students in conducting oral histories with people they either knew personally or came to know made history come alive."[20]

For the full effect of the oral tradition, the language of the indigenous people must be used. Language was the necessary vehicle of communication, and the usage of certain words and phrases cannot be exactly translated to the same precise meaning in another language. The danger for Native oral tradition is the threat that the languages may be lost. At the end of the twentieth century an estimated 213 Native languages existed throughout the United States, of which 176 were living languages still spoken by Indian communities. Unfortunately thirty-five Indian languages have become extinct in the postmodern era, establishing a dangerous trend for the future of Indian languages. These statistics are uncertain due to factors such as accurately counting the number of language speakers, the changing of languages with other dialects and completely different languages, and the revitalization of languages. By 2010 an estimated 209 Native languages are spoken in North America and roughly 275 Indian languages are spoken in South America.[21]

Languages are verbal tools for transporting indigenous knowledge of the past from one generation to the next. In the process languages have evolved into new dialects, although they have remained basically the same as the original language. With each change in language the words change, meaning that a story is changed slightly, but the basic fabric of it is the same.

Moreover, men and women differ in how they tell the same stories. Women have a language within the language when they tell stories in the oral tradition. Women tell stories to others while they sew, make pottery, and do their work. Cherokee folklorist Rayna Green wrote: "Thus the women have always kept the stories, in clay or reeds, in wool or cotton, in grass or paint or words to songs."[22] They provide much more detail than do male storytellers. Therefore their listeners would hear the story in a slightly different way. The usage of certain words, gesticulation, and the roles of women slightly shift the story too. In fact, female storytellers often tell short stories within the larger story.

Stories produce a sociocultural history about the community in general, conveying values, ideas, and beliefs as well as additional insight about the people. As a result cultural information and ethnographic data are products of the oral tradition. For example, women among the Muscogee Creeks and Seminoles in Oklahoma experienced a different reality than their male counterparts. Their perception and recollection of events presented a different view and a different reality in conjunction with the reality of their menfolk. Since even fewer historical documents accurately convey how Native women view their experiences and surroundings than is the case for men, trying to research this perspective on reality is even more challenging.

Oral communication is supplemented by other ways of communicating, especially among the Pueblo groups of the Southwest. The Pueblo groups held dances by clowns who mocked individuals and other cultures to demonstrate their comprehension and opinion. Tewa anthropologist Alfonso Ortiz explained that "pueblo dramatizations, performed in their Native languages, serve to transform what might have been unique and disruptive historical events into a part of the ongoing, internal, cultural dialogue of the people." Ortiz explained that the clowns depicted the arrival of the Spanish and later encounters with U.S. bureaucrats, missionaries, and anthropologists. All the depictions illustrated self-worth and cultural continuity. The ceremonial demonstrations rendered a Pueblo version of history; the clowns acted as agents of history, much like field historians, by interpreting current events and the present values of other cultures.[23]

The Pueblo clown dances are outside of the various kinds of oral traditions. Oral historian Ruth Finnegan noted that "broadly one can list three main classes of oral tradition: recognized literary forms, generalized historical knowledge, and personal recollections."[24] Each of these types exists in American Indian oral tradition and is much the same in other oral cultures.[25]

In examining the Indian oral tradition, the creation stories of two groups can be compared for similarities.[26] Scholars have found that the Pima and Zuni emergence myths both had "a common stock of characters, including a pair of male culture heroes, the sun, and mankind . . . [and] overall [the] interpretation is that the tribes share a dual concept of culture hero."[27] Among other groups, coming from the earth is common. How the people came to be was never forgotten as the creation stories established the tribal identities of various Native communities.

Telling stories regularly provides continuity for Native people. Some stories are told at certain times of the year. Some are told during particular seasons, at times of the month, or at ceremonies. Other stories are told when necessary. The stories, parables, myths, songs, and the like making up the oral tradition have been told again and again. Repetition was necessary for the people to remember, thus also decreasing the possibility for error.[28]

Among the Muscogee Creeks, observing rituals, following cultural norms, and obeying laws served to maintain order in society and respect for the metaphysical. In all four cardinal directions the forces of fire confronted the people, and they had to make a decision. From the south a blue fire faced the people, a black fire burned in the west, and a white fire was aflame in the east, but the people chose the red and yellow fire from the north.[29] The fire of the north warmed the people and provided light over the world. It enabled the plants to grow, so that the Muscogee Creeks learned to respect all of the elements for life, and they celebrated the harvest of the green corn (busk) in ceremonials. Should the people fail in their respect for nature and forget the busk ceremonies, the people would disappear from the land and it would fall beneath the waters of the ocean.

The Muscogee Creeks stressed the importance of community, and generations of ceremonialism reinforced it. As the ceremonies became ritualized, the Muscogees developed ceremonial laws to maximize the community's confirmations of successful ceremonies and thus confirmed that the Creek way of life was the correct one.[30]

From this tale of origin, the Muscogees articulated and developed codes or tribal laws ranking their clans in a hierarchy, mirroring Asif Agha's social relations defined through language. The Creeks had clans to carry out tribal laws to make sure their people obeyed them. Hence the tribal police came from certain clans placed in charge. For example, the highest clan was the Wind people, so that the *mekkos* or kings came from the Wind clan. The clan animals that could fly like the eagle, which was carried on the breath of the Master of Breath, were regarded as higher than those clan animals that could not fly. In a Muscogee community or *tvlvn*, the higher-ranked clans provided the leadership for war, peace, or medicine. People of the Medicine Way of knowledge typically came from certain clans, like the Bear clan, thus their word carried much weight in decision making in councils. Stories about the clans and how they came to be are part of the oral tradition of the Creeks, and other Native groups have similar accounts. Due to the clans being identified with animals, many stories are about nonhumans.

A common story among many tribes is a myth of the Great Flood when water covered the entire earth. The Iroquois believe in a turtle that swam down deep into the waters and came up to the surface with some earth between its claws. The earth's surface was made from this material. Thus the turtle was the "hero" and became a respected clan animal. It was also recognized for its durability and long life. Living so long made the turtle wise and full of knowledge that was a gift from the Great Manitou (Great Spirit).

In Choctaw oral tradition the story is told about two brothers, Chataw and Chickasa, who divided the people into two groups. Chickasa led his followers northward, and they camped finally on the bank of the Lower Mississippi River. Chataw led his people eastward, as they were influenced by the guiding power of a pole that had become sacred to them. Ultimately they camped at an area in present-day northern Mississippi, and Chataw's people built a mound and called it Nanah Waya.

The stories of many tribes involve a "trickster" who is responsible for disorder and calamities in people's lives or in a community. As many as thirty-six indigenous communities call the trickster Coyote and blame him for all unpredictable events. But among the Iroquois the trickster is a Great Hare. Some tribal creation stories include the trickster. Usually the Coyote trickster is called a "cultural hero," and he can exist in human or animal form as he pleases. Among some tribes Coyote is female. Other Native groups believe that Coyote has special powers and that he can bless a people or curse them by making them suffer.

The trickster figure provides the balance in the lives of Native people and in their communities. Because people believe in the powers of spirits within their environmental surroundings, Coyote serves as the psychological pivot for unexplained phenomena. Oral tradition often focuses on the generic Indian trickster and worldview of each tribal people in principal stories. These accounts demonstrate how the people see their surroundings and how what cannot be explained is blamed on the trickster.

The narrative process of oral tradition provides an oral history of many experiences, and it reminds Native people who they are. Narrative carries the story's plot. "The written and the spoken narrative are two distinct artistic creations," wrote oral historian Caoimhin O'Danachair. He added, "Each has its own conventions, forms, characteristics. Those of the oral tradition are largely influenced by the method of their transmission and usually recognizable as such."[31] The role of storyteller usually lies with the tribal elders as their life experiences consist of numerous stories and wisdom conveyed through oral tradition that becomes Native oral history.

Biographer David Dunaway has suggested that "oral biography, a life narrative researched primarily through interviews, has been used to democratize history by incorporating vantage points of those often excluded from the historical canon: women and minority-group members. Sociologists have used orally gathered survey data to create composite portraits of a people, as well as regional or national biographical overviews."[32] As Dunaway notes, "Anthropologists have turned to intensive oral interviewing to establish a 'life history,' narrated biographies of the infamous and the historically disenfranchised, those individuals whose lives of quiet, community-oriented distinction leave no wake of speeches, news articles, and published letters."[33] In terms of content, "oral history, in other words, brings out the narrative (and mythic) character of history most clearly because it explicitly comprises a group under investigation, an informant and a listener. They form relationships."[34]

Jan Vansina observes in his widely cited *Oral Tradition as History*: "Without oral traditions we would know very little about the past of large parts of the world, and we would not know them from the inside."[35] On the bias inherent in the telling and writing of history, Vansina concluded, "The historian interprets from perspectives he knows."[36] Thus the history discipline has the responsibility to learn about other perspectives as well as to learn about the importance of oral tradition among indigenous peoples.

Oral history has greater expression than written history because the person interviewed can express different accounts of the past, and the same person can later provide a retrospective view of events witnessed earlier. Studs Turkel's World War II oral history, *The Good War*, won the Pulitzer Prize in 1984, but for the most part mainstream historians have not fully recognized oral history for its contributions to history.[37] Due to its flexible nature without permanent documentation, it has been rejected by professional historians as unreliable. Mainstream historians claim that each person presenting oral history tells how a particular individual remembers it and that it varies each time it is told.[38] However, to traditional Indians the indefiniteness of oral history was not an important variable. They considered all versions valid while focusing on the basic facts being recalled.[39] They valued each account as potentially adding more information that could also be beneficial in some way to understanding a past experience.

In the process of the oral tradition, Native people spoke of nonhuman entities as being human. Native people humanized all things so that an order of communication was established within the tribal language. Thus Native languages carried the responsibility of maintaining ethos and the conveyance of reality in the Medicine Way. In order for oral tradition to function effectively, the use of language had to be accurate, since an entire tribal community depended upon verbal communication as its foundation for sharing information and knowledge.[40] The natural surroundings provided an order of home space that assisted language through points of reference. Words and phrases were needed to describe all things in the surroundings of a Natural Democracy. The Medicine Way functioned in this inclusive manner, as language conveyed Native logic and the rationale for decision making.

Words are like stones used in constructing the foundation of a community's structure. By using linguistics to study a community, more information can be ascertained about a group, such as knowledge about their environment.[41] Scholars can obtain information about the Native environment's flora and fauna and the importance of such flora and fauna to the tribal worldview.[42]

Studying historical linguistics can also provide chronological data about a Native group. Accurate dates can be obtained from linguistic evidence by using techniques of glottochronology. This method of studying the spread of languages keeps track of the number of cognates from a list of basic vocabulary of the Native group. By comparing the language with a similar language, more information can be obtained about the group in question. At what point the two languages were separated and what similarities remain can be ascertained from this approach of comparative study.[43]

However, the foundational knowledge of the myth or story depends on the ability of the translator—a common problem. Nuances within the language are often lost in translation, giving a slightly different meaning to the myth or story. Over time the meanings of traditional stories and myths may be lost as people accept the newer accounts. "Every natural language contains terms for judging conduct, and every natural human group shares a system for common judgment, but between languages and between groups judgments are frequently incompatible (or incommensurable)," according to educator Murray Wax.[44]

In recalling his early experiences at Carlisle Indian School, Luther Standing Bear, a noted Lakota writer, described the importance of the Native language, oral tradition, and perception: "Every true student, every lover of nature has 'the Indian point of view,' but there are few such students, for few white men approach nature in the Indian manner. The Indian and the white man sense things differently because the white man has put distance between himself and nature; and assuming a lofty place in the scheme of things has lost for him both reverence and understanding. Consequently the white man finds Indian philosophy obscure—wrapped, as he says, in a maze of ideas and symbols which he does not understand."[45]

Oral tradition requires a background setting, and the story being told references a time, a season, or something that provides a context. How the storyteller uses language is relevant to the actions told in the story, which might include tricksters, animals, and spiritual beings. Simultaneously "place" is an important element of the story and helps provide a cultural context for the action being described. If the story has a purpose, it is retold regularly and becomes part of a tribe's oral tradition. When the account has no useful purpose for being retold, it is oral history.

Historian Louis Gottschalk observed that oral history "provides a truer and more realistic dimension, yet one must always be aware of the subjectivity of the information. . . . Oral history can record the opinions of people who are seldom heard."[46] In support of this point, he further noted that "the facts of history are derived from testimony and therefore are facts of meaning. They cannot be seen, felt, tasted, heard, or smelled. They may be said to be symbolic or representative of something that once was real, but they have no objective reality of their own. In other words, they exist only in the observer's or historian's mind (and thus may be called 'subjective')."[47]

Narrative and oral tradition are tools for building a bridge between the two interpretations of history addressed in these chapters. Typically, Indian history is written from a window perspective about Indians. Within the present generation of scholarship, historians and insightful scholars are at last addressing the dynamics of cross-cultural experiences between Indians and whites. But what is needed is a bridge of innovative theory and methodology to understand Native history from an indigenous perspective.

Stories are a large part of Indian life today. Friends and relatives, usually elders, tell stories in the oral tradition. They talk mainly about what happened to someone whom everyone knew. And they usually identify who these people's relatives are. Contrary to the historic stereotype of the "silent Indian" or the "stoic Indian," Indian people talk a lot. The storytellers use narrative in developing an oral tradition that consists of stories, myths, and legends. A good storyteller is known for providing a brief history of kinship of the person(s) involved, presenting the plot of what happened, and usually speculating as to why it happened. Sometimes the stories are serious; bad things happened. Sometimes they are funny, and the humor breaks tension and brings people together by making them laugh.

Stories possess power, a kind of emotional energy that can produce tears of laughter or sadness. Among the Seminoles and Creeks, and among many Indian groups, stories are usually about what happened to someone as an experience. They are not normally about someone's great deeds of personal victory, or a battle, or the signing of a treaty. Most stories are simply about people.

Oral tradition produces a kind of social history and also reveals much about the culture of a people. The social history tells what the people are like, their preferences, and what they think is important in their lives. This sociocultural accounting is also a kind of community history of oral tradition, and these stories bond community members together. The stories, as they are told, weave a fabric of continuity, holding the community together and giving a sense of place, time, people, feeling, and identity. Indian people enjoy good stories and good humor, but they are also affected by the bad stories, by bad things that have happened to people. Instead of writing about a particular group from the window of a library or from archives using historical documents, oral tradition allows people to "feel" the history of the past and share a sense of time and place with the people.

Oral tradition does not function with the sole purpose of becoming oral history, although it frequently does so. As mentioned, the oral tradition becomes a sociocultural history of the community, and it may contain some biographical history, culture hero history, women's history, environmental history, and metaphysical history.

Configured more on a daily basis, the oral tradition consists of stories that are about people and what happened to them, and perhaps about "what they did," but not necessarily about "what they accomplished." This kind of oral tradition weaves a fabric about the community. As certain stories are repeated, and others are not, the sorting out process of oral tradition shapes collective memory. This demonstrates what is significant to the community and what the needs of the people are. As people's needs change over time, some stories are less used, then almost forgotten. Native people change, but only on the basis of their decision to change.

Over time American Indians have supplied some written evidence of their natural world and events. Early written evidence includes pictographs, rock writing or rock art, and hide paintings.[48] During the early nineteenth century the invention of Sequoyah's syllabary enabled the writing of Cherokee documents in their Native language. Additional written evidence has been left in the form of picture-writing and Navajo sandpaintings. These forms often are derived from the memory of an individual but can also include the subconscious dream, for example, or a historical experience.

Winter counts provided accounts of important events. These counts were often drawn according to the seasons of the year and related what happened during these periods. They depicted battles, supernatural phenomena, and other special events deemed important by the person recording the winter count. In addition, items used in daily life were somewhat like winter counts, for each one had a story. For pottery, for example, this might involve who made it, when, where, and other information. Symbols used in winter counts and on pottery and other household objects represented clues to the Indian past. Such symbols were often part of a system that needs to be deciphered, and this can best be done by understanding the Medicine Way.[49]

By learning about the oral tradition of a community, scholars can begin to understand the Third Dimension made possible by Native speech communities within an indigenous paradigm. Speech and language are an introduction into the reality of the Native community and how the people function in their Native context. Listening carefully is imperative to understanding. The oral tradition is like a metaphorical key for opening a door to understanding a community and how its people think, conceptualize their logic, and draw conclusions based on their prior knowledge. In a way this is a cultural reorientation to crossing the cultural bridge of understanding and entering the Third Dimension reality in which Native people and their community exist.

Part of passing through the door to the other side includes understanding the thought process of indigenous people and the mainstream scholars' willingness to take the risk of which Homi Bhabha's hybridity has warned us (see preceding chapter). For Native groups who are closer to their historic traditions, their sense of logic is related to a circular thinking process. Unlike the linear process of western society, the circular process addresses items as to their relationships within a system or base of knowledge. Basic elementary functions of perception, causality, and reality work in a circular fashion that does not differentiate time and historical events, so that the conscious knowledge becomes a part of the subconscious knowledge.

This kind of thought and logic thereby influence how Indians see and understand the world. For them it is a reality of the conscious and subconscious, a combination of the physical and the metaphysical. The real world and the surreal world form a dialectical relationship.

Reality for Indian people and their communities is very different from the reality of non-Indians. This combined reality of the physical environment and metaphysical environment reflects the people's belief in a combined reality. Stories convey this reality of spiritual beings interacting with people on a regular basis. Nature and its metaphysical phenomena interact with people in a nonconcrete fashion that western society usually dismisses. This metaphysical and physical combined reality is natural to Indian people, part of their daily lives and the realm within which their community functions. This is the other side of the equation of the history of Indian-white relations.

Oral history has been a conduit for Native communities. During the Great Depression years, the Works Progress Administration directed the collection of a large body of interviews with Indians. The interviews were made available as the Indian Pioneer Papers at the University of Oklahoma. These data provide important insight into the ways in which tribal communities maintained their traditional ethos while surrounded by the modern values of the white mainstream.

Since the 1970s American Indian communities have begun developing tribal archives, usually housed at tribal government headquarters. Although much of the collected holdings consists of written or printed documents by non-Indians, tribal archives have also collected oral history interviews. The Cherokees and Chickasaws in Oklahoma are examples of tribes concerned with preserving the past, and there are about a dozen other tribal archives in the state. Institutes and organizations also hold oral history collections; for example, the American Indian Studies Institute at the University of South Dakota houses the largest American Indian oral history collection.

Several oral Indian history projects and collections were developed at about the same time throughout the country. The Doris Duke family funded a number of oral Indian history projects, which are housed at various universities: the University of South Dakota, Vermillion; Western History Collections at the University of Oklahoma; University of Utah; University of Illinois; California State University, Fullerton; and the University of Florida. The Intertribal Friendship House in Oakland, California, houses an Indian oral history collection. Native American Services Education College in Chicago and the D'Arcy McNickle Center for the History of the American Indian at the Newberry Library in Chicago house the Chicago Urban Indian Oral History Project of some thirty interviews.

Indians are deeply connected to the earth, and their continuing communities have hosted the ongoing traditions of storytelling. Indians remember stories and retell the same ones that a grandmother or grandfather told them, and these accounts relive life while transcending time as the past becomes part of the present. "Old stories continue to be told, and new stories are created," said ethnohistorian Peter Iverson in describing Indian life.[50] Indian people are noted storytellers, for this is how they share information and knowledge, and it is their way of life. In the indigenous paradigm individual memory and community memory are much the same. Historian David Thelen stated, "since the memory of past experiences is so profoundly intertwined with the basic identities of individuals, groups, and cultures, the study of memory exists in different forms along a spectrum of experience, from the personal, individual, and private to the collective, cultural, and public."[51]

The Medicine Way of history is including stories of tribal oral traditions in writing about the Indian past. In bringing together the indigenous paradigm and the western paradigm, a weaving process would be in order. With oral tradition representing the traditional Native way of recording history and analyzing research representing the western approach, a compromise is needed to use both and afford them equal status.

One scholar noted that "one might call this [weaving approach] the search for a 'braided' narrative, since it interweaves analysis with storytelling."[52] At the same time, careful conduct is in order in writing about oral tradition and a tribal community, as something is being borrowed from them. Respect for all is part of using oral tradition. As has been suggested, "in the tribal world that is still inhabited by many of the residents of rural American Indian communities, the appraisal of conduct proceeds differently. The ethical analyses of modern philosophers fit but poorly within the processes of reflection in Indian and many other communities."[53]

The oral tradition is part of the reality and ethos of Indian people. It must be understood in its proper role within indigenous cultures, and it can be used as a source of additional evidence and to challenge previous notions about a case study, tribe, or individual.[54] Stories are the basis of oral tradition, and storytelling is one of the means that makes Indians who we are. Story has power, and when exercised by a storyteller, the story brings the past, present, and future into one continuum of time. Thus it is important to keep in mind that time becomes less important and the message of the story is most relevant in the Indian way of thinking.

Oral tradition is not oral history but replaces it as the main venue for passing on history from one generation to the next. This communal trove remains a true source of information and knowledge about Native peoples. If scholars and writers will listen, and listen with Indian ears, they will learn much about Indian people. To listen in a non-Indian way is to take stories out of the cultural context of Indian reality. Conclusively oral tradition is the foundation of real Indian history.

All things begin with a story about the beginning. Like the Muscogee Creeks, who struggled from below to the face of *Ekv nv*, the earth, Native people survived and learned to prosper. Their way of learning about life through nature requires that they never forget where they came from, and thus their emphasis on oral tradition is pertinent to being connected to the past. For Indians, this is a lesson that our identity and who our people are must not be forgotten, and the ways of our people are found in our stories.

8

Power of Earth and Woman

Among the Lakota people, the prophecy of the White Buffalo Calf Woman is told. Ages before the coming of the white man, the Lakota tell a story of prophecy when their people suffered from starvation due to the cold of winter. For months, this suffering lasted until the camp's elders summoned two warriors to find food for their people. The two warriors set out to hunt. In their exhausting pursuit with no luck, a white buffalo appeared in the distance. As the white buffalo approached them, it turned into a beautiful maiden dressed in white. One warrior desired to be with the maiden and made his intention known. The other warrior was cautious and he became afraid by the transformation of the buffalo into a woman. The first warrior left with the maiden, and an overpowering fog shrouded them from sight. When the fog cleared the second warrior found his friend being eaten by worms. The young beautiful woman told the second warrior to return to his people and announce that she was coming to them. While in dire hunger, the people waited. The white buffalo woman arrived and gave the Lakota the sacred pipe for spiritual strength. Next, she told them where to find food, and said that she would return as a white buffalo 600 years later. She warned them that as long as the people live in the right way, they would prosper, but if not, then all would suffer and the end would come. The white buffalo woman said that she had been sent to help them to learn to survive, and now they were on their own.[1]

The "sense of place" is integral to American Indians for it represents homeland and the people who are a part of it. As the earth bonds all things together in kinship, then all things are related, according to many tribal beliefs. That is, we are related to the earth, meaning all things of the earth—the sky, rivers, mountains, a piñon tree, and a blade of grass—and we are related to one another. All things are a part of each other. Native people are connected to the earth. The earth is the mother to Indians and to all humans, including our enemies, so that we are all related. The earth gives life each day and it is the essence of existence. The mother defined Native people's lives, gave them lessons to live by, and shaped their cultures.[2] The earth is known by many names—Earth Mother, Mother Earth, Grandmother, Changing Woman, and Earth Woman—and she represents the natural environment for it is a part of her.

American Indian history has slowly changed in its scholarly analysis of Indian people. As we have seen, it has long been written from the right side of the equation of Indian-white relations. New scholarship in American Indian history must look inside Indian communities as the initial step toward fully understanding Native reality and ethos. Native reality involves environmental influences impacting Indian life. Since the postmodern era, Indian life and the status of indigenous peoples have changed considerably.[3] Much of Indian daily life and the indigenous worldview is influenced by forces outside tribal communities.[4] As Native people continue to adjust to modernity, they will alter their cultures by continually borrowing technology from the mainstream. Simultaneously American Indians are still very much part of the natural world.[5] Historically the natural people of the Americas were Indians, who envisioned life based on environmental influences.[6] Their adaptation to the natural environment shaped their culture and identity.[7]

Indians have noticed the influence of nature on their lives for many centuries.[8] And this is something that the mainstream has forgotten or given lower priority. In other words, nature is constant, moving generally in steady patterns and rotations, and scholars themselves need to realize their relationship with the out-of-doors environment (see figure 8, in chapter 5).[9]

Due to the importance of the symbolism of Mother Earth, women's studies, environmental studies, and the sense of place in American Indian history have much in common. Some scholars in the first two fields have focused on the cultural importance of women in American Indian communities. In essence, women's studies can help to explain the physical and symbolic roles of Native women in Indian societies. In light of earth-woman maternalism, environmental historical studies can explain how the earth is an integral part of Native worldviews and how Indian communities see themselves. Public historian John Jackson informs all of us that our place of origin and its natural environment secure our identity.[10]

Stories in the oral tradition explain how the earth is the source of creation and this power of life is special. Certain places on earth are empowered and are considered sacred. Among the Diné (Navajo), elder Mamie Salt said, "The whole land is sacred. . . . People also identify zones and spots on the larger land forms and in the surrounding country (commonly entire hills, mountains, and canyons) that some people say have too much sacred power for residence, grazing and other everyday uses." More specifically, Salt observed that many places exist as land forms that interact with certain natural forces. For example, mountaintops are where the first rays of the sun are seen, and "they gather the rain for the surrounding country." High points like mountains are "favored for prayers that relate to the surrounding country within view and the growing things" upon it.[11]

Special land forms on earth transfer spiritual energy and Native people respect such sites. As described in the last chapter, the Muscogee Creeks tell a creation story of the people emerging from *Ekv nv*—Mother Earth. The people are symbolically united in the Earth Mother's womb. For it is from *Ekv nv* that the Creeks say they come, like many Indian groups of a similar oral tradition. Their stories in myths and legends say that the earth is the mother of their people—their point of origin and life.

The Diné believe in an Earth Mother called Changing Woman,

who created their people, according to Diné mythology. Changing Woman created the four original clans, and she was the first to be honored with *Kinaalda*, a girl's puberty ceremony. Changing Woman was the mother of "hero twins," who saved the world from monsters. She symbolizes the four seasons of the year by representing the young girl changing from youth to age and returning to youth. Called the Earth Mother, Changing Woman represents the gift of life and its phases.[12]

Changing Woman gave other important things to the Diné. To women the Earth Mother gave the responsibility of protecting the Earth Bundle. The bundle contained soil from four or six sacred mountains and its power of renewal. The power of rendering life came from within the Earth Bundle, and the Diné used the bundle in their most important ceremony, called the Blessingway.[13]

The sacred mountains—Mount Blanca to the East, Mount Taylor to the South, San Francisco Peaks to the West, and Mount Hesperus to the North—uphold the universe of the Diné. Within these boundaries lie the sacred power of Changing Woman and her blessing upon the Navajo. For other Indian groups, special places of the landscape are empowered, and these sites share their power to help the people. The home called earth is the natural environment and animals as well as plants have a purpose. We should realize these purposes in life.[14]

John Rogers, an Ojibwe, recalled going to his grandmother's as a child and walking in the woods. During his journeys the plants and animals talked to him: "Grandmother's house was some six miles distant on a different trail. We traveled slowly, but enjoyed every step of the way. The call of the birds and the voices of other wild things were like music to my ears. It seemed that the trees and shrubs were whispering messages and that the Great Spirit hovered very near on this trail where the shadows were deep. Now and then we would see a deer or a rabbit, or perhaps, it would be a squirrel that would scamper up the tree and scold us for intruding upon his peaceful domain."[15]

As Rogers's story demonstrates, Indians humanize everything according to the indigenous ethos of each tribe, and thus all things have a human quality in the Natural Democracy. Communication,

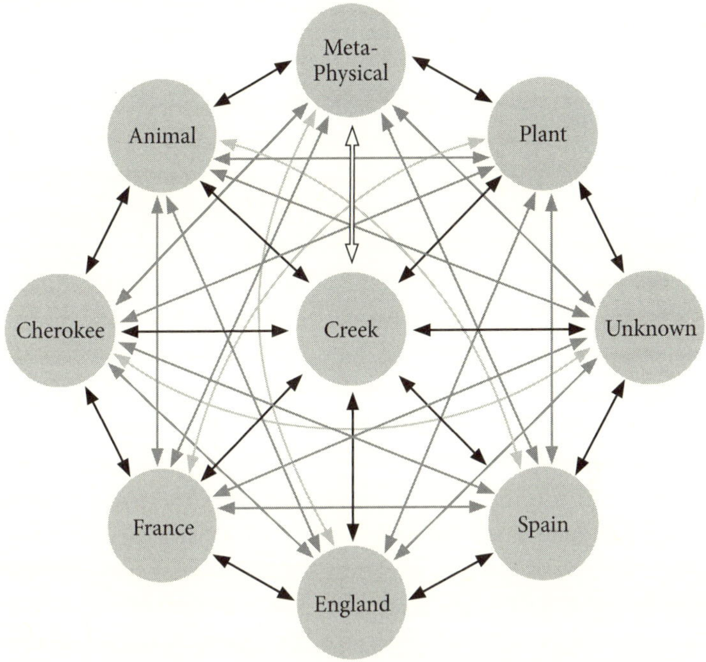

FIGURE 10. In the Natural Democracy matrix in an Indian reality, the totality concept involves each community possessing reciprocal relationships with all other communities, except for the one-way connection with the metaphysical community.

even without words but through sounds, produces a generic language that helps to bond entities and spiritualizes the natural environment. In these Native speech communities, all understand the indigenous ethos. The Medicine Way is not a religion; it is a way of life. In this totality is the Medicine Way (see figure 10).

Mother Earth is integral to most Indian communities of various regions. In case studies, archaeology has proven the early existence of Native communities and has helped to establish their identities long ago. To understand Indian people one must learn from the earth and be patient. The earth has power, especially in important sites, that engages with human memory in a process anthropologist Keith Basso calls "earth stalking." In his work with the Western Apache, Basso found that certain sites reminded people of stories and power related to sacred places in Apacheland.[16]

According to the mythology of Indian groups, the Creator exists in various forms. Some regard the Creator as a spiritual power with no shape, but other groups maintain that the Creator has shape in the form of a great animal. Some tribes believe the Creator is a female entity, including the Shawnees, who believe in *Moneto*, an ancient grandmother in the sky.

Among the many Native nations the Creator has many names, much as God has many names among Christian and non-Christian groups. As examples, the Creator is *Usen*, according to the Apaches, *Gitchimanitou*, as described by the Ojibwes; *Begochiddy*, the Great God of the Diné; First Maker or Person Above by the Crows; *Hesaketvmese* (Master of Breath) by the Muscogee Creeks; and *Nuakolahe* (One Who Made the Earth) among the Kiowa Apaches.[17] All tribes have their name for the Great Mystery.

It is believed that the Creator assigned roles and responsibilities to the Indians and their communities. Stories in the oral tradition cite moral lessons for Indians to act as stewards of the earth, like taking care of one's grandmother. Metaphorically the grandmother is responsible for giving the grandchild life via the mother; therefore a similar responsibility for caring is reciprocated.

The ancient people of the Americas also looked to the stars in the heavens in an attempt to understand their lives.[18] These fire beings were the same stars that later Indians studied and looked to for guidance, since things so old had great knowledge of the universe. The stars and the planets in the heavenly sky, like the earth, were the oldest beings known to the Indians for they existed before humans, plants, and animals. Stories about life were related to the stars, and some groups, like the Seminoles, believed that the Milky Way was the path to the spiritual world.

The Indians' universe included the earth and all of its elements here and above in the Natural Democracy. All things were related in the totality, causing indigenous philosophies to be holistic and circular in nature. This complex adaptive system involved the Native people learning about the universe and their environmental surroundings and developing their cultures accordingly. All entities were a part of daily life such that the universe, like Native reality, was the physical and the metaphysical combined.

As mentioned, symbolically many indigenous groups came from the womb of Mother Earth. Among some groups, some of their people or beings remained underground. Their mythological stories tell of the underground as another world in which not all is good.

Among the Pueblo communities of the Southwest, the Kachina religion dates back to about 1350. The Pueblos believe that their ancestors were reborn in the underworld. Their ancestors became beings or spirits that interpreted life for the people as well as for all living things because the gods of the Pueblos wanted the people to know certain things.[19] Pueblo author Joe Sando wrote: "The people came from the north to their recent areas of residence, from the place of origin at Shibapu, where they emerged from the underworld by way of a lake."[20]

The Mayas also believe in an underworld. The art historian Jacinto Quirarte proclaimed that much of Maya art and iconography depicts the underworld and the afterlife for the Maya people.[21] The underworld represents the unborn of the world. This is the home of wrongdoers, and they hold the secrets and knowledge that sometimes punishes those above. The underworld of darkness poses a constant threat, and people fear that they might fall into the darkness. The underworld among the Mayas is obviously important, as other scholars have found that "[Jacinto] Quirarte is undoubtedly correct in his interpretation that much of Maya art and iconography pertains to the underworld, the afterlife."[22] His observation demonstrates that good earth knowledge versus bad earth knowledge is among the dichotomies within the indigenous paradigm.

Like the grandmother described earlier as the earth and giver of life, symbolism is humanized and integrated into indigenous knowledge. Such symbolism explains what the rational western mind cannot. In communal life and tradition the grandmother is always present. Her womanly powers and strength are in the blood, which provides life to her children, and their future children are also a part of the bloodline. The woman and grandmother are the lifelines for people and the central element of many oral traditional stories.

Tradition has taught Native men to respect the role of women, especially elderly Indian women. Through the ages, the Indian woman has symbolically represented the earth and all of the lessons to be learned. The powers of the Earth Mother are great. Activist spokesman Russell Means of the Lakota expressed his supportive view of the role of the Earth Mother in his own people's lives and heritage: "We are the children of the Earth," said Means, the noted urban warrior and co-leader of the American Indian Movement. "She is our Mother, and it's our right and duty to protect her." He added, "There are forces in the universe beyond anything Europeans can imagine. From our traditional ways, we know that we do not have the right to degrade our Mother and that we must live in harmony with all creation. . . . If humanity keeps abusing Mother Earth, she will retaliate, and her abusers will be eliminated . . . many of our prophecies tell us that. I strongly believe in the power of mothers. If we have anything to convey to non-Indians, it is the true sense of this power and its sacredness."[23] Deep down, Indians know the earth as a woman in the spiritual humanization of all things. In her own way she provided all of the medicine that Native people would need. Nature's way is the Medicine Way.

In the Southwest the importance of women in Pueblo culture is demonstrated by their role in controlling the crops coming up from the earth. The people work with the earth, praying to it for good crops. Customarily the Pueblo men harvest the corn and then give it to their women for distribution to the community.[24]

Joseph Bruchac, an Abenaki storyteller, explained that "native women had control over their own lives. They could decide who they would or would not marry, they owned their own land, they had true reproductive freedom (including herbal methods of birth control), and they had political power. In New England, women chiefs were not uncommon, and throughout the Northeast there were various arrangements giving women direct control in choosing chiefs among the Iroquois."[25]

Unlike the emphasis on patrilineality in the mainstream, many Native groups stress matrilineality. From the mother flows the power of life, and the children are connected through blood with direct care given to them by the mother. Like the earth, women have the power to create, and this virtuous gift is not taken for granted. This view also gives women status in the community, especially female elders who become matriarchs.

Female elders are expected to be the first level of curers, taking care of their children's headaches, toothaches, stomachaches, and the like. As a storehouse of knowledge, the earth provides medicines to heal and to cure. Its plants and herbs are made into modern western medicines by pharmaceutical companies. For Native people the earth is a natural pharmacopeia and offers them at least 170 kinds of medicines.[26] Sick people knowing they were being cured represent the same kind of positivism as going to a medical doctor with the expectation of getting better. Faith in the healing qualities of the earth became an integral component of the indigenous ethos. Curing herbs used in a certain manner and ritual symbolically added to the optimism of the sick, who believed that they were going to get better. There was power in hope generated from belief, which is a part of the Medicine Way.

The symbolism is natural, as a part of life and the understanding of life in tribal communities due to the healing medicine powers. Woman is the giver of life as her sex was created to give birth, just as the earth yields flora and fauna, and the rivers and the mountains, and all things. This belief that woman is the provider of life is a powerful characteristic among Indian people. Women's biological ability to reproduce is part of nature's blessed gift to Indian women and all women. This ability to give life symbolizes the past, present, and future so that time always seems the same in a continuum. The heritage of the people derives from the traditional role of the Indian woman.

Yet Indian women see themselves as different from white American women, and most individual Indian women did not participate in the mainstream feminist movement. In her study of cross-cultural relations in the late nineteenth and early twentieth century, historian Margaret Jacobs observed that while white women attempted to help improve the lives of American Indian women, the two groups remained different due to cultural backgrounds.[27] Native women have been more accepting of their role in their tribal communities due to the respected status derived from a Natural Democracy. Furthermore, Native men respect the life-giving power of women, and a majority of Native societies are matrilineal.

The importance of symbolism is represented in many tribes' oral tradition. Told in stories, myths, and legends, the role of the woman is much more than the engendered female of Indian society. Many Indian groups have stories and tales and prophecies about women who have played an integral part of the community and its future. Women were mothers and wives, sisters and aunts, healers and prophets, and in some cases they were warriors and leaders.

During the nineteenth century on the plains, Native women played a crucial role in keeping their people alive. Anthropologist Oscar Lewis described the woman warrior among the North Piegan Blackfeet rising to the occasion due to need. Afterward, the woman warrior held special status in the community.[28] Perhaps the best known woman warrior was Lozen among the Apache. She fought alongside her brother until his capture by soldiers. Afterward Lozen fought with Geronimo against the Americans. She possessed the ability of a prophet to see far away and anticipated the approaching of the enemy.[29] Close to the earth and their natural surroundings, the Apaches learned to adapt to the demanding ways of the desert and mountains of their natural environment and homeland. Lozen represented the flexibility and strength of Apache women to endure while acting to defend the home space of her people, as if she was fighting for her grandmother—the earth.

Indian life is about adaptation and seeking balance. According to anthropologists, "sometime between AD 1110 and 1600 a group of Athapaskan-speaking tribes migrated from northwestern North America into the southwestern United States, where most eventually came to be referred to as Apaches . . . [with] their general style of adaptation to the Southwest."[30] The Apaches recall stories of such movement and adaptation by their people.

Among the Lakota people the prophecy of the White Buffalo Calf

Woman presented at the beginning of the chapter is told and retold. White Buffalo Calf Woman represents a manifestation of the earth for she is a part of it and of the natural environment, which often tests people. The story tells about the moral way of good and bad to provide balance for the Lakota people. Maintaining balance in life is a journey of many personal experiences. Each person faces daily decisions; however, stories of the oral tradition help set cultural norms and provide lessons about human behavior and a healthy tribal outlook on life.

It is extraordinary that the complex adaptive systems of Indian communities and their cultures were able to endure so much change. This ability was required in order to survive the rigors of the earth's demands on human life. For example, Plains Indian families expected hardship from the cold winters, especially during blizzards. Through her aged eyes of wisdom, the White Buffalo Calf Woman watched the suffering Lakota. Human life became vulnerable, especially among the young and the very old. They would become stronger. She taught them to adapt. This threatening situation compelled the Plains Indians to adopt the horse, to become nomadic to pursue the buffalo, and to develop tipis that could be quickly taken down and put up.[31]

Philosophical and religious beliefs were products of the changes forced upon the complex adaptive systems of the Plains Indians and other Native groups living in harsh lands of Earth Woman, such as those living in her deserts of the Southwest. Due to their ability to adapt, Indians have survived, have continued to alter their communities and cultures, and have flourished.

In the family or extended family the Indian woman provided stability. She was always there for her children and her husband. She was and remains the constant in people's lives. While her husband might be away hunting, or even lost in war, the Native woman was the caretaker for her family, as in the necessity of Indian women working in contemporary times.

While women were important in a tribal community, the people did not see all women as the same. Within the community the Indian woman had special status according to her family's status due to her mother or father. The success of the woman's husband as a warrior and as a provider of food and shelter could help to improve her status. The Indian woman could earn special status as a woman among others in the community. How well she sewed or cooked as well as her generosity toward others impacted an individual woman's status. These were her roles in societal relations.

While mainstream historians have generally neglected Native women, this is not the case for Indian history written or told by Indians. Women held together the social and cultural fabric of a community by acting as keepers of culture and society. Since the adoption of an ethnohistorical approach by modern American Indian historians, increasing numbers of biographies of Indian women have appeared in print. A helpful brief biography is David E. Jones, ed., *Sanapia: Comanche Medicine Woman* (1972), and an early classic is Frank B. Linderman, ed., *Red Mother* (1932), published later as *Pretty-Shield, Medicine Woman of the Crows* (1972). A helpful compilation of most of the literature on Indian women is Gretchen M. Bataille and Kathleen Mullen Sands, *American Indian Women Telling Their Lives* (1984). Two insightful books are Theda Perdue, *Cherokee Women: Gender and Culture Change, 1700–1835* (1998), and Michelene E. Pesantubbee, *Choctaw Women in a Chaotic World* (2003).

Along with biographies of Native women, Indian female autobiographies have risen significantly with the emergence of the Indian academic voice in the late 1960s. Since the early 1970s such autobiographies have included Maria Campbell, *Halfbreed* (1973); Ruth Underhill, ed., *Papago Woman, Maria Chona* (1979); Crying Wind, *Crying Wind* (1977); Beverly Hungry Wolf, *The Ways of My Grandmothers* (1980); Nancy Oestreich Lurie, ed., *Mountain Wolf Woman, Sister of Crashing Thunder: The Autobiography of a Winnebago Indian* (1961); Vada R. Carlson, ed., *No Turning Back: A True Account of a Hopi Girl's Struggle to Bridge the Gap between the World of Her People and the World of the White Man* (1964); and Mary Crow Dog with Richard Erodes, *Lakota Woman* (1990).

The burden of Indian women as keepers of the family and caregivers to the children has continued during the cultural transition to urbanization. Even after the turn of the twenty-first century, with more than two-thirds of the Indian population living in cities, one out of every four Indian households was run by Indian women without a father figure and with an average of two children.

Indian women have always been present, in war, famine, crisis, and in need. They have served as both parents when the father was away, even in modern times. Although women are seriously underrepresented in history written by academics, Native people have a great amount of respect for their women, and should give more.[32] Fatigued from her day's work and chores, the Indian woman found enough strength to put her children to bed at night, while singing a lullaby or telling a story or simply rocking her children in her weary arms until they fell fast asleep. Like a reed, the Indian woman would bend to weather even the worst storm, but she would never break even if it meant sacrificing her life. Although never given enough credit by non-Indian writers, the Indian woman carried a heavy burden.

Early Euroamericans looked down upon Native women and stereotyped them as slaves and drudges. While Native women worked hard, their men respected them for fulfilling their demanding roles. The role of Native men was also demanding, but women served as the foundation of tribal communities. Indian women have been vastly misrepresented and misunderstood as long as non-Indians have written about Native people without knowing them; learning the truth of who they are reveals the misconceptions, brings their significance to light, and affords them recognition as the heart of the family.

A young Indian girl learns from her mother, aunts, and grandmother about the significance of her place in society and how this will change. She learns that she and others will carry on the next generation. Her role becomes the same as her mother's and grandmother's. Her lessons derive from past cultural norms as she is taught her place and responsibility in the community. Her role is a cultural constant that helps to provide infrastructure to Native society. Yet she must possess the instinct to change when needed to meet the needs of her family.

Many of the stories from tribal oral traditions and relating to the earth are part of the Earth Woman. As the woman goes about carrying out her responsibilities and personal burdens, she is watched and studied by others. She is the symbol of life itself, like the earth with its many powers, of which the greatest is to reproduce and to give life. Not only do women bear children; they play perhaps the most significant role in raising them to young adulthood.

The Indian woman was also a teacher, like her mother and grandmother. As she had been taught by her mother and aunts, she passed along knowledge and wisdom. She taught her children the cultural ways of her people as well as the particular way in which she carried out her daily activities. Community helper, individual performer meeting family needs, and instructor for life, the Indian woman was the source for knowledge and advisor with wisdom, and as she grew older her wisdom increased. The expectations for a Native woman define her life and reality in the community. In addition, her traditional role has expanded in the twentieth and twenty-first centuries as she remains the keeper of the family. Today many Indian women are single parents with the burden of raising their children, sometimes with the help of their parents.

Normally the grandmother of the family served as the focal point of authority and security. She imbued strength, representing stability and continuity of the family. In her aged wisdom was the security of identity for her relatives and how they were related according to kinship. Many Indian communities were based on matrilineal descent for status and membership in their tribes.

A special bond existed between mother and daughter. Daughters almost always went to their mothers for advice and support. Learning to do things for her family, the mother also learned her role and status in the community. The same special bond occurred between the grandmother and grandchildren. The grandmother would sacrifice in order to protect and provide for her grandchildren, because they were also a part of her. In case of the death of a mother, the grandmother stood ready to assume the upbringing of the grandchildren. Grandmother always seemed to know what was best due to her many years of experiences and wisdom.

The grandmother is a common symbol in the oral tradition for many Indian tribes. In a Shawnee myth, the Creator is Grandmother. Named *Moneto*, she has a dog living with her in her lodge high above earth. As she makes a blanket—the universe of stars and the sun and the moon—she lays her sewing down periodically to cook and do other chores. The dog pulls certain objects from the blanket or places them on the blanket, and such objects become a part of earth.

Centuries of observation of plants and animals provided Natives with enough evidence for them to realize the importance of the process or power in creation. Learning about Indian life requires learning about the earth because Native people are heavily influenced by their natural environment. In attempting to learn about early Indian life before Indian-white relations, one must entertain a theory of reconstructing Indian communities. As noted earlier, archaeology provides a means for this analytical approach. The unsettling situation of a lack of evidence in written form for historians should not be a dead-end or an excuse to stop pursuing the full scope of Indian history. Rather, theory and archaeology can be helpful as additional evidence to environmental and women's studies.

By studying archaeology we can approach Indian places or Native sites in a scientific way. This is an acceptable method, if the proper questions and a respectful cultural protocol are followed as the archaeological study is carried out. Archaeology can provide clues in reconstructing a historic Indian reality and culture. Metaphysical influences on Indian life cannot be documented by academics who retain their cultural biases.[33] And sometimes what an archaeologist might see must simply be believed, especially pertaining to the excavation of ancient ruins where sacred power abounds.

Life is movement in the form of fluctuating change called energy. Indians call this changing motion spirituality. Since all things are of the Earth Mother, such things are empowered with life or a spirit. As the earth is life itself, all things of the earth are life—a flowing river, falling snow, a meadow of flowing grass, a mountain, or even a small rock. All things have a spiritual life force. And life is sacred, according to Native beliefs.

Among the Muscogee Creeks the power of life is the movement of wind or breath that we take in and exhale. The power of life is the action and state of inaction of a larger process that involves movement. In a universal context, the wind blowing over the earth is the breathing of the earth, including windstorms and hurricanes.

The Native woman is the earth in a metaphorical sense to Native people. Creation stories frequently include powerful female entities. Such female powers are generally positive, but they can also be destructive. For example, the White Buffalo Calf Woman of the Lakota oral tradition took the life of the sinful warrior, but the story provided a lesson of how to live life for the Lakota.

Acts of nature are manifestations of powers from Earth Woman. Storms, earthquakes, volcanic eruptions, or even a spring rain remind us that nature has the power to create and to destroy. Violent acts of nature are extraordinary, and they are part of the metahistory of Indian people and are recorded in stories. For example, an eclipse occurred on September 17, 1811, at the height of the Shawnee Prophet's metaphysical power. This turbulent time also endured earthquakes, shooting stars, and violent storms, and the Mississippi River even flowed backward due to earthquakes. On August 12, 1833, the Lakota recorded in their winter counts that the stars fell. In the twentieth century Mother Earth exhibited the Mississippi River flooding from heavy rainstorms that killed 246 people in 1927. In 1935 the Yangtze River in China flooded from excessive rains, which killed over 100,000 people.

In more recent times violent rainstorms produced the largest hail on record for the United States. A hailstone 18.75 inches in circumference was found after a storm that hit Aurora, Nebraska, on June 22, 2003. This display was almost equaled on July 23, 2010, when hail measuring 18.62 inches stoned Vivian, South Dakota.[34]

In a paper presented to the National Academy of Sciences in 1979, ecological anthropologist John W. Bennett pointed out the two common characteristics among all peoples and the land. He identified them as space and place. Bennett concluded that "space is where humans live. . . . The land that constitutes a group's space encompasses a range in which people, among other things, acquire their livelihoods, and which they are willing to defend. Place on the other hand, refers to some spot or spots within the larger range in which domiciles and other objects created by humans, or given definitions and meanings by humans, are located, such as storage facilities, ceremonial centers, sacred places, and the like."[35]

Many places exist throughout the continental United States that are considered sacred to the American Indians. In studying the Pueblo people, New Mexico State Historian Erna Ferguson stressed that the Pueblos "lived close to the earth" and "their religion is of earth and the things of earth."[36] The earth hosted special places of power that Indians learned to respect. There are many recognized sacred sites in America and at least forty-four that are endangered. Among the many nations of Indians, sacred places include the Devil's Tower for the Kiowa and Cheyenne, Blue Lake for the Taos, and Pyramid Lake for the Paiute. Other places include the San Francisco Peaks near Flagstaff, Arizona, for the Hopis and Mount Taylor for the Acomas.[37]

As more becomes known about American Indian sacred sites, the endowed power of such places could be vulnerable to misuse by both non-Indians and Indians.[38] Such places need protection by the tribes and through legislation by the U.S. government.

Certain sites have been empowered by the Creator. Some places of power are good and some are bad, or cursed by evil. Indians do not live at such sites, although they traditionally visited these places such as Rainbow Bridge for empowerment or to try to learn more about the supernatural.[39]

The power of place in the supernatural transcends cultures and races. The power of place has an awing effect with a spiritual presence, reminding us that there is a greater power than people. Fred McTaggart, a non-Indian scholar who studied the Mesquakie Indians of Iowa and collected their stories, began to feel the spiritual environment of the Indians. On their reservation during the winter, he wrote:

> I was still shivering but I continued to stand there in the wind, listening carefully and looking out across the clearing to my left. The timber was directly behind me and I could feel its presence vividly. By now, the sound that had stopped me was not important. In the land to my left and the woods behind me was a feel-

ing that demanded attention. As anxious as I was to get inside that warm house, I felt compelled to listen and to look. There were spirits in the land, I had been told, the spirits of the people, animals, plants, dreams, and stories that belonged to this piece of ground. I was romantic enough to accept and believe the mysticism of the Mesquakies. But it was still mysticism. Until now.[40]

McTaggart had witnessed the spiritual awareness as a part of the Medicine Way all around us.

There are places of power on land and water. Certain waters have special powers, or they are sites for evil. The Muscogee Creeks believe in the water king, who lives at the bottom of clear and calm water, such as in lakes and in rivers. It still lurks there. The Seminoles share in this belief of a water king. The Ojibwes believe in a water monster who lives at the bottom of Lake Superior or Lake Michigan. Ships wrecked by storms, canoes capsized, and people swept from bridges are the crimes committed by the water monster, according to the Ojibwes.

Rivers like the Columbia, Mississippi, Missouri, Ohio, and others remain spiritually important to Native people. Early Native people built effigies like the serpent mound north of the Ohio River. The mound has a symbolic connection between the serpent and the river, representing the continuity of life and death.

In a valley in the Southwest, ancient Indians lived centuries ago, and their presence is still felt. Historian Calvin Martin described a personal experience of a presence engulfing him. "I straightened up and stepped away from the pictroglyphs, idly casting my eye over the pebbly floor, wondering whether there might be another projectile point lying hereabout," wrote Martin. He continued, "In an instant there was a terrific report, like the sound of a gunshot immediately at my back, and I whirled around. There before me stood a whirlwind being, in stature, as best I recollect, slightly taller than me. Confronting me. . . . I had willfully asked to be found by a sacred object—and had been. Was I to be surprised at finding myself face to face with a wind spirit?"[41]

Like rivers of water flowing across the land, there are zones that are dangerous, evil riverlike zones meandering across the landscape, and local Indians tend to avoid them. These are distinct routes of positive and negative zones that travelers and hunters, both Indian and non-Indian, come to acknowledge. Positive areas are valleys and meadows and surrounding areas that emit a beauty that the human spirit finds comforting. For example, long ago the Shawnees called many areas of Kentucky the land of the spirits because they radiated an abundance of grasses and trees filled with birds and animals. It was as if the Creator had made these places special, and the Shawnees believed that they should treat these flowing areas with respect.

Rivers on the earth were often negative zones where hunters and travelers met with accidents, got lost, or lost their lives. Danger dwells in such rivers on the land, and the human spirit finds discomfort in such negative areas. The instinctive response is anxiety and fear. These feelings cause panic, and thus one easily falls into the trap of such dangerous places of calamity. The Muscogee Creeks and Seminoles believe that the metaphysical can trap one's mind momentarily in a mental state called *e ho sa*. In this state of being caught between the physical and metaphysical, people lose their sense of time and of where they are trapped. Then suddenly they are set free when the metaphysical releases its grip.

The majestic heights evoke awe from Indians, who often call such places sacred. Due to the respect for the beauty of mountains, names are given to them, and it is believed that such places are where spirits live. From high areas the spirit of a mountain, or a spirit residing there, appears before the people in visions and in dreams. Such mountains are empowered by the Creator for they are gigantic and they harness much power, which can be a blessing or a danger for Indian people living in the area.

Many mountains are sacred places for Indian people. As earlier noted, Mount Taylor is a boundary marker for the Diné. Mount Adams is relevant to the Yakama people of Washington, and other mountains are important to various tribal cultures. Mountains are part of the metahistory of Indians, serving as a liaison between the physical and metaphysical worlds.

Deserts test the human spirit. For life to exist there, the human spirit learns adaptability, resourcefulness, and patience. Indian people living in such regions are great students of nature's most challenging areas. Life is sparse with limited rainfall, causing the body and the mind to become imbalanced. Illusions from the subconscious challenge the conscious mind. Physical thirst and hunger punish the body simultaneously, until one learns to live in Earth Woman's desert environment and to learn the lessons of discipline and patience in life.

Native peoples of the basin and range area of the West learned about the desert. They learned how to survive there as the environment challenged them. The challenge compelled them to adapt by using their acquired knowledge, and they lived with the environment by not changing it. Whether we move to another place or a place has been described in literature that we have read, our mind has invented a place. As more descriptions are available, this place in mind becomes vivid with colors and distinction of outline with all kinds of details. The human mind creates illusions about a place, and a relationship is developed with the place.

Such a place is a home, consisting of a house or lodge and the landscape. The landscape is of the earth, so that the illusion of place in mind allows us to return home. Hence we identify with this place in mind that is a part of us, "our first exposure to life, the place where we come to know the world," in the words of public historian Robert Archibald.[42] All things in the Medicine Way, including one's natural surroundings and home space, are within the Natural Democracy.

Furthermore, the spirits of the people and the place establish a relationship that is constant. Because the people have lived in a certain place, or sung or danced there for a long time, the relationship between human and place is empowered with a spiritual presence in such a way that some people might say such places are haunted. In reality the power of the relationship is great enough to be heard or smelled, and aberrations sometimes appear, thereby designating the empowerment of such ethnogeographic places.

The interaction with spirits is best understood through Native logic. It requires thinking like Native people, which is different for a

Navajo or Comanche or Mohawk, although all three accept the presence of spirits and the power of medicine. In reconstructing the indigenous past and reality, Native logic is integrally involved. Finding evidence for understanding Native logic is not an easy task.

Many prehistoric cultures have left evidence for the future. For example, like the Old World scribes and artists, the early Native people called the Anasazi left drawings in their cliff dwellings. These pictures are tremendously valuable because along with the archaeological materials left behind, they are virtually the only evidence we have of these cultures. How can we interpret the meanings of these drawings? In order to understand their meanings, current scholars need to think like the Anasazi, if possible. By understanding the values and communal structure of the ancient ones, we can decipher something of their cultures and histories. This would mean re-creating the historical reality of the Anasazi by examining all sources of evidence for the period and place in question. Then, using Anasazi logic and decision making, we would come closer to understanding the drawings.

When all of us think about who we are, we think about where we come from. Simultaneously, we think logically about the place that we call home, and where we were born, where we were raised, and where our people are.[43] Place is identity that is native to Indian people. Harold Isaacs asserted that the land has defined group identity. He stressed that the relationship is infinite: "The physical characteristics that bear on group identity extend in critical ways to the place, the land, the soil to which the group is attached, literally, historically, [and] mythically."[44] The longevity of this relationship extends from the past to the present and to the future.

Place provides all of us with a sense of history. In the western mind, history represents a series of events and great deeds, usually about men. Within the last few decades of scholarship in the academy, historians have produced impressive works in social history, cultural history, and other fields. But more is to be done in the area of Native history. Although the environment is also the homeland, place is usually disregarded or deemphasized. In the Indian's mind, however, place is important to the understanding of life and the past.[45] Tribal communities have such home places such as the Turquoise House that the Twins searched for and the Rainbow Bridge that allowed them to cross over to find home.

Place provides us with a sense of reality that is our own; from that we have a Native perspective that yields a view of the world manifesting our values and attitudes toward all things. All that is called ethos comes from the power of place, as was experienced by Black Elk standing high on Harney Peak, weeping in the rain, while realizing the power of beauty that was natural.

Steeped in the powers of the womanly earth, indigenous people believed that the Earth Woman empowered them and all things. Yet the people learned to survive as their community confronted greater external forces like floods, famine, and drought and as military enemies confronted them. These forces challenged the internal bonding influences of their communities' social units of persons, extended families, clans or societies, community, tribe, and spirituality. Such forces challenged the infrastructure and cohesion of a Native community. For example, the Tewa world changed but became stronger due to external forces threatening the internal forces within their community—internal forces such as their ability to remain united, possessing effective leadership, and having sufficient resources with which to respond. In the end, internal forces helped to change the Tewa people, who learned to survive change by changing.[46]

In the indigenous worldview the earth and woman are one and the same. Symbolically they are an integral part of the Circle of Life. They give life and nourish it for the continuity of the earth and for people. Even the animal and plant worlds follow the same philosophy of gender differences as one of the natural laws of the indigenous universe. Life proceeds with the seasons in a cycle, not in a linear manner. This is a fundamental concept of circularity that people seem to take for granted and forget. Although most modern Indian people have highly valued the role of their women, this has not always been the situation; in the last half of the twentieth century national attention focused on Native women as victims of violence and abuse. Contemporary domestic violence has occurred on reservations, and charges were raised of sexism within the American Indian Movement during the 1970s. Yet Indian women remain strong, the forces in society who give life and nurture it; who protect, feed, clothe, and sacrifice for their children in order to perpetuate the life to which they have given birth.

Among the Lakota, the White Buffalo Calf Woman taught the people about the Circle of Life and how animals and plants were a part of the earth. As the White Buffalo Calf Woman story was passed down, it taught the Lakota valuable lessons. It also prophesied the future, for the beginning and the end are the same in the Circle of Life and for those Indian people who believe in the old ways.

In Janesville, Wisconsin, on August 20, 1994, the white buffalo calf returned. Named Miracle by the white farmers who owned her, the white buffalo attracted the attention of many Native people, who journeyed there to see her. They prayed to the white buffalo and left prayer offerings. She changed colors from white to black, red, yellow and brown. Miracle, the white buffalo, died of natural causes on September 19, 2004. Her life continues to be celebrated by Native people and others, but what of the prophecy in connection to the birth of the white buffalo called Miracle?

The Lakota belief in the White Buffalo Calf Woman came true, connecting myth and reality. Knowing that she would return, the Lakota felt blessed with this knowledge. Having faith in myths is a part of the Medicine Way of embracing the tandem of the metaphysical and physical as one. Miracle was proof to them that the ancient myth was true.

9

Coming Full Circle

Like the seasons changing in cycles every year and the rotational change from day to night, the Circle of Life includes all things, according to traditional Indian belief. The past is a part of the present such that in Indian awareness, history represents a continuum without a beginning or an end. One young Indian person said:

> "The broken circle suggested to me what I felt in my heart and the feelings other people have in their hearts. Because the circle has been around for thousands of years, and now it's come apart because people are forgetting about the ways of the spirit and the ways of kindness to people. They're greedy and money hungry and want power, and that won't do much when they get to the spirit world. . . . If people's visions vanish and our way of life isn't like a growing, healthy tree, then we will all vanish. . . . That's the philosophy of Indian life. It is centered around the spirits and around the Creator. All of it.[1]

Teaching and writing the history of American Indians is an overwhelming experience of tackling multitudinous histories of many tribal communities and academically proclaiming that a single history represents all of them. In short, trying to teach American Indian history is like teaching the histories of many civilizations during various eras in a single course. As of the year 2010, the federal government recognized 566 tribes, so teaching Indian history is like covering the histories of nearly 600 nations, compounded by trying to convey both men's and women's perspectives. Writing Indian history is equally challenging due to the complex nature of the subject.

Many scholars and writers have been academically, romantically, or politically inspired to write American Indian history. But in each case the author faces serious concerns of what focus to adopt, problems of organization, the unforeseen plethora of research sources housed at various sites, and simply where to begin and when to end. These challenges pose additional concerns as one begins to think further about the various responsibilities of writing American Indian history.[2]

The challenges of reconceptualizing and rewriting American Indian history have been explored throughout this book. In an effort to meet these challenges, I have attempted to push readers to rethink the pedagogy and writing of American Indian history; specifically, I have proposed the Medicine Way as a response to the current state of the field. Three paramount points have been introduced and explained.

The first major point is that the binary equation of the Indian-white relationship can be used as a model to introduce Native reality as it once flourished and continues to exist, according to the period and tribe being studied. This Indian-white equation is a theoretical model demonstrating that (1) Native people have been written about mostly by non-Indians, (2) a shared history developed, incorporating both the Indian and white perspectives and centering on areas in which the two sides shaped history together, such as in battles or at boarding schools, and (3) there is a Native point of view based on an indigenous ethos and reality.

The binary Indian-white equation can be used to illustrate a tribal community's various relationships. The initial step is to imagine a single binary of a white mainstream perspective and an Indian perspective, and a shared experience. These three views are separate dimensions of contextualization. With this in mind, a cross-cultural bridge of understanding develops from exploring the range of the Indian-white binary. This allows us to realize and comprehend the various stages of Native history, First Dimension, Second Dimension, and Third Dimension. It helps to imagine a bridge having three sections, connecting the three phases of Indian history described in the Medicine Way.

The second major point is the internal-external model that addresses the infrastructure of a tribal community. Within a community, this inside-to-outside approach suggests that sociocultural units of the Native person, extended family, clan or society, community, tribe, and spirituality hold the community together. Balance and harmony are the purposes in life for all units as they exist as one community in a natural environment. It is theorized that each tribal community consists of these integral parts and solidifies in times of need to thwart the outside influences of war, famine, federal policy, and other external threats.

The third major point is the realization that in the Third Dimension, a tribal community has multiple human and nonhuman relationships in an indigenous paradigm that exists in physical-metaphysical reality. Each tribal community has this multiplicity of relationships that I call a Natural Democracy.

Each of these three paramount points has served for a millennium or more within the totality called a Natural Democracy, an Indian reality and ethos—the Indian world. Furthermore, the Natural Democracy theory is applicable to other indigenous communities in the world. As a starting point, this Natural Democracy model can be applied to indigenous communities who respect their natural surroundings in Australia, India, New Zealand, and throughout the world. Acceptance of the indigenous Medicine Way theory is a route to begin decolonizing the western mode of imperial thinking. Some things have to be taken for granted to entertain the first step in crossing the cultural bridge of the Medicine Way—for example, that matters metaphysical warrant inclusion. Indeed, in the mainstream we unconsciously take many things for granted—for example, that matters metaphysical warrant exclusion.

In order to understand and to write about Indian life, one should imagine the entirety of a people—their completeness—heroes, oral tradition, society, community, ceremonials, battles, issues, and so on. In writing about the Maya of Mexico, Norman Hammond and Gordon R. Willey note: "Maya cultural history and cultural processes cannot be understood in terms of the Maya alone[;] a Maya world, a Maya idea set, a Maya tradition, or whatever one wishes to call it, must always first be taken into account."[3] The big picture of American Indians has to be visualized prior to the arrival of Columbus. Next, the large context has to be imagined: how contact with Europeans and Americans has caused Native people to reinvent their identities, compromise their cultures, and preserve their worldviews.

In order to improve and revise our thinking about doing Indian history, historians need to be open to accepting the challenge to rethink how we analyze and write on the subject. This book invites historians and other scholars who write Indian history to accept an alternative logic and set of concepts about the subject.

First of all, we need to think deeply about what Indian reality was like during the time periods we are investigating. The bottom line is to try to reconstruct the reality of the people. This is not a small task. The typical way of approaching Indian history is to research the existing documents on the subject. Unfortunately, this leaves holes in the reconstruction process, since Native people left only a limited amount of written evidence compared to the plethora of paper produced about them.

Yet over time Indians have supplied multiple kinds of records of their natural world and events. Early evidence includes petroglyphs, rock art, and hide paintings. During the early nineteenth century the invention of Sequoyah's syllabary enabled the Cherokee to produce their own documents. Additional accounts have been left in the form of picture-writing and Navajo sandpaintings. These forms were often derived from the memory of an individual but can also include the subconscious, such as dreams, or historical events and experience.

Recorded Native evidence is also found in the form of winter counts. Plains Indian groups in particular recorded important experiences of the past. These counts were often drawn according to the seasons of the year, and they related what happened during these periods. They depicted battles, supernatural phenomena, and other special experiences deemed important by the person recording the winter count.

Another source of research data is photographs and images such as drawings and paintings. The *American Indian Culture and Research Journal* published a special edition, "The Shadow Catcher," in 1996. The volume addresses the opportunities and insights provided by Indian photographs and images. In libraries and archives at universities and historical societies, collections of Indian images and photographs offer this valuable window into Native life and tribal cultures. Such helpful collections include the photographs in the Western History Collections of the University of Oklahoma. This visual evidence serves as an additional source of clues to the reality of the Indian past, although one must consider that the photographs are of Indians taken by non-Indians.

A major objective of this revisionary process is understanding the ethos of Indian people according to their tribal worldview. Chapter 2 lays the foundation for seeing in the Native way, and one does not have to be Indian in order to accomplish this exercise.[4] The learning process of seeing involves understanding how Indian people of a particular tribe relate to everything in their lives. Seeing is acknowledging everything in one's environment, with respect for each entity in the Natural Democracy. The quest requires examining everything we can to try to understand what Native people thought about Indian history.

The minds and lives of American Indians are immeasurably complex in relationship to the nontangible. Indian history is not merely a human history in the Americas. As writer Mary Roberts has noted, "implicitly contrasting Indians with white, the Indian mind is not literal, specific, scientific—it is philosophical, vague, and poetic."[5] Native historical reality represents a matrix of inter-relational alliances, acknowledging medicine power everywhere, visualizing the connection between the physical and metaphysical, and understanding the cycles of the natural world where human beings, nonhuman beings, animals, and plants are all kin interacting in a Natural Democracy.

In 1961 noted anthropologist Fred Eggan observed that "the major contribution of ethnohistory in the next decades may well be in the revision of American Indian history. We are proud of the historians who have written on the American Indian. But, with some exceptions, they have been primarily concerned with the significance of the Indians for American history. Even where, like Grant Foreman or Angie Debo, they had a deep sympathy with the Indian, they had only a general familiarity with his cultural patterns and values. The future writers on Indian history will give us the other side of the coin emphasizing the Indian's view of his world and of the events which have transpired—as well as the changes wrought in White society and culture."[6]

Eggan's call for change began to be attempted only in the last two decades of the twentieth century. The history profession could not accomplish this task alone, nor could any other discipline. The labyrinth-like complexity of American Indian history challenged the academic disciplines and influenced the professional discipline of anthropology as it was practiced in the United States.

Even at this point it was crucial to acknowledge the rising Indian voice in Native history. This is part of the Indian-white equation introduced in chapter 2 as the basis of Indian history and where it is moving in terms of interpretation. Anthropologists were the first academics to take Indian views seriously as they studied tribal communities. The efforts of anthropologists studying Native people in the field have provided crucial ethnographic data for anthropology and other disciplines.

The collaboration of anthropology and history did not entail the collapse of either discipline but rather the birth of a new field called ethnohistory. In a timely manner, ethnohistory has contributed to the field of American Indian history by assisting in the revision of the mainstream approach. "Ethnohistory was not invented suddenly when the society devoted to it was organized," Francis Jennings recalled of the American Society for Ethnohistory. He continued, "Like most complex intellectual efforts, it had progenitors who were at work even in the latter nineteenth century. . . . They, however, were ethnologists and museologists who conceived their work as a branch of anthropology; and what they wrote reflects the outlook of the anthropology of that era."[7] The partnership of anthropology and history was struck in the agreement that both disciplines have something to contribute to the study of indigenous people. History and anthropology were not alone in this collaboration, as other disciplines like archaeology and linguistics had already become involved in the study of American Indians.

The synergy of history and anthropology in particular is a strategic partnership of the new Indian history that Robert Berkhofer called for in 1971. Berkhofer observed that "American Indian history must move from being primarily a record of white-Indian relations to become the story of Indians in the United States (or North America) over time."[8]

Four years later historian David Edmunds assessed the change in Indian history and the surge of academic interest in Indians. He noted that "several factors have contributed to this phenomenon. During the late 1960s many young Americans became increasingly disenchanted with the deteriorating environment and the lack of progress in solving urban problems. Searching for an alternate life-style, these young people rejected the traditional white belief that man should always dominate nature. Instead they turned toward Indian philosophies of living in harmony with the environment."[9] Instead of Indian history being simplified, the opposite happened. Whereas Indian history, culture, and archaeology had seemed to be the integral parts of understanding Native people, scholars increasingly realized that they needed to add the natural environment into the mix.

In 1991 Richard White asserted in his award-winning *The Middle Ground* that Indians should be at center stage, equal partners in defining and shaping history. As scholars have continued to grasp at understanding of the multi-relational complexity of American Indian history, ethnohistorians have come the closest to writing in the Third Dimension.

Native scholars have also been busy trying to shift the mainstream paradigm of how Indian history has been perceived and written. Since the 1980s Indians have also written about themselves and have produced an impressive amount of literature, including by the prolific Lakota scholar Vine Deloria Jr. and the Cherokee writer Robert Conley. Cherokee-Creek historian Tom Holm has authored *Strong Hearts, Wounded Souls: Native American Veterans of the Vietnam*

War (1996) and *The Great Confusion in Indian Affairs: Native Americans and Whites in the Progressive Era* (2005). Like Vine Deloria, Conley, and Holm, Philip Deloria has written about Indians in general with two significant contributions, *Playing Indian* (1998) and *Indians in Unexpected Places* (2004).

Shoshone historian Steven J. Crum wrote *Po'I Pentun Tammen Kimmappeh, The Road on Which We Came: A History of the Western Shoshone* (1994). Choctaw historian Clara Sue Kidwell produced two salient books about her people, *Choctaws and Missionaries in Mississippi, 1818–1918* (1995), and *The Choctaw Indians of Oklahoma: From Tribe to Nation, 1855–1970* (2007). Interestingly, most Native historians have written about their own people. For example, Donna Akers published *Living in the Land of Death: The Choctaw Nation, 1830–1860* (2004). Edward Charles Valandra wrote about his Lakota people and termination in *Not Without Our Consent: Lakota Resistance to Termination, 1950–59* (2006). Ned Blackhawk, a Shoshone historian, produced an award-winning book, *Violence over the Land: Indians and Empires in the Early American West* (2006). William Bauer has written about his people on his reservation in *We Were all Like Migrant Workers Here: Work, Community and Memory on California's Round Valley Reservation, 1850–1941* (2010).

Other Native historians have also added to this Native-authored bibliography. In 2009 a special edition of the *American Indian Quarterly* produced several essays and two commentaries by Native scholars writing from their homelands as the framework of their scholarship.[10] One of the Native scholars in this issue, Malinda Maynor Lowery, published her award-winning book *Lumbee Indians in the Jim Crow South: Race, Identity, and the Making of a Nation* in the following year. In the same light as this discourse of the Medicine Way, Native scholars are coming home, so to speak, to write their people's histories from the inside perspective after having been trained in mainstream universities.

These Native-authored publications largely written after the turn of the twenty-first century have generated some attention in the history discipline and given it pause. One important question is where does the Medicine Way of Indian history fit into the larger historiography? Indeed, the Medicine Way is a parallel paradigm to the western orientation of history. When Robert Berkhofer called for a new Indian history in the early 1970s, scholars writing about Native people began to move them toward center stage in the production of history, as outlined in the discussion of the Second Dimension. This occurred during the rise of ethnic studies programs across the country and in Canada. One might call this part of the new social history movement that proliferated in the late 1970s and was soon joined by new western history in the 1980s.

However, Medicine Way history is actually much older; its *longue durée* pre-dates the arrival of Columbus in the western hemisphere. As Benedict Anderson has contended, prior to the late fifteenth century, civilizations in North America developed outside and separate from western influence.[11] Like Māori indigenous history, Native African history, and others representing 370 million indigenous people of 5,000 communities in 72 countries as of 2010, American Indians had their own version of history, and it was and is further divided into more than 500 tribal histories. True, postcontact western influence has altered the Medicine Way; yet it remains as a parallel paradigm housed within Natural Democracy.

Western-oriented scholars have also provided theoretical concepts that can help non-Indians understand the Medicine Way. Leopold von Ranke helps explain it for understanding the truth of the Indian past—as it happened in a Native context. The Medicine Way is beyond a human-oriented history, and it is broader in scope than the French Annales School interpretation, which includes all of human social interaction. In effect expanding upon the Annales approach, the Medicine Way includes nonhuman entities of the flora and fauna and the natural environment. Because of the metaphysical component of the Medicine Way, fundamental aspects of it can be partially explained by Edward Said. His discussion of othering helps establish a parallel paradigm that tells the rest of the academy a lot about itself. Again, the abstract of Indian metaphysics is difficult to grasp and can feel like trying to nail jelly to the wall, but Michel Foucault's understanding of power as empowerment from structuralism is helpful in demonstrating established human authority. However, instead of human-constructed institutions, if one applies the earth as a natural structure with the work of Keith Basso in mind, indigenous understanding of power derives from the infrastructure of Earth Woman's natural environment. The power of nature—in the form of lightning, an earthquake, or a tsunami, for example—is much greater than human-created power, although they are not quite the same kind of power. The Medicine Way includes human and supernatural powers.

Science in the twenty-first century can indeed help explain the Medicine Way of human-nonhuman history, but this indigenous paradigm has a course of its own within Natural Democracy. In this indigenous context the Medicine Way falls outside the continuous debate over history, if the academy is willing to entertain history as existing only within its categorical box. By natural design, the Medicine Way is not linear but rather cyclical, and it extensively involves the abstract that so disquiets empiricists. To begin to place or wedge the Medicine Way into historiography requires willingness to entertain a history of theoretical, abstract nature within its own paradigm of tangibles and nontangibles.

Ironically the study of American Indians is coming full circle, but the circle is not quite completed by Indian books written from the left side of the equation in the Third Dimension. In our digital era of cloud computing, growing dependence on computer technology to create and distribute images and information is in some ways comparable to the mode whereby Indian youth experienced traditional learning via stories of the oral tradition. Indian scholars in increasing numbers in all academic disciplines and more Indian studies programs are fully participating in the scholarship and are sharing knowledge about their people rather as earlier generations once shared knowledge around campfires. Abenaki storyteller Joseph Bruchac has observed: "If you see things in terms of circles and cycles, and if you care about the survival of your children then you begin to engage in commonsense practices. . . . The circle is the way to see. The circle is the way to life, always keeping in mind the seven generations to come, always asking: how will my deeds affect the lives of my children's children's children?"[12]

Native history needs to be viewed in the broadest way possible using spherical imagination to envision the multiple relationships of tribal communities, and historians need more tools at their disposal. Native literature offers another resource. Alun Munslow has noted: "By the late 1990s new historicism had . . . a much wider cultural analysis."[13] By taking a cultural and new intellectual approach of analyzing the works of Native writers, such as Leslie Silko's groundbreaking novel *Ceremony*, James Welch's *Fools Crow*, and other indigenous literature, more insight into Native reality can be revealed.

With the twentieth century ended, thorough assessments of the historiography of the American Indian are in order if we are to improve our understanding of Indian people, their complex ways, and their histories.[14] One insightful Native person stated, "We're looking for truth about our people, it's not in the textbooks and it's not anywhere we can pop it up on a computer, the way the white man's education wants us to do—the white system wants us to hurry up and find something and read it and go take a test and pass it and, suddenly, you know it and you're smart."[15]

To claim that mainstream history represents all of the American experience is not justifiable, and to presume that it comprehensively meets all societal needs is to commit a gross error.[16] American Indian history is not just a human history, and a call for change is needed to understand the complete past of Native people.

As the youth warned in the opening to this chapter, when Indian values are broken, the circle is broken. Visions vanish, and living life becomes difficult. Our health becomes threatened. We must seek balance and secure our place in the circle of our community and become a part of the circle, for it goes on. This Circle of Life in the universe is the seasons changing, day and night continuing as a part of this circle, and it is an Indian way of understanding life.

It is from this perspective that Fred Eggan, Dee Brown, Robert Berkhofer, Vine Deloria and others have at various times called for a change in Indian history to hear the Native voice. Respectfully to all, the cross-cultural bridge of understanding across the Three Dimensions to a Natural Democracy demonstrates the Medicine Way of American Indian history for everyone.

Finally, the complexity of the experiences of the tribal nations encompasses all things in the universe as their histories. The Circle of Life continues. Native people functioning within indigenous cultures were fully cognizant of the scope of life, and they continually tried to keep this in perspective. Tribal philosophies developed from relationships with nature and the environment, enabling the understanding that human beings were an integral part in a system created by a superior force. In this grand order of life all parts were inter-related, with no single dimension—economics, militarism, religion, or ideology, for example—determining the course of evolution.

One last point is that many Native people believe in "talking circles" to discuss important issues. Historically, councils were called for great decisions to be made. The single purpose of this book is a call for change, a call for anyone interested in Indian history and Native studies to begin talking about indigenous ethos and Native reality being central to teaching and writing American Indian history. We might all regard ourselves as a kind of talking circle. The Medicine Way is a different way of thinking altogether from our accustomed western style of thought. As I and the two colleagues mentioned at the opening of this book continue teaching courses surveying Indian history, I usually end the last lecture with the same maneuver. Typically I tell my undergraduates that I do not care whether they remember anything about Indian history from the course; this catches their attention. Then I tell them I hope, instead, that they have thought deeply about American Indian history. Most of the time at that point there is a collective silence, and then some begin to nod their heads and then others.

Notes

1. The Complexity of American Indian History

1. Brown, *Bury My Heart at Wounded Knee*, xviii.
2. Innes, "Introduction: Native Studies and Native Cultural Preservation."
3. In Montgomery's *An Elementary American History*, chapter 1 is "The Discovery and Naming of America" (1000–1507); Tindall, in *America: A Narrative History*, attempts to correct the error of European discovery of North American by listing chapter 1 as "The Collision of Cultures," but it has a subtitle: "European Visions of America." In Bailey and Kennedy's *The American Pageant*, chapter 1 is called "New World Beginning" and excludes "Discovery," although the New World is new to Europeans at the time, not to Indians. Norton and colleagues, in *A People and a Nation*, shed light on contact history, calling chapter 1 "The Meeting of Old World and New, 1491–1650." In Foner's *Give Me Liberty!* chapter 1, "A New World," most accurately describes European expansion to an already populated Americas.
4. Hough, *Out of Place*, 3.
5. See Spivak, *Can the Subaltern Speak?*
6. Glassberg, *Sense of History*, 22.
7. Susman, *Culture as History*, 17.
8. Geertz, *Interpretation of Cultures*, 14.
9. Black Elk is quoted in Neihardt, *Black Elk Speaks*, 194–95; the quote is also in Hill, *Words of Power*, xi.

2. Native Ethos of "Seeing" and a Natural Democracy

1. Neihardt, *Black Elk Speaks*, 36.
2. An earlier version of this chapter was presented as an invited paper

for a public lecture, "Themes in Life: Learning from American Indian History," presented at Adrian College, Adrian, Michigan, March 12, 1993.

3. As of July 1999 the federal government recognized 547 American Indian tribal groups, and a year later in July 2000 a total of 558 federally recognized tribes existed. There are 564 tribes as of 2010.
4. McGaa, *Native Wisdom*, 36–37.
5. Vine Deloria Jr. addresses these elements in *The Metaphysics of Modern Existence*.
6. For Black Elk see Neihardt, *Black Elk Speaks*; for Lame Deer see Lame Deer and Erodes, *Lame Deer, Seeker of Visions*, and Neihardt, *Black Elk Speaks*, 36; and for Severt Young Bear see Young Bear and Theisz, *Standing in the Light*, and McGaa, *Native Wisdom*, 36–37.
7. An introduction to American Indians studying the universe is in Williamson, *Living the Sky*, and Miller, *Stars of the First People*.
8. Young Bear and Theisz, *Standing in the Light*, 27.
9. Anthropologist William Sturtevant pointed out that "most historians, and many cultural anthropologists, argue that one cannot thus sharply distinguish 'empirical' from 'speculative' history—all historiography is speculative to a degree, and historical evidence is varyingly empirical." See Sturtevant, "Anthropology, History, and Ethnohistory," 4.
10. Jacobs, "The Indian and the Frontier," 44.
11. An estimated twenty-seven tribes as of 1993 had no written history about them; see Hale, *Researching and Writing Tribal Histories*.
12. Webb, *Chronological List of Engagements*.
13. Fixico, "The Struggle for Our Homes," 35.
14. For some clarification about Black Elk's power vision, and real life being in the hereafter world, see Neihardt, *Black Elk Speaks*, 21–46.
15. For a full range of myths and legends of various tribes, see Erodes and Ortiz, *American Indian Myths and Legends*. For legends specifically on the Senecas of the Iroquois, see Kelsey, *Tales To Tell*. On prophecy of the coming of whites see Nabokov, *Native American Testimony*, 6–31.
16. Flores, *The Natural West* 3; in his discussion of animals and humans as nature's children, he uses the term *human animals*, p. 28.
17. For information on the structure of community and society, see Murdock, *Social Structure*.
18. Tinker, "An American Indian Theological Response to Ecojustice," 159–60.

19. For the importance of the circle as a concept and important part of cultures, see Conn, *Circles of the World*; Rita L. Irwin, *A Circle of Empowerment*; Lee, *The Circle Is Sacred*; McNab, *Circles of Time*; Mischke, *Circles, Consciousness and Culture*; Shumaker, *The Circle of Totems*; and Kenneth Walker, *The Circle of Life*.
20. Said, *Orientalism*, and Berkhofer, *The White Man's Indian*.
21. Isaacs, *Idols of the Tribe*, 21.

3. The First Dimension of Indian-White Relations

1. Mendy Mayberry, "Body Found in Woods," *Sapulpa Herald*, vol. 71, no. 127, February 10, 1984. In this case, the little people known by the Euchees were tricksters; for a general introduction to the trickster role, see Radin, *The Trickster*.
2. Reconstructed diary of Christopher Columbus, including letter, ca. 1492, in Fuson, trans., *The Log of Christopher Columbus*.
3. Vaughan, "From White Man to Redskin," 921.
4. Vaughan, "From White Man to Redskin," 921.
5. Vaughan, "From White Man to Redskin," 925.
6. Pearce, "From the History of Ideas to Ethnohistory," 89.
7. Martin, *In the Spirit of the Earth*, 123. For further insight, see Garn, *Human Races*.
8. Quoted in Merrell, "Some Thoughts on Colonial Historians," 96.
9. Hoxie, "Problems of Indian History," 392.
10. Hanke, "American Historians and the World Today."
11. Hanke, "American Historians and the World Today."
12. Gilbert, "The American Indian and United States Diplomatic History," 229–30.
13. Gottschalk, *Understanding History*, 41. Herbert Butterfield has written extensively on the foundations of professional history; see Butterfield, *The Origins of History*, *Man on His Past*. For an early work, see Flint, *History of the Philosophy of History*. See also Danto, *Analytical Philosophy of History;* Klibansky and Paton, *Philosophy and History*; Meyerhoff, *The Philosophy of History*; Shotwell, *The History of History*; Teggart, *Theory and History*; and Thompson, *A History of Historical Writings*.

    The definition of history is addressed in Childe, *What Happened in History*; Breisach, *Historiography*; Carr, *What Is History?*; Childe, *History*; Dray, *Laws and Explanation in History*; Elton, *The Practice of History*; Fischer, *Historian's Fallacies*; and Gardiner, *The Nature of Historical Explanation*.

14. Pitt, *Using Historical Sources*, 9.
15. Axtell, *Beyond 1492*, and see Iggers, "The Image of Ranke."
16. Carr, *What Is History?* 5–6.
17. See Anderson, *Conquest of Texas*; Blackhawk, *Violence over the Land;* and Jacoby, *Shadows at Dawn.*
18. Middlekauff, "Narrative History and Ordinary Life," 8.
19. For example, see Kenyon, *The History Men*, and Beale, "The Professional Historian."
20. Hagan, *Theodore Roosevelt and Six Friends of the Indian*, 4, originally quoted in Hagerdorn, *Roosevelt in the Bad Lands*, 355.
21. Horsman, "Scientific Racism and the American Indian," and Bieder, *Science Encounters the Indian.*
22. Adams, "Ethnoarchaeology as a Merging," 294.
23. Adams, "Ethnoarchaeology as a Merging," 293.
24. Berkhofer, "Political Context of a New Indian History."
25. See Axtell, *Beyond 1492*. The philosophy of writing history has inspired the works of Barzun, "Where Is History Now?"; Dray, *Philosophy of History*; Field, "Some Problems of the Philosophy of History"; Gallie, "The Historical Understanding"; Gardiner, *The Philosophy of History*; Joynt and Rescher, "The Problem of Uniqueness in History"; Mandelbaum, *Anatomy of Historical Knowledge*; and Walsh, *Philosophy of History: An Introduction.*
26. Axtell, *Beyond 1492*. Theoretical approaches toward history include Romein, "Theoretical History."
27. Gary B. Nash, "Whither Indian History?"
28. Standing Bear, *Land of the Spotted Eagle.*
29. See Blackhawk, *Violence over the Land.*
30. Ewers, "When Red and White Men Met."
31. Forbes, "Frontiers in American History."
32. Forbes, "Frontiers in American History."
33. Horsman, *Race and Manifest Destiny*, 25–42.
34. Jennings, "A Growing Partnership," 95.
35. Bruce Trigger, a skilled ethnohistorian, addressed issues of mainstream bias and chauvinism: "Today it is increasingly being realized that many activities of Euroamerican settlers cannot be understood adequately without a sound understanding of native history." Trigger continues, "Francis Jennings (1975) was puzzled by seeming anomalies in understanding the behavior and motives of the native peoples of New England that were posed by traditional accounts of the colonial history of that region in the 17th century. . . . This led

him to realize that historians had erroneously accepted at face value the contemporary accounts of European colonists concerning their relations with native peoples and neighboring colonies." See Trigger, "Ethnohistory: Problems and Prospects," 15.

36. Curti, *Growth of American Thought*.
37. Horsman, *Race and Manifest Destiny*, 189.
38. Said, *Orientalism*.
39. For a general estimate of Indian wars, refer to Keenan, *Encyclopedia of American Indian Wars*.
40. Thornton, *American Indian Holocaust*, 30.
41. Sheehan, *Seeds of Extinction*.
42. Drinnon, *Facing West*, xvii.
43. Jacoby, *Shadows at Dawn*, 2.
44. Turner, "Significance of the Frontier."
45. For additional information about stereotypes regarding American Indian, see Haan, "Another Example of Stereotypes."
46. Keen, *The Aztec Image*.
47. See Hanke, "American Historians and the World Today."
48. Merrell, "Some Thoughts on Colonial Historians," 95.
49. Wilbur R. Jacobs, "The Indian and the Frontier," 43–44.
50. Forbes, "Manipulation of Race, Caste and Identity," 1. Reconstructed diary of Christopher Columbus, including letter, ca. 1492, in Fuson, trans., *The Log of Christopher Columbus*.

4. *The Second Dimension of Interacting Indian-White Relations*

1. Tecumseh's Speech at Vincennes, August 20, 1810, in Klinck, *Tecumseh*, 73, originally quoted in Marshall, *History of Kentucky*, 482–83.
2. An earlier version of this chapter is from my paper "Traditional Knowledge and Indian Intellectualism in Indian History," presented at Stanford University, January 29, 1990.
3. The ability of the mind to recall events as history is addressed in Kammen, *Mystic Chords of Memory*; Nagel, *Structure of Science*; Bernstein, *Beyond Objectivism and Relativism*; Emery, *Systems Thinking*; Marshack, *Roots of Civilization*; and Jennings, "A Growing Partnership," 96.
4. Kuhn, *Structure of Scientific Revolutions*, 109–10.
5. Axtell, "Ethnohistory: An Historian's Viewpoint," 5.
6. Olafson, "Narrative History and the Concept of Action," 284–85; originally from White, *Foundations of Historical Knowledge*, 259.
7. Jennings, "A Growing Partnership," 96.

8. James Axtell reminds us that "essentially, there are three ways to approach the history of Indian-white relations in colonial America. The predominant approach since the seventeenth century has been to view the meeting of cultures from the colonial side of the frontier. Eurocentric histories of this kind are usually written from the perspective of the English capitals—London, Jamestown, Boston, Philadelphia, Charleston—through the eyes of English policymakers, governors, explorers, missionaries, soldiers, and traders. The reasons are not hard to find. One is that most of the sources (at least the obvious and most accessible sources residing in libraries) were written by these people, and the Indians did not develop a system of writing, the art of printing, or the institutional preservation of records by which they could pass on their own versions of the colonial story. A second reason is that the character of Anglo-Indian relations has been assigned a minor part in the scenario of colonial America." See Axtell, "Bronze Men and Golden Ages," 664.
9. The publications of the Indian Historian Press of San Francisco, especially the newspaper *Wassaja* and the journal the *Indian Historian*, frequently stake this claim. For other expressions of the "Indian" perspective, see Grinde, *The Iroquois*; Brown, *Bury My Heart at Wounded Knee*; Armstrong, *I Have Spoken*; Ortiz, "Requirements for a 'New History.'" Two tribal histories, Quam, *The Zunis*, and Slickpoo, *Noon-Nee-Me-Poo (We, the Nez Perces)*, are essentially collections of traditional stories, legends, and myths, challenging other historians to become sensitive to the categories employed by traditionalist native peoples in thinking about their past. See Alfonso Ortiz, "Some concerns Central to the Writing of 'Indian' History."
10. Axtell, "Bronze Men and Golden Ages," 664.
11. Forbes, "Manipulation of Race, Caste and Identity," 10.
12. Nancy Lurie observed that "ethnohistory" is not a new method or area of investigation, . . . it is as old as ethnology itself," in Trigger, "Ethnohistory: Problems and Prospects," 2.
13. Axtell, "Bronze Men and Golden Ages," 664.
14. Trigger, "Ethnohistory: Problems and Prospects," 2.
15. Sturtevant, "Anthropology, History, and Ethnohistory," 3.
16. "And yet," wrote historian Bernard Sheehan, "despite all the sanguine hopes and enthusiastic forecasts, the Indian proved intractable." Historian Calvin Martin continued this observation, stating that "He [the Indian] remained, alas, a drunkard, a murderer, a pauper, a pagan, and the rest of it. The Indian's inherent degeneracy, so

contemporaries thought, coupled with the powerful vices of the frontier environment nullified the goodwill of the Jeffersonian incorporationist plan. The only alternative, for Thomas L. McKenney, Lewis Cass, John C. Calhoun, Andrew Jackson, and others was to move the tribesmen west, beyond the Mississippi, out of harm's way." See Martin, "Ethnohistory" 48.

17. "The historian, although not blinded by an elaborate theoretical scheme like the anthropologist, was just as victimized by his implicit assumptions in trying to see beyond the tribe or the reservation to the internal dynamics of Indian life and politics. Even when the historian thought he was portraying the Indian 'side' in his writing, he adopted implicitly either the white view of his sources or, equally invidious, the assumption that the outcome of his story was determined more by the white side than by the Indian side." See Berkhofer, "Political Context of a New Indian History," 364.
18. Berkhofer, "Political Context of a New Indian History," 364.
19. Berkhofer, "Political Context of a New Indian History," 364.
20. Jamake Highwater's work *The Primal Mind* is a philosophical study of the American Indian; the author demonstrates how Indians differ in their thinking from the dominant society. See also Fixico, *The American Indian Mind*.
21. O'Neil, "Commentary" on "Perspectives on the Writing of Indian History," 38.
22. Studies that point out the different perspective of Indians from the mainstream include Breuing, "Hopi Perspectives on Formal Education," and Lowry, "Differences in Visual Perception and Auditory Discrimination."
23. Some years ago anthropologist Judith Kleinfeld observed that children of the Tlingit Indian village of Angoon frequently crowded the local cinema and could recall minute details of the films they had watched. This extraordinary visual ability is applied as a learning technique among American Indian groups. See Fuchs and Havighurst, *To Live On This Earth*, 122.
24. Historian James Merrell noted that "studies of colonial New England have long ignored native influence on the development of that region, and farther south, where the Indians' presence in colonial times was still more pervasive, the scholarship's silence speaks even louder." See Merrell, "Some Thoughts on Colonial Historians," 99–100.
25. James Axtell suggested that "by emphasizing that each culture must be understood in its own terms, as these change over time, ethnohis-

tory ensures that the history of the frontier will cease to be (in one traditional historian's words) the short 'pathetic' story of the 'inevitable' triumph of a 'booming' White 'civilization' over a 'fragile' 'primitive' culture." See Axtell, "Ethnohistory: An Historian's Viewpoint," 3.

26. "An awareness of the importance of understanding native cultures subsequent to European contact gradually developed within American anthropology in the context of studies of acculturation[;] the original goal of these studies in retrospect was a patronizing one. . . . Anthropologists sought to learn more about how native cultures had responded to different forms of European domination so that they might help government agencies to formulate more effective and also more humane policies for dealing with native peoples. . . . As a result of these studies, some anthropologists became aware of the need to understand native cultures in an historical perspective and concluded that native history was a subject worthy of study in its own right. . . . Works such as Robert Redfield, Ralph Linton and M. J. Herskovits' (1936) 'Outline for the Study of Acculturation,' Linton's (1940) *Acculturation in Seven American Indian Tribes*, and Edward Spicer's monumental *Cycles of Conquest* (1962) and his *Perspectives in American Indian Cultural Change* (1961) were milestones in the development of studies of acculturation into what by the 1950's had widely come to be called ethnohistory." See Trigger, "Ethnohistory: Problems and Prospects," 4.

27. Marc Bloch observed that "the variety of historical evidence is nearly infinite. Everything that man says or writes, everything that he makes, everything he touches can and ought to touch can and ought to teach us about him." See Bloch, *The Historian's Craft*, 66.

28. Patrick Gardiner observed that "the historian, unlike the natural scientist, does not seek to explain events by correlating them with other events in the light of some well-attested uniformity or general law; his aim is rather to uncover their inner rationale, and this can only be done—[R. G.] Collingwood argues—by 're-enacting' within his own mind the thoughts of the person or persons with whose activities he is dealing." See Gardiner, *The Philosophy of History*, 5.

29. As J. W. Goethe remarked, "history must from time to time be rewritten, not because many new facts have been discovered, but because new aspects come into view, because the participant in the progress of an age is led to standpoints from which the past can be regarded and judged in a novel manner." See Teggart, *Theory and Processes of History*, 15.

30. In *The Idea of History* Glyn Daniel observed that "the first man to use the word prehistory seems to have been Daniel Wilson, and this was just over a hundred years ago, in 1851, in the title of his book, *The Archaeology and Prehistoric Annals of Scotland*. . . . 1851 was the first time that prehistory was introduced into the English language. The *Oxford English Dictionary* records the stages by which the word came into respectable and general usage. Sir Edward Tylor was using it in his *Primitive Culture* in 1871" See Daniel, *Idea of Prehistory*, 1.
31. Berkhofer, *A Behavioral Approach to Historical Analysis*, 252–53.
32. Magnaghi, "Herbert E. Bolton," 46.
33. See Whorf, "An American Indian Model of the Universe."

5. *The Third Dimension of Physical and Metaphysical Reality*

1. Nabokov, *Native American Testimony*, 125.
2. I presented an earlier version as a paper, "The Metaphysical Reality of American Indian History," at the 25th Anniversary of D'Arcy McNickle Center at the Newberry Library, Chicago, on September 13, 1997.
3. Coe, *Red Patriots*, 29, and Wickman, *Osceola's Legacy*, 5.
4. Wickman, *Osceola's Legacy*, 72–74.
5. Wickman, *Osceola's Legacy*, 72–74.
6. For more information on consciousness please refer to Louch, *Explanation and Human Action*, chap. 7, 134–58.
7. Scientist Martin Rees observed that "for life like us to evolve, there must be time for a least one generation of stars to have evolved and aided, to produce the heavy element, and then time for the Sun to form and for evolution to proceed for several billion years on a planet orbiting around it. When the expanding Universe is that old, it will of course be several billion light years across. . . . Astronomers have also noted apparent coincidences involving the basic physical laws and rations, where there is a rather delicate balance [that] often seems to prevail." Rees, "The Anthropic Universe," 45.
8. The causes of events, according to science, are addressed in Wesley C. Salmon, *Scientific Explanation*.
9. The study of culture that defines the reality of a community of people is addressed in Barber and Berdan, *The Emperor's Mirror*; Rouse, "The Strategy of Culture History"; Sears, "Study of Social and Religious Systems"; Childe and Kegan, *Society and Knowledge*; Murdock, *Social Structure*; Sahlins, *Tribesmen*; and Service, *Primitive Social Organization*.

10. See Mannheim, *Ideology and Utopia.*
11. For further information on native realities, see Carpenter, *Eskimo Realities*; Gibson, *Perception of the Visual World*; and Kleinfeld, "Visual Memory."
12. In his study of American Indians classified as "primitive man," Paul Radin noted that the primitive man is "pre-eminently a man of practical common sense. . . . This tough-mindedness leads to a recognition of all types of realities, realities which primitive man sees in all their directness and ruggedness, stripped of all that false and sentimental haze so universal among civilized peoples . . . primitive man is endowed with an overpowering sense of reality and possesses a manner of facing this reality, which to a western European implies an almost complete lack of sensitiveness." See Radin, *Primitive Man as Philosopher*, 19.
13. Jack Forbes observed that "many anthropologists write books about natives but ignore archival research, or ignore some other important source of information. Some sociologists produce community studies which lack any meaningful time-depth perspectives. And many historians have written books about Indians or about native-European relations which totally lack an understanding of native culture and viewpoints." See Forbes, "The Ethnohistorian in the Southwest," 433.
14. See Hämäläinen, *The Comanche Empire.*
15. James Vanstone stated: "The widespread existence of the *nakhani* belief had also been attributed to a fear of the dangers in the woods that almost every Indian experiences at one time or another. Apparently, it is not the woods as such that are frightening, but the unknown disasters that lie within the forest depths." See Vanstone, *Athapaskan Adaptations*, 63–64.
16. Carl Gustavson has argued that there are six social forces—economic, religious, technological, institutional, ideological, and military forces—"which generate dynamic energies in society; they furnish the power for the loom of history. . . . The problem of causation is inextricably connected with the whole question of movement and change in history, and some facility in dealing with it is indispensable for an understanding of the course of events." See Gustavson, *A Preface to History*, 52, 56.
17. Vanstone, *Athapaskan Adaptations*, 63–64.
18. Robert Berkhofer Jr. stated: "Thus both the missionaries and Handsome Lake had new value-orientations for the demoralized Senecas.

. . . Obviously, the adherents of both sides perceived the path to social salvation differently—but both sides sought social salvation!" See Berkhofer, "Faith and Factionalism among the Senecas," 106.

19. Calvin Martin observed that "hunters cultivated a relationship with individual plants and animals, not with nature—an important point"; Martin, *In the Spirit of the Earth*, 54.
20. Irwin, "Cherokee Healing."
21. Mooney, *Myths of the Cherokee*, 229.
22. Sue Ellen Jacobs, "Gender Roles at San Juan Pueblo," 181.
23. Regarding the analysis of "space" by various cultural viewpoints, see Kent, *Analyzing Activity Areas*.
24. For information on other indigenous concepts of space, see Li, "Constituting Tribal Space," 149.
25. Lefebvre, *The Production of Space*, 1–67.
26. Connerton, *How Societies Remember*, 3, 10, 11; this is a volume in a series related to the Frankfort School of thought, which invoked transdisciplinary studies on social issues.
27. Tylor, *Religion in Primitive Culture*, x.
28. Tylor, *Religion in Primitive Culture*, xi.
29. Conley, *Cherokee Medicine Man*, 93–94, and Lossiah, *Cherokee Little People*.
30. Vanstone, *Athapaskan Adaptations*, 63–64.
31. Linderman, *Old Man Coyote*, 35.
32. Linderman, *Old Man Coyote*, 35.
33. "The Little People of the Seneca," in Hardin, *Legends and Lore*, 82.
34. Salisbury, "The Indians' Old World," 440.
35. Bruce Trigger noted: "In recent years a growing number of archaeologists have come to agree with the philosopher and archaeologist R. G. Collingwood that 'no historical problem should be studied without studying . . . the history of historical thought about it.' Historical investigations of archeological interpretation have multiplied and more sophisticated methodologies have been adopted"; Trigger, *A History of Archaeological Thought*, 1–2.
36. Firth, *Man and Culture*, 1, 58.
37. In his approach Karl Figlio relates the importance of understanding one's state of mind while interpreting oral history, which would also pertain to analyzing conventional history from interpreting documents; see Figlio, "Oral History and the Unconscious," 121–30.
38. Conrad Arensberg noted that "our genealogical charts, refined as kinship diagrams, mark such sequences faithfully enough for suc-

cessive generations, but our treatments of nonkinship do not. Instead they often use correlation models in one form or another, seeking to relate to kinship data a kind of such nonkinship data: household, residence, access to fields, gifts and presentations, etc. without regard to sequential occurrence, but timelessly, simultaneously. There is much power in this; and we have learned a great deal from it, as we have also learned from the uncovering, by componential and formal analyses, of the timeless internal logics of kinship nomenclature systems." Arensberg, "Culture as Behavior," 20.

39. Radcliffe-Brown observed that "the idea is that in a given society we can isolate conceptually, if not in reality, a certain set of actions and interactions amongst persons which are determined by the relationships by kinship or marriage, and that in a particular society these are interconnected in such a way that we can give a general analytical description of them as constituting a system." Radcliffe-Brown, *Structure and Function in Primitive Society*, 6, 53.
40. Swanton, "Social Organization and Social Usages," and *Notes on the Creek Indians*, 132–36, 139–41. J. Leitch Wright Jr. listed Fox and Potato clans among non-Muscogee towns, which belonged to the Creek Confederacy; see Wright, *Creeks and Seminoles*, 18–19.
41. Murdock, *Social Structure*, 68, 70; in the same work see also his chapter "The Clan," 65–78. For additional information on American Indian clans see chapter 5, "A Family Writ Large—The Clans," in Reid, *A Law of Blood*, 35–48; Kaut, "The Clan System"; and Stipe, "Eastern Dakota Clans."
42. Lowie, *Primitive Society*, 111.
43. See Geertz, *Interpretation of Cultures*.
44. Kaut, *The Western Apache Clans System*, 82.
45. Irwin, "Cherokee Healing," 242.
46. Irwin, "Cherokee Healing," 244.
47. de Baillou, "A Contribution to the Mythology," 95.
48. Irwin, "Cherokee Healing," 247.
49. Rasnake, *Domination and Cultural Resistance*, 4.
50. Neihardt, *Black Elk Speaks*, 49.
51. Martin, "Metaphysics of Writing Indian-White History," 153.
52. Martin, "Metaphysics of Writing Indian-White History," 154.
53. Martin, "Metaphysics of Writing Indian-White History," 158.

6. A Cross-Cultural Bridge of Understanding

1. "At the Rainbow's End," Indian Legend.com, copyright 2003, http://

www.indianlegend.com, accessed September 23, 2010. See also Hassell, *Rainbow Bridge*. The story of the Twins' journey is elaborated at great length in Matthews, *Navajo Legends*, 104–59.

2. Description of Rainbow Bridge in 1913 by Theodore Roosevelt, *A Book Lover's Holiday in the Open*, 29.
3. Marquis, *Wooden Leg*, 364–65.
4. Bhabha, *The Location of Culture*, 277.
5. Gadacz, "Language of Ethnohistory," 152.
6. Forbes, "The Ethnohistorian in the Southwest," 430.
7. Fenton, "Ethnohistory and Its Problems," 2.
8. Axtell, "The Ethnohistory of Early America," 113.
9. Axtell, "The Ethnohistory of Early America," 113.
10. Gottschalk, *Understanding History*, 48–49.
11. Some works for historical methods are Krupat, *Ethnocriticism*; Hughes, "The Historian and the Social Scientist"; Shafer, "History Not Art"; Lowie, "Survivals and Historical Method"; Harry Elmer Barnes, *A History of Historical Writing*; and McClelland, *Causal Explanation and Model Building*.
12. Le Goff and Nora, *Constructing the Past*, 4.
13. Forbes, "The Historian and the Indian," 349.
14. Berkhofer, "Cultural Pluralism versus Ethnocentrism," 37.
15. For helpful discussion, see Barry Barnes, *Scientific Knowledge and Sociological Theory*.
16. The importance of culture as a foundation to society is addressed generally in Benedict, *Patterns of Culture*; Hatch, *Theories of Man and Culture*; Kroeber, *The Nature of Culture*; Sahlins and Service, *Evolution and Culture*; Steward, *Theory of Cultural Change*; Wagner, *The Invention of Culture*; Wallace, *Culture and Personality*; Wissler, *Man and Culture*; Leslie A. White, *The Science of Culture*, and *The Concept of Cultural Systems*.
17. The notion of reconstructing cultures is aided by the works of V. Gordon Childe, *Piecing Together the Past*; Alfred L. Kroeber, "The Culture-Area and Age-area Concepts of Clark Wissler"; and Harvey C. Moore, "Cumulation and Cultural Process."
18. Hume, *Historical Archaeology*, 4.
19. Hagan, "On Writing the History of the American Indian," 149.
20. Fogelson, "The Ethnohistory of Events and Nonevents," 134.
21. As examples of philosophy with possible insight into Indian life, refer to Merrilee H. Salmon, *Philosophy and Archaeology*, and Smart, *Philosophy and Scientific Realism*.

22. Ronald Horowitz noted that "some group identities may be lost by 'assimilation,' the process of erasing the boundary between one group and another. There are two principal varieties of assimilation. Two or more groups may unite to form a new group, larger and different from any of the component parts. This we refer to as 'amalgamation.' . . . Alternatively, one group may lose its identity by merging into another group, which retains its identity. This we call 'incorporation.'. . . The moving force of assimilation and differentiation is the sense of similarity and difference from others sharing the same space. . . . 'Parkinson's Law' . . . by which group identity tends to expand or contract to fill the political space available for its expression." Horowitz, "Ethnic Identity," 115, 137.
23. Linton, *The Tree of Culture*, v.
24. Berkhofer, *A Behavioral Approach to Historical Analysis*, 5.
25. Berkhofer, *A Behavioral Approach to Historical Analysis*, 56.
26. Refer to Nadel, *The Foundations of Social Anthropology*, and Radcliffe-Brown and Srinivas, *Method in Social Anthropology*.
27. Trigger, "Ethnohistory and Archaeology," 17.
28. The ethnohistory of American Indian literature is plentiful in works combining history and cultural anthropology since the 1950s.
29. Twenty-eight pages of Alfred Kroeber et al., *Culture: A Critical Review of Concepts and Definitions* (1952) are devoted to a partial listing of definitions proposed for culture. Tylor, "The Science of Culture," 1.
30. Tylor, *The Origins of Culture*, 1.
31. Tylor, *The Origins of Culture*, 1.
32. Theodora Kroeber, *A. L. Kroeber*, 131.
33. Martin, "Ethnohistory," 41.
34. Lowie, *History of Ethnological Theory*, 3.
35. Radcliffe-Brown, *Structure and Function in Primitive Society*, 2.
36. Studies that emphasize the importance of the family structure include Stauss, "The Study of American Indian Families," and Price, "The Native American Family." Family life and clans are stressed in Trigger, *The Huron*.
37. Munslow, *Deconstructing History*, 18–19.
38. For examples, see Harris, *Rise of Anthropological Theory*; Hodder, *The Present Past*; Honigmann, *Development of Anthropological Ideas*; Redman, *Research and Theory in Current Archeology*; and the much earlier work Lowie, *The History of Ethnological Theory*.
39. See Hämäläinen, *Comanche Empire*, and Barr, *Peace Came in the Form of a Woman*.

40. Barr, *Peace Came in the Form of a Woman.*
41. Trigger, "Ethnohistory and Archaeology," 22.
42. Examples are Blackhawk, *Violence over the Land*, and Bauer, *We Were All Like Migrant Workers.*
43. For example, see Dobyns, "More Methodological Perspectives on Historical Demography."
44. Dobyns, *Their Numbers Become Thinned*, and Thornton, *American Indian Holocaust.*
45. Robert W. Fogel observed that "the mathematical approach, [cliometrics] has developed most rapidly within the field of economic history"; see Fogel, "The Limits of Quantitative Methods in History," 331.

7. Oral Tradition and Language

1. Swanton, "Social Organization and Social Usages."
2. As more universities have grasped the importance of American Indian history, they have hired progressively more historians who study American Indian history; many universities have done this since the mid-1970s.
3. Ritchie, *Doing Oral History*, 85.
4. McTaggart, *Wolf That I Am*, 185.
5. McTaggart, *Wolf That I Am*, 186.
6. Martin, *In the Spirit of the Earth*, 115. A related study is McNeill, *Mythistory and Other Essays.*
7. Vanstone, *Athapaskan Adaptations*, 63–64.
8. Burke, *History and Social Theory*, 101.
9. William McNeill compared oral tradition and history as follows: "Our common parlance reckons myth to be false while history is, or aspires to be, true. . . . But what seems true to one historian will seem false to another, so one historian's truth becomes another's myth, even at the moment of utterance. . . . The principal source of historical complexity lies in the fact that human beings react both to the natural world and to one another chiefly through the mediation of symbols. . . . Resort to symbols, in effect, loosened up the connection between external reality and human responses, freeing us from instinct by setting us adrift on a sea of uncertainty." See McNeill, "Mythistory, or Truth, History, Historians," 1–2.
10. McNeill, "Mythistory, or Truth, History, Historians," 1–2.
11. Pueblo writer Joe Sando has written that "the [Pueblo] people tell the story of their history, 'from the beginning,' with all the artistry of

the traditional storyteller, complete with age-old mythology and beliefs formalized into narrative, from the Hegira to the invasion by the Europeans." See Sando, *The Pueblo Indians*, 17.

12. Jumperz, "The Speech Community," 382.
13. Agha, *Language and Social Relations*, especially the chapters "From Referring to Registers" and "Register Formations."
14. See information about the Doris Duke Indian Oral History Project in Ellis, "The Duke Indian Oral History Collection."
15. Ellis, "The Duke Indian Oral History Collection."
16. Connerton, *How Societies Remember*, 6–40. Archaeologist William Hampton Adams has explained that "oral historians soon began investigating less prominent individuals and collecting the slave narratives in the 1930's. Since then oral history has grown tremendously in popularity." Adams, "Ethnoarchaeology as a Merging," 295.
17. Early differences between Anglo Americans and Native Americans in a new environment for the former are addressed in Jones, *O Strange New World*.
18. Martin, *In the Spirit of the Earth*, 92.
19. Woody, "Earth Is Richer for This Voice," 19.
20. Long, "The Personal Dimension in Doing Oral History," 310–11. See also Ilisevich, "Oral History in Undergraduate Research," and Ebner, "Students as Oral Historians."
21. "American Indian Languages," http://anthropology.si.edu/outreach/indbib/americanindianlanguages.pdf, accessed September 8, 2011. Other sources on American Indian languages are Campbell, *American Indian Languages*; Goddard, *Handbook of North American Indians*, vol. 17: *Languages*; and Mithun, *Languages of Native North America*.
22. Rayna Green, *That's What She Said*, 3.
23. Pueblo writer Joe Sando wrote that "in reverent narration, through the art of ritual dance and mime, the Pueblo people related their traditional history, passing the story down from generation to generation." See Sando, *The Pueblo Indians*, 15–17.
24. Finnegan, "A Note on Oral Tradition," 195.
25. Finnegan, "A Note on Oral Tradition," 195.
26. Finnegan, "A Note on Oral Tradition," 195.
27. Bahr, "On the Complexity of Southwest Indian Emergence Myths," 318, 347. Additional case studies include Levin, *Ethnicity and Aboriginality*, and Jett, "Pueblo Indian Migration."
28. Debo, *The Road to Disappearance*, 15.

29. For the origin of the Muscogee Creeks, see Swanton, *Early History of the Creek Indians*, and "Social Organization and Social Usages."
30. For a discussion of Muscogee Creek traditions and other members of the Five Civilized Tribes in the late nineteenth century, see Perdue, *Nations Remembered*, 87–115. For history and cultural information about the Creeks, see Debo, *The Road to Disappearance*; Michael Green, *The Politics of Indian Removal*; Wright, *Creeks and Seminoles*. For cultural information on the Seminoles of Oklahoma, refer to Howard and Lena, *Oklahoma Seminoles*.
31. O'Danachair, "Oral Tradition and the Printed Word," 36.
32. Dunaway, "The Oral Biography," 256–57.
33. Dunaway, "The Oral Biography," 256–57.
34. Figlio, "Oral History and the Unconscious," 121.
35. Vansina, *Oral Tradition as History*, 198.
36. Vansina, *Oral Tradition as History*, 198.
37. See Terkel, *The Good War*.
38. Thelen, *Memory and American History*, ix.
39. Thelen, *Memory and American History*, ix.
40. Sturtevant, "Anthropology, History, and Ethnohistory," 38.
41. Sturtevant, "Anthropology, History, and Ethnohistory," 38.
42. Sturtevant, "Anthropology, History, and Ethnohistory," 38.
43. Sturtevant, "Anthropology, History, and Ethnohistory," 40.
44. Wax, "The Ethics of Research," 433.
45. Standing Bear, *Land of the Spotted Eagle*, 195–96.
46. Quoted in Seligman, "Is Oral History a Valid Research Instrument?" 182.
47. Gottschalk, *Understanding History*, 42.
48. Early native societal infrastructure is addressed in Hoebel, *Man in the Primitive World*; Jochim, *Hunter-Gather Subsistence*; and Pagden, *The Fall of Natural Man*.
49. See Dunnell, *Systematics in Prehistory*; and Hodder, *Symbols in Action* and *Symbolic and Structural Archaeology*. Richard Erodes and Alfonso Ortiz have compiled a wide range of tribal myths and legends in *American Indian Myths and Legends*. Another insightful compilation is Jay Miller, *Earthmaker*. A similar compilation with geographic representation is Hardin, *Legends and Lore*. Indian oratory and commentary consisting of speeches on a variety of subjects are in Vanderwerth, *Indian Oratory*; Colin G. Calloway, *The World Turned Upside Down*; Mintz, *Native American Voices*; Arlene Hirschfelder, *Native Heritage*; and Nabokov, *Native American Testimony*. While Calloway's and Mintz's editions stress Indian accounts

during the colonial era, Hirschfelder collected more or less contemporary personal accounts about basic areas of life. Nabokov gives the fullest range of individual Indian perspectives from those of historical leaders to those of contemporary spokespersons.

50. Peter Iverson, commentary on session, "Tribal Sovereignty in the Twentieth Century," American Society for Ethnohistory, Annual Meeting, Mashantucket, Connecticut, October 23, 1999.
51. Thelen, *Memory and American History, vii.*
52. Burke, *History and Social Theory*, 163.
53. Wax, "The Ethics of Research," 433.
54. See Basso, *Wisdom Sits in Places*, for a work that incorporates oral tradition.

8. *Power of Earth and Woman*

1. The White Buffalo Calf Woman story is commonly told. This version is in Walker, *Lakota Belief and Ritual*, 109–12.
2. Bamforth, *Ecology and Human Organization*, 85–192.
3. Historian Gary Nash suggested that "instead of additional studies organized around questions of White-Indian policy we need examinations of internal change in Indian communities during three centuries of contacts with Europeans." See Gary B. Nash, "Whither Indian History?"
4. Buffalohead, "Farmers, Warriors, Traders," 236, 240.
5. Richard White, "Discovering Nature in North America," 882.
6. Wissler, *The Relation of Nature to Man*; Fairchild, *The Noble Savage*; and the early work of Huxley, *Man's Place in Nature.*
7. Studies on human adaptation to environment include Altman and Wohlwill, *Behaviour and the Natural Environment*; Kaplan and Kaplan, *The Experience of Nature*; Roderick Nash, *Wilderness and the American Mind*; Moran, *Human Adaptability*; Friscancho, *Human Adaptation*; and Kluckhohn and Murray, *Personality in Nature.*
8. Refer to Butzer, *Environment and Archaeology*; James V. Wright, "A Regional Examination"; and Nazarea, *Ethnoecology.*
9. L. C. Birch observed that "it is necessary first to indicate the sense in which we are using the word 'nature.' All of us are conscious of an awareness of the world around us. Some would consider the channels of that awareness as limited to the so-called five senses. But whether we admit of five or fifty senses, awareness is an awareness of something. When we ask, 'What is nature?, we are asking What is the general character of that something? The person who looks at a

sunset or a flower experiences nature. There is in his object of experience both a qualitative and a quantitative component: the redness of the glow; and the electromagnetic waves by which science explains the phenomenon." See Birch, "Concept of Nature," 295.

10. Jackson, *A Sense of Place*, 157.
11. Kelley and Frances, "Places Important to Navajo People," 157, 159, 160.
12. Shepardson, "Gender Status of Navajo Women," in Klein and Ackerman, *Women and Power*, 160.
13. Shepardson, "Gender Status of Navajo Women," 172.
14. Murray Wax stated, "Where the rational man of the Western science conceives of the universe as inanimate, that is, composed of matter in motion, these Indians conceive of their environment as social responsive," said Wax. "Not only animals but even plants and rocks are, or may be, sentient beings affected by human actions who may in their turn affect human actors. When the numbers of a human group are healthy and prosperous, they are enjoying a harmonious relationship with these other beings." See Wax, "The Ethics of Research," 434.
15. See Steinberg, *Down to Earth*.
16. See Basso, *Wisdom Sits in Places*.
17. Brant, *Jim Whitewolf*, 123.
18. In addition archaeology and astronomy have collaborated as a new field in studying American Indians. Collectively the use of archaeology and astronomy might be called archaeoastronomy. It began seriously in 1894 with the publication of Sir J. Norman Lackyer's *Dawn of Astronomy*. To support this suggestion, oral history is related as native people stored their knowledge in stories told in their oral traditions. In a broader way, oral tradition of stories can inform us about all of native life. See Eliade, *Cosmos and History*, and Hadingham, *Early Man and the Cosmos*.
19. Margaret D. Jacobs, *Engendered Encounters*, 5.
20. Sando, *The Pueblo Indians*, 17.
21. Hammond and Willey, *Maya Archaeology*, xvi. See also León-Portilla, *Time and Reality*.
22. Gordon R. Willey and Norman Hammond, "Introduction," in Hammond and Willey, *Maya Archaeology*, xvi.
23. Forward by Russell Means in Weaver, *Defending Mother Earth*, xii.
24. Originally quoted in Margaret D. Jacobs, *Engendered Encounters*, 7. Also see Dozier, *Pueblo Indians of North America*, 133–34, 137–38, 145–48, 163–66.
25. Inter Press Service, comp., *Story Earth*, 11.

26. Vogel, *American Indian Medicine*, 3–12.
27. Margaret D. Jacobs, *White Mother to a Dark Race*, xxxi.
28. Lewis, "Manly-Hearted Women among the North Piegan."
29. Aleshire, *Warrior Woman*, 71–85.
30. Tweedie, "Notes of the History and Adaptation of the Apache Tribe," 1132.
31. The term *complex adaptive systems* was introduced to me by Chris Newman, and this section owes much to his paper "A Complex Adaptive Systems Analysis of Post Contact Change of Native Americans," presented at the Organization of American Historians Midwest Regional Conference, Iowa State University, Ames, September 4–6, 2000. Also see Lewin, *Complexity*; Gumerman and Gell-Mann, *Understanding Complexity*; and Tainter and Tainter, *Evolving Complexity and Environmental Risk*.
32. Native women have also been the victims of disrespect and violence; see Bachman, *Death and Violence on the Reservation*, and Perry, *Silent Victims*.
33. For archaeological theory for interpreting early cultures, see Bayard, "Science, Theory, and Reality"; Childe, *Piecing Together the Past*; Dunnell, "Evolutionary Theory and Archaeology"; Fitting, *Development of North American Archaeology*; Gould, *Explorations in Ethnoarchaeology*; Hole and Heizer, *An Introduction to Prehistoric Archaeology*; Hudson, *A Social History of Archaeology*; Laet, *Archaeology and Its Problems*; Lowther, "Epistemology and Archaeological Theory"; Shanks and Tilley, *Re-Constructing Archaeology*; Trigger, *A History of Archaeological Thought*; Wheeler, *Archaeology from the Earth*; and Willey and Phillips, *Method and Theory in American Archaeology*.
34. "Hazardous Weather Education," http://stormsector.com/severe_weather.php, accessed October 5, 2010.
35. Bennett, "Land as Space, Place, and Commodity," quoted in Jorgensen, "Land Is Cultural," 2.
36. Quoted in Margaret D. Jacobs, *Engendered Encounters*, 92.
37. Sando, *The Pueblo Indians*, 17.
38. See Sears, *Sacred Places*, and Milne, *Sacred Places in North America*.
39. A helpful study is Gallagher, *The Power of Place*.
40. McTaggart, *Wolf That I Am*, 107.
41. Martin, *In the Spirit of the Earth*, 26–27.
42. Archibald, *A Place to Remember*, 15.
43. William Brandon observed that "the traditional view of Indians in American history sees them as natural features of the land, rather

like mountains or rivers or buffalo or troublesome, if colorful, wild varmints, affecting American history only by occasionally impeding the civilizing progress of advancing settlers. . . . This traditional view remains overwhelmingly in evidence even though in recent years a great deal of important work has been done in local and regional Indian history, enhancing the value of basic historical contributions from earlier (and for the most part anthropological) writers such as George Bird Grinnell, J. P. Dunn, Frederick Webb Hodge, John R. Swanton, James Mooney, and others." See Brandon, "American Indians and American History," 16.

44. Isaacs, *Idols of the Tribe*, 51.
45. For history and identity of places among the Navajos, see Lindford, *Navajo Places*.
46. Sue Ellen Jacobs, "Gender Roles at San Juan Pueblo," 210.

9. Coming Full Circle

1. Guardipee, "Mending the Broken Circle," 28.
2. Fixico, "Ethics and Responsibilities in Writing American Indian History."
3. Hammond and Willey, *Maya Archaeology*, xvii.
4. Danver, "Why Should a Non-Indian Write Indian History?"
5. Margaret D. Jacobs, *Engendered Encounters*, 89.
6. Eggan, "Some Anthropological Approaches," 8.
7. Jennings, "A Growing Partnership."
8. Berkhofer, "Political Context of a New Indian History," 357.
9. Edmunds, "The Indian in the Mainstream," 243.
10. Hill and McCallum, "Guest Editors' Remarks."
11. Benedict Anderson, *Imagined Communities*, 69.
12. Inter Press Service, comp., *Story Earth*, 12–13.
13. Munslow, *Deconstructing History*, 30.
14. For a limited assessment of ethnohistory on American Indians, see Hoxie, "What's Your Problem?"
15. *All Roads Are Good*, 184.
16. Jack Forbes made this point in 1963, and mainstream historians have continued to write in the same "conqueror-consciousness" even beyond 1992 (500 hundred years after Columbus's arrival), still purporting an Anglo-American interpretation of this country. Forbes argued further that European influence has affected much of the Anglo-American genre of historical writing, so that colonial American history is perceived as an extension of British history; see Forbes, "The Historian and the Indian," 349, 350.

Bibliography

Unpublished Sources

"American Indian Languages." http://anthropology.si.edu/outreach/indbib/americanindianlanguages.pdf, accessed September 8, 2011.

"At the Rainbow's End." Indian Legend.com, copyright 2003, http://ww.indianlegend.com, accessed September 23, 2010.

Bennett, John W. "Land as Space, Place, and Commodity." Paper in "Report of the Committee on Soil as a Resource in Relation to Surface Mining," National Academy of Sciences, Washington DC, 1979.

Brueing, Robert C. "Hopi Perspectives on Formal Education." PhD diss., University of Kansas, 1973.

Fixico, Donald L. "Realities of American Indian Life and History." Keynote address, Northern Plains History Annual Meeting, Sioux Falls, South Dakota, October 2, 1998.

"Hazardous Weather Education." http://stormsector.com/severe_weather.php, accessed October 5, 2010.

Iverson, Peter. Commentary on session, "Tribal Sovereignty in the Twentieth Century." American Society for Ethnohistory, Mashantucket CT. October 23, 1999.

Newman, Chris. "A Complex Adaptive Systems Analysis of Post Contact Change of Native Americans." Paper presented at Organization of American Historians Midwest Regional Conference, Iowa State University, Ames, September 4–6, 2000.

Ortiz, Alfonso. "Some Concerns Central to the Writing of 'Indian' History." Commentary presented at American Historical Association Meeting, Chicago, 1974.

Ortiz, Roxanne Dunbar. "Requirements for a 'New History' of American Indian-United States Relations." Paper presented at American Historical Association Meeting, Washington DC, 1980.

Turner, Frederick J. "The Significance of the Frontier in American History." Paper presented at American Historical Association meeting, Chicago, July 12, 1893. In *Annual Report of the American Historical Association for 1893*, 199–227.

Published Sources

Adams, William Hampton. "Ethnoarchaeology as a Merging of Historical Archaeology and Oral History." *North American Archaeologist* 4, no. 4 (1983): 293–305.

Agha, Asif. *Language and Social Relations*. Cambridge: Cambridge University Press, 1986.

Akers, Donna L. *Living in the Land of Death: The Choctaw Nation, 1830–1860*. East Lansing: Michigan State University Press, 2004.

Aleshire, Peter. *Warrior Woman: The Story of Lozen, Apache Warrior and Shaman*. New York: St. Martin's Press. 2001.

All Roads Are Good: Native Voices on Life and Culture. Washington DC: Smithsonian Institution Press, 1994.

Altman, Irwin, and Joachim F. Wohlwill, eds. *Behaviour and the Natural Environment*. New York: Plenum Press, 1983.

American Indian Culture and Research Journal 20, no. 3 (1996).

Anderson, Benedict. *Imagined Communities: Reflections on the Origin and Spread of Nationalism*. London: Verso, 1983.

Anderson, Gary Clayton. *The Conquest of Texas: Ethnic Cleansing in the Promised Land, 1820–1875*. Norman: University of Oklahoma Press, 2005.

Archibald, Robert R. *A Place to Remember: Using History to Build Community*. Walnut Creek CA: AltaMira Press, 1999.

Arensberg, Conrad M. "Culture as Behavior: Structure and Emergence." *Annual Review of Anthropology* 1 (1972): 1–26.

Armstrong, Virginia Irving, comp. *I Have Spoken: American History through the Voices of the Indians*. Chicago: Sage Books, 1971.

Axtell, James. *Beyond 1492: Encounters in Colonial North America*. New York: Oxford University Press, 1992.

———. "Bronze Men and Golden Ages: The Intellectual History of Indian-White Relations in Colonial America." *Journal of Interdisciplinary History* 12, no. 4 (Spring 1982): 663–75.

———. "The Ethnohistory of Early America: A Review Essay." *William and Mary Quarterly* 35, no. 1 (January 1978): 110–44.

———. "Ethnohistory: An Historian's viewpoint." *Ethnohistory* 26, no. 1 (Winter 1979): 1–13.

———. *The Invasion Within: The Contest of Cultures in Colonial North America*. New York: Oxford University Press, 1985.

———. "A North American Perspective for Colonial History." *History Teacher* 12, no. 4 (August 1979): 549–62.

Bachman, Ronet. *Death and Violence On the Reservation: Homicide, Family Violence, and Suicide in American Indian Populations*. New York: Auburn House, 1992.

Baerreis, David A. "The Ethnohistoric Approach and Archaeology." *Ethnohistory* 8, no. 1 (Winter 1961): 49–77.

Bahr, Donald M. "On the Complexity of Southwest Indian Emergence Myths." *Journal of Anthropological Research* 33, no. 3 (Fall 1977): 317–49.

Bailey, Thomas A., and David M. Kennedy. *The American Pageant: A History of the Republic*, 7th ed., vol. 1. Lexington MA: D. C. Heath and Company, 1984.

Bamforth, Douglas B. *Ecology and Human Organization on the Great Plains*. New York: Plenum Press, 1988.

Barber, Russell J., and Frances F. Berdan. *The Emperor's Mirror: Understanding Cultures through Primary Sources*. Tucson: University of Arizona Press, 1998.

Barnes, Barry. *Scientific Knowledge and Sociological Theory*. London: Routledge and Kegan Paul, 1974.

Barnes, Harry Elmer. *A History of Historical Writing*. Norman: University of Oklahoma Press, 1937.

Barr, Juliana. *Peace Came in the Form of a Woman: Indians and Spaniards in the Texas Borderlands*. Chapel Hill: University of North Carolina Press, 2007.

Barzun, Jacques. "Where Is History Now?" *Proceedings of the Massachusetts Historical Society* 95 (1983): 142–53.

Basso, Keith H. *Wisdom Sits in Places: Landscape and Language among the Western Apache*. Albuquerque: University of New Mexico Press, 1996.

Bataille, Gretchen M., and Kathleen Mullen Sands. *American Indian Women Telling Their Lives*. Lincoln: University of Nebraska Press, 1984.

Bauer, William Jr. *We Were All Like Migrant Workers Here: Work, Community and Memory on California's Round Valley Reservation, 1850–1941*. Chapel Hill: University of North Carolina Press, 2010.

Bayard, D. T. "Science, Theory, and Reality in the New Archaeology." *American Antiquity* 34 (1969): 376–84.

Beale, Howard. "The Professional Historian." *Pacific Historical Review* 22, no. 3 (August 1953): 227–55.

Benedict, Ruth. *Patterns of Culture*. Boston: Houghton Mifflin, 1934.

Berkhofer, Robert F. Jr. *A Behavorial Approach to Historical Analysis*. New York: Free Press, 1969.

———. "Cultural Pluralism versus Ethnocentrism in the New Indian History." In *The American Indian and the Problem of History*, ed. Calvin Martin, 35–45. New York: Oxford University Press, 1987.

———. "Faith and Factionalism among the Senecas: Theory and Ethnohistory." *Ethnohistory* 12, no. 2 (1965): 99–112.

———. "The Political Context of a New Indian History." *Pacific Historical Review* 40, no. 3 (August 1971): 357–82.

———. *The White Man's Indian: Images of the American Indian from Columbus to the Present*. New York: Vintage Books, 1979.

Bernstein, Richard J. *Beyond Objectivism and Relativism: Science, Hermeneutics and Praxis*. Philadelphia: University of Pennsylvania Press, 1983.

Bhabha, Homi. *The Location of Culture*. London: Routledge, 1994.

Bieder, Robert Eugene. *Science Encounters the Indian, 1820–1880: The Early Years of American Ethnology*. Norman: University of Oklahoma Press, 1986.

Biolsi, Thomas, and Larry J. Zimmerman. eds. *Indians and Anthropoligists: Vine Deloria Jr. and the Critique of Anthropology*. Tucson: University of Arizona Press, 1997.

Birch, L. C. "Concept of Nature." *American Scientist* 39, no. 2 (1951): 294–302.

Blackhawk, Ned. *Violence over the Land: Indians and Empires in the Early American West*. Cambridge: Harvard University Press, 2006.

Bloch, Marc. *The Historian's Craft*. New York: Vintage Books, 1953.

Brandon, William. "American Indians and American History." *American West* 2, no. 2 (Spring 1965): 14–25, 91–92.

Brant, Charles S., ed. *Jim Whitewolf: The Life of a Kiowa Apache Indian*. New York: Dover Publications, 1969.

Breisach, Ernst. *Historiography: Ancient, Medieval and Modern*. Chicago: University of Chicago Press, 1983.

Breuing, Robert C. "Hopi Perspectives on Formal Education." PhD diss., University of Kansas, 1973.

Brown, Dee. *Bury My Heart at Wounded Knee: An Indian History of the American West*. New York: Holt, Rinehart and Winston, 1970.

Buffalohead, Priscilla K. "Farmers, Warriors, Traders: A Fresh Look at Ojibway Women." *Minnesota History* 48, no. 6 (Summer 1983): 266–44.

Burke, Peter. *History and Social Theory*. Ithaca: Cornell University Press, 1993.

Butterfield, Fox. "Why They Excel." *Parade Magazine* (South Bend IN), January 21, 1990.

Butterfield, Herbert. *Man on His Past: The Study of the History of Historical Scholarship*. Cambridge: Cambridge University Press, 1955.

———. *The Origins of History*. London: Eyre Methuen, 1981.

Butzer, Karl W. *Environment and Archaeology: An Introduction to Pleistocene Geography*. Chicago: Aldine Publishing Company, 1964.

Cajete, Gregory. *Native Science: Natural Laws of Interdependence*. Santa Fe: Clear Light Publishers, 2000.

Caldwell, E. K. *Dreaming the Dawn: Conversations with Native Artists and Activists*. Lincoln: University of Nebraska Press, 1999.

Calloway, Colin G., ed. *New Directions in American Indian History*. Norman: University of Oklahoma Press, 1988.

———. *The World Turned Upside Down: Indian Voices from Early America*. Boston: St. Martin's Press, 1994.

Campbell, Lyle. *American Indian Languages: The Historical Linguistics of Native America*. New York: Oxford University Press, 1997.

Campbell, Maria. *Halfbreed*. Toronto: McClelland and Stewart, 1973.

Carlson, Vada R., ed. *No Turning Back: A True Account of a Hopi Girl's Struggle to Bridge the Gap between the World of Her People and the World of the White Man*. Albuquerque: University of New Mexico Press, 1964.

Carmack, Robert M. "Ethnohhistory: A Review of Its Development, Definitions, Methods, and Aims." *Annual Review of Anthropology* 1 (1972): 227–46.

Carpenter, Edmund. *Eskimo Realities*. New York: Holt, Rinehart and Winston, 1973.

Carr, Edward H. *What Is History?* New York: Vintage, 1967.

Champagne, Duane. *American Indian societies: Strategies and Conditions of Political and Cultural Survival*. Cambridge MA: Cultural Survival, 1989.

Childe, Vere Gordon. *History: What Is History?* London: Cobbett, 1947.

———. *Piecing Together the Past: The Interpretation of Archaeological Data*. London: Routledge, 1956.

———. *What Happened in History*. Baltimore: Penguin Books, 1942.

Childe, Vere Gordon, and Paul Kegan. *Society and Knowledge: The Growth of Human Traditions*. New York: Harper, 1956.

Coe, Charles. *Red Patriots: The Story of the Seminoles*. 1898; facsimile ed., Gainesville: University Press of Florida, 1974.

Conn, Richard. *Circles of the World: Traditional Art of the Plains Indians*. Denver: Denver Art Museum, 1982.

Connerton, Paul. *How Societies Remember*. New York: Cambridge University Press, 1989.

Conley, Robert J. *Cherokee Medicine Man: The Life and Work of a Modern-Day Healer*. Norman: University of Oklahoma Press, 2005.

Cronon, William. *Changes in the Land: Indians, Colonists, and the Ecology of New England*. New York: Hill and Wang, 1983.

Crow Dog, Mary, with Richard Erodes. *Lakota Woman*. New York: Harper Perennial, 1990.

Crum, Steven. *Po'I Pentun Tammen Kimmappeh, The Road on Which We Came: A History of the Western Shoshone*. Salt Lake City: University of Utah Press, 1994.

Crying Wind. *Crying Wind*. Chicago: Moody Press 1977.

Curti, Merle. *Growth of American Thought*. New York: Harper, 1951.

Daniel, Glyn. *The Idea of Prehistory*. London: C. A. Watts and Company, 1962.

Danto, Arthur Coleman. *Analytical Philosophy of History*. Cambridge: Cambridge University Press, 1965.

Danver, Steven L. "Why Should a Non-Indian Write Indian History?" In Donald L. Fixico, ed. "Writing American Indian History," *Journal of the West* 49, no. 4 (Fall 2010): 52–55.

de Baillou, Clemens. "A Contribution to the Mythology and Conceptual World of the Cherokee Indians." *Ethnohistory* 8, no. 1 (Winter 1961): 93–102.

Debo, Angie. *The Road to Disappearance: A History of the Creek Indians*. Norman: University of Oklahoma Press, 1941.

Deloria, Philip J. *Indians in Unexpected Places*. Lawrence: University Press of Kansas, 2004.

———. *Playing Indian*. New Haven: Yale University Press, 1998.

Deloria, Vine Jr. *The Metaphysics of Modern Existence*. San Francisco: Harper and Row, 1979.

Dicke, Robert H. *Gravitation and the Universe*. Philadelphia: American Philosophical Society, 1970.

Dobyns, Henry F. "More Methodological Perspectives on Historical Demography." *Ethnohistory* 36, no. 3 (Summer 1989): 285–99.

———. *Their Numbers Become Thinned: Native American Population Dynamics in Eastern North America*. Knoxville: University of Tennessee Press; 1983.

Dozier, Edward P. *Pueblo Indians of North America*. New York: Holt, Rinehart and Winston, 1970.

Dray, William H. *Laws and Explanation in History*. London: Oxford University Press, 1957.

———. *Philosophy of History*. Englewood Cliffs NJ: Prentice-Hall, 1964.

Drinnon, Richard, ed. *Facing West: The Metaphysics of Indian-Hating and Empire Building*. New York: New American Library, 1980.
Dunaway, David King. "The Oral Biography." *Biography* 14, no. 3 (Summer 1991): 256–66.
Dunnell, Robert C. "Evolutionary Theory and Archaeology." *Advances in Archaeological Method and Theory* 3 (1980): 35–99.
———. *Systematics in Prehistory*. New York: Free Press, 1971.
Dymond, David Percy. *Archaeology and History: A Plea for Reconciliation*. London: Thames and Hudson, 1974.
Ebner, Michael H. "Students as Oral Historians." *History Teacher* 9, no. 2 (February 1976): 196–201.
Edmunds, R. David. "The Indian in the Mainstream: Indian Historiography for Teachers of American History Surveys." *History Teacher* 8, no. 2 (February 1975): 242–64.
Eggan, Fred. "Some Anthropological Approaches to the Understanding of Ethnological Cultures." *Ethnohistory* 8, no. 1 (Winter 1961): 1–11.
Eliade, Mircea. *Cosmos and History: The Myth of the Eternal Return*. New York: Harper and Row, 1959.
Ellis, Richard. "The Duke Indian Oral History Collection at the University of New Mexico." *New Mexico Historical Review* 48 (July 1973): 259–63.
Elton, Geofrey Rudolf. *The Practice of History*. London: Methuen, 1967.
Emery, Frederick Edmund, ed. *Systems Thinking: Selected Readings*. New York: Harmondsworth, 1969.
Erodes, Richard, and Alfonso Ortiz, eds. *American Indian Myths and Legends*. New York: Pantheon Books, 1984.
Ewers, John C. "When Red and White Men Met." *Western Historical Quarterly* 2, no. 2 (April 1971): 133–50.
———. *Indian Life on the Upper Missouri*. Norman: University of Oklahoma Press, 1968.
Fairchild, Hoxie Neale. *The Noble Savage: A Study in Romantic Naturalism*. New York: Columbia University Press, 1928.
Fenton, William N. "Ethnohistory and Its Problems." *Ethnohistory* 9, no. 1 (Winter 1962): 1–23.
——— "Field Work, Museum Studies, and Ethnohistorical Research." *Ethnohistory* 13, nos. 1–2 (Winter–Spring 1966): 71–85.
Field, G. C. "Some Problems of the Philosophy of History." Annual Philosophical Lecture, 1938. *Proceedings of the British Academy* 24 (1938): 55–83.
Figlio, Karl. "Oral History and the Unconscious." *History Workshop Journal* 26 (1988): 120–32.

Finnegan, Ruth. "A Note on Oral Tradition and Historical Evidence." *History and Theory* 9 (1970): 195–201.

Firth, Raymond William. *Man and Culture: An Evaluation of the Work of Bronislaw Malinowski.* London: Routledge and Kegan Paul, 1957.

Fischer, David H. *Historian's Fallacies: Toward a Logic of Historical Thought.* London: Routledge and Kegan Paul, 1971.

Fitting, James Edward, ed. *The Development of North American Archaeology.* Garden City: Anchor Books, 1973.

Fitzgerald, J. A., and W. W. Ludeman. "The Intelligence of Indian Children." *Journal of Comparative Psychology* 6 (August 1926): 319–28.

Fixico, Donald L. *The American Indian Mind in a Linear World: American Indian Studies and Traditional Knowledge.* New York: Routledge, 2003.

——— "Ethics and Responsibilities in Writing American Indian History." *American Indian Quarterly* 20, no. 1 (Winter 1996): 29–39.

———. "The Muscogee Creeks: A Nativistic People." In *Between Two Worlds: The Survival of Twentieth Century Indians*, ed. Arrell M. Gibson, 30–43. Oklahoma City: Oklahoma Historical Society, 1986.

———. "The Persistence of Identity in Indian Communities of the Western Great Lakes.". In *American Indians: Social Justice and Public Policy*, ed. Donald E. Green and Thomas V. Tonnesen, 109–48. Milwaukee: University of Wisconsin System Institute on Race and Ethnicity, 1991.

———, ed. *Rethinking American Indian History.* Albuquerque: University of New Mexico Press, 1997.

———. "The Struggle for Our Homes: Indian and White Values and Tribal Lands." In *Defending Mother Earth: Native American Perspectives on Environmental Justice*, ed. Jace Weaver, 29–46. Maryknoll NY: Orbis Books, 1996.

Flint, Robert. *History of the Philosophy of History, Vol. 1.* Edinburgh: William Blackwood and Sons, 1893.

Flores, Dan. *The Natural West: Environmental History in the Great Plains and Rocky Mountains.* Norman: University of Oklahoma Press, 2001.

Fogel, Robert William. "The Limits of Quantitative Methods in History." *American Historical Review* 80, no. 2 (April 1975): 329–50.

Fogelson, Raymond D. "The Ethnohistory of Events and Nonevents." *Ethnohistory* 36, no. 2 (Spring 1989): 133–47.

Foner, Eric. *Give Me Liberty! An American History*, vol. 1. New York: W. W. Norton, 2005.

Forbes, Jack D. "The Ethnohistorian in the Southwest." *Journal of the West* 3, nos. 1–4 (1964): 430–36.

———. "Frontiers in American History and the Role of the Frontier Historian." *Ethnohistory* 15, no. 2 (Spring 1968): 203–35.

———. "The Historian and the Indian: Racial Bias in American History." *Americas* 19, no. 4 (April 1963): 349–62.

———. "The Manipulation of Race, Caste and Identity: Classifying Afroamericans, Native Americans and Red-Black People." *Journal of Ethnic Studies* 17, no. 4 (Winter 1990): 1–51.

Frisch, Michael. *A Shared Authority: Essays on the Craft and Meaning of Oral History and Public History*. Albany: State University of New York Press, 1990.

Friscancho, A. Roberto. *Human Adaptation: A Functional Interpretation*. St. Louis: C. V. Mosby, 1979.

Fuchs, Estelle, and Robert Havighurst. *To Live on This Earth: American Indian Education*. Garden City: Anchor Press, 1973.

Furet, Francois. *In the Workshop of History*. Chicago: University of Chicago Press, 1984.

Fuson, Robert H., trans. *The Log of Christopher Columbus*. Camden ME: International Marine Publishing, 1992.

Gadacz, Rene R. "The Language of Ethnohistory." *Anthropologica* 4, no. 2 (1982): 147–65.

Gallagher, Winifred. *The Power of Place: How Our Surroundings Shape Our Thoughts, Emotions and Actions*. New York: Harper Perennial, 1994.

Gallie, W. B. "The Historical Understanding." *History and Theory* 3, no. 1 (1963): 144–202.

Gardiner, Patrick L. *The Nature of Historical Explanation*. London: Oxford University Press, 1952.

Gardiner, Patrick L., ed. *The Philosophy of History*. London: Oxford University Press, 1974.

Garn, Stanley M. *Human Races*. Springfield IL: Charles C. Thomas Publisher, 1961.

Geertz, Clifford. *The Interpretation of Cultures: Selected Essays*. New York: Basic Books, 1973.

Gibson, James Jerome. *The Perception of the Visual World*. Boston: Houghton Mifflin, 1950.

Gilbert, Arthur N. "The American Indian and United States Diplomatic History: A Reader in the Study of Symbols and Meanings." *History Teacher* 8, no. 2 (February 1975): 229–41.

Glassberg, David. *Sense of History: The Place of the Past in American Life*. Amherst: University of Massachusetts Press, 2001.

Glazer, Nathan, and Daniel P. Moynihan, eds. *Ethnicity: Theory and Experience*. Cambridge: Harvard University Press, 1958.

Goddard, Ives, vol. ed. *Handbook of North American Indians*, vol. 17: *Languages*. William C. Sturtevant, general ed. Washington DC: Smithsonian Institution Press, 1996.

Gottschalk, Louis. *Understanding History: A Primer of Historical Method*. 1950; repr., New York: Alfred A. Knopf, 1967.

Gould, Richard A., ed. *Explorations in Ethnoarchaeology*. Albuquerque: University of New Mexico Press, 1978.

Green, Michael. *The Politics of Indian Removal: Creek Government and Society*. Lincoln: University of Nebraska Press, 1982.

Green, Rayna, ed. *That's What She Said: Contemporary Poetry and Fiction by Native American Women*. Bloomington: Indiana University Press, 1984.

Grinde, Donald A. *The Iroquois and the Founding of the American Nation*. San Francisco: Indian Historian Press, 1977.

Grinnell, George Bird. *Pawnee Hero Stories and Folk-tales*. Lincoln: University of Nebraska Press, 1971.

Guardipee, Norman. "Mending the Broken Circle." In *Dreaming the Dawn: Conversations with Native Artists and Activists*, ed. E. K. Caldewell, 25–32. Lincoln: University of Nebraska Press, 1999.

Gumerman, George J., and Murray Gell-Mann, eds. *Understanding Complexity in the Prehistoric Southwest*. Reading MA: Addison-Wesley, 1994.

Gustavson, Carl G. *A Preface to History*. New York: McGraw-Hill, 1955.

Haan, Richard L. "Another Example of Stereotypes on the Early American Frontier: The Imperialist Historians and the American Indian." *Ethnohistory* 20, no. 2 (Spring 1973): 143–52.

Hadingham, Robert. *Early Man and the Cosmos*. New York: Walker and Company, 1984.

Hagan, William T. "On Writing the History of the American Indian." *Journal of Interdisciplinary History* 2 (1971–72): 149–54.

———. *Theodore Roosevelt and Six Friends of the Indian*. Norman: University of Oklahoma Press, 1997.

Hagerdorn, Herman. *Roosevelt in the Badlands*. Boston: Houghton Mifflin Company, 1921.

Hale, Duane Kendall. *Researching and Writing Tribal Histories*. Grand Rapids: Michigan Indian Press and Grand Rapids Tribal Council, 1991.

Hämäläinen, Pekka. *The Comanche Empire*. New Haven: Yale University Press, 2008.

Hammond, Norman, and Gordon R. Willey, eds. *Maya Archaeology and Ethnohistory*. Austin: University of Texas Press, 1976.

Hanke, Lewis. "American Historians and the World Today: Responsibilities and Opportunities." *American Historical Review* 80, no. 1 (February 1975): 1–20.

Hardin, Terri, ed. *Legends and Lore of the American Indians*. New York: Barnes and Noble Books, 1993.

Harris, Marvin. *The Rise of Anthropological Theory: A History of Theories of Culture*. New York: Crowell, 1968.

Hassell, Hank. *Rainbow Bridge: An Illustrated History*. Logan: Utah State University Press, 1999.

Hassrick, Royal B. *The Sioux: Life and Customs of a Warrior Society*. Norman: University of Oklahoma Press, 1964.

Hatch, Elvin T. *Theories of Man and Culture*. New York: Columbia University Press, 1973.

Hauptman, Laurence M. *Tribes and Tribulations: Misconceptions about American Indians and Their Histories*. Albuquerque: University of New Mexico Press, 1995.

Henige, David P. "'In possession of the Author': The Problem of Source Monopoly in Oral Historiography." *International Journal of Oral History* 1 (1980): 181–94.

Higham, John. "The Future of American History." *Journal of American History* 80, nos. 3–4 (March 1994): 1289–1309.

Highwater, Jamake. *The Primal Mind*. New York: Harper and Row, 1981.

Hill, Jonathan D., ed. *History, Power and Identity: Ethnogenesis in the Americas, 1492–1992*. Iowa City: University of Iowa Press, 1996.

Hill, Norbert S., ed. *Words of Power: Voices from Indian America*. Golden CO: Fulcrum Publishing, 1994.

Hill, Susan M., and Mary Jane Logan McCallum, eds. "Guest Editors' Remarks." Special Edition, "Writing From Home." *American Indian Quarterly* 33, no. 4 (Fall 2009): ix–xix, 427–560.

Hirschfelder, Arlene, ed. *Native Heritage: Personal Accounts by American Indians, 1790 to the Present*. New York: Macmillan, 1995.

Hodder, Ian. *The Present Past: An Introduction to Anthropology for Archaeologists*. London: Batsford, 1982.

———. *Symbols in Action: Ethnoarchaeological Studies of Material Culture*. Cambridge: Cambridge University Press, 1982.

Hodder, Ian, ed. *Symbolic and Structural Archaeology*. Cambridge: Cambridge University Press, 1982.

Hoebel, Edward Adamson. *The Cheyennes: Indians of the Great Plains*. 2nd ed. New York: Holt, 1978.

———. *Man in the Primitive World: An Introduction to Anthropology*. New York: McGraw-Hill, 1949.

Hole, Frank, and Robert F. Heizer. *An Introduction to Prehistoric Archaeology*. 2nd ed. New York: Holt, Rinehart and Winston, 1969.
Holm, Tom. *The Great Confusion in Indian Affairs: Native Americans and Whites in the Progressive Era*. Austin: University of Texas Press, 2005.
———. *Strong Hearts, Wounded Souls: Native American Veterans of the Vietnam War*. Austin: University of Texas Press, 1996.
Honigmann, John J. *The Development of Anthropological Ideas*. Homewood IL: Dorsey, 1976.
Horowitz, Ronald L. "Ethnic Identity." In *Ethnicity: Theory and Experience*, ed. Nathan Glazer and Daniel P. Moynihan, 111–40. Cambridge: Harvard University Press, 1958.
Horsman, Reginald. *Race and Manifest Destiny: The Origins of American Racial Anglo-Saxonism*. Cambridge: Harvard University Press, 1981.
———. "Scientific Racism and the American Indian in the Mid-Nineteenth Century." *American Quarterly* 27 (1975): 152–68.
Hough, Michael. *Out of Place: Restoring Identity to the Regional Landscape*. New Haven: Yale University Press, 1990.
Howard, James H., in collaboration with Willie Lena. *Oklahoma Seminoles: Medicines, Magic, and Religion*. Norman: University of Oklahoma Press, 1984.
Hoxie, Frederick E. "The Problems of Indian History." *Social Science Journal* 25, no. 4 (1988): 389–99.
———. "What's Your Problem? New Work in Twentieth-Century Native American Ethnohistory." *Ethnohistory* 47, no. 2 (Spring 2000): 469–81.
Hudson, Charles. "The Historical Approach in Anthropology." In *Handbook of Social and Cultural Anthropology*, ed. John J. Honigmann, 111–41. Chicago: Rand McNally College Publishing Company, 1973.
Hudson, Kenneth. *A Social History of Archaeology: The British Experience*. London: Macmillan, 1981.
Hughes, H. Stuart. "The Historian and the Social Scientist." *American Historical Review* 66, no. 1 (October 1960): 20–46.
Hume, Ivor Noël. *Historical Archaeology*. New York: Alfred A. Knopf, 1969.
Hungry Wolf, Beverly. *The Ways of My Grandmothers*. New Rork: William Morrow, 1980.
Huxley, Thomas Henry. *Man's Place in Nature and Other Anthropological Essays*. New York: Appleton and Company, 1896.
Iggers, Georg G. "The Image of Ranke in American and German Historical Thought." *History and Theory* 2, no. 1 (1962): 17–40.
Ilisevich, Robert D.. "Oral History in Undergraduate Research." *History Teacher* 6 (November 1972): 47–50.

Innes, Robert Alexander. "Introduction: Native Studies and Native Cultural Preservation, Revitalization, and Persistence." Special Edition: New Interpretations of Native Cultural Preservation, *American Indian Culture and Research Journal* 34, no. 2 (2010): 1–9, 10–164.

Inter Press Service, comp. *Story Earth: Native Voices on the Environment*. San Francisco: Mercury House, 1993.

Irwin, Lee. "Cherokee Healing: Myth, Dreams, and Medicine." *American Indian Quarterly* 16, no. 2 (Spring 1992): 237–57.

Irwin, Rita L. *A Circle of Empowerment: Women, Education, and Leadership*. Albany: State University of New York Press, 1995.

Isaacs, Harold R. *Idols of the Tribe: Group Identity and Political Change*. New York: Harper and Row, 1975.

Jackson, John. *A Sense of Place, a Sense of Time*. New Haven: Yale University Press, 1994.

Jacobs, Margaret D. *Engendered Encounters: Feminism and Pueblo Cultures 1879–1934*. Lincoln: University of Nebraska Press, 1999.

———. *White Mother to a Dark Race: Settler Colonialism, Maternalism, and the Removal of Indigenous Children in the American West and Australia, 1880–1940*. Lincoln: University of Nebraska Press, 2009.

Jacobs, Sue Ellen. "Gender Roles at San Juan Pueblo." In *Women and Power in Native North America*, ed. Laura F. Klein and Lillian A. Ackerman, 177–213. Norman: University of Oklahoma Press, 1995.

Jacobs, Wilbur R. "The Indian and the Frontier in American History—A Need for Revision." *Western Historical Quarterly* 4, no. 1 (January 1973): 43–56.

———. "Native American History: How It Illuminates Our Past." *American Historical Review* 80, no. 3 (June 1975): 595–609.

Jacoby, Karl. *Shadows at Dawn: An Apache Massacre and the Violence of History*. New York: Penguin Books, 2008.

Jennings, Francis. "A Growing Partnership: Historians, Anthropologists, and American Indian History." *History Teacher* 14, no. 1 (November 1980): 87–104.

———. *The Invasion of America: Indians, Colonialism, and the Cant of Conquest*. Chapel Hill: University of North Carolina Press, 1975.

Jett, Stephen C. "Pueblo Indian Migration: An Evaluation of the Possible Physical and Cultural Determinants." *American Antiquity* 29, no. 3 (1962): 281–300.

Jochim, Michael A. *Hunter-Gatherer Subsistence and Settlement: A Predictive Model*. New York: Academic Press, 1976.

Johnson, Jay K., ed. *The Development of Southeastern Archaeology*. Tuscaloosa: University of Alabama Press, 1993.

Jones, David E., ed. *Sanapia: Comanche Medicine Woman*. Prospects Heights IL: Waveland Press, 1972.

Jones, Howard Mumford. *O Strange New World: American Culture, The Formative Years*. New York: Viking Press, 1964.

Jorgensen, Joseph G. "Land Is Cultural, So Is a Commodity: The Locus of Differences among Indians, Cowboys, Sod-Busters, and Environmentalists." *Journal of Ethnic Studies* 12, no. 3 (Fall 1984): 1–21.

———. "On Ethics and Anthropology." *Current Anthropology* 12, no. 3 (June 1971): 321–34.

Joynt, Carey B., and Nicholas Rescher. "The Problem of Uniqueness in History." *History and Theory* 1, no. 2 (1961): 150–62.

Jumperz, John J. "The Speech Community." In *International Encyclopedia of the Social Sciences*, 381–86. New York: Macmillan, 1968.

Kammen, Michael G. *Mystic Chords of Memory*. New York: Alfred A. Knopf, 1991.

Kaplan, Abraham. "Philosophy of Science in Anthropology." *Annual Review of Anthropology* 13 (1984): 25–39.

Kaplan, Rachel, and Stephen Kaplan. *The Experience of Nature: A Psychological Perspective*. New York: Cambridge University Press, 1989.

Kaut, Charles R. "The Clan System as an Epiphenomenal Element of Western Apache Social Organization." *Ethnology* 13, no. 1 (January 1974): 45–70.

———. *The Western Apache Clans System: Its Origins and Development*. Albuquerque: University of New Mexico Press, 1957.

Keen, Benjamin. *The Aztec Image in Western Thought*. New Brunswick NJ: Rutgers University Press, 1971.

Keenan, Jerry, ed. *Encyclopedia of American Indian Wars, 1492–1890*. New York: W. W. Norton, 1977.

Kelley, Klara, and Harris Francis. "Places Important to Navajo People." *American Indian Quarterly* 17, no. 2 (Spring 1993): 151–70.

Kelsey, Morton T. *Tales to Tell: Legends of the Senecas*. Pecos NM: Dove Publications, 1978.

Kent, Susan. *Analyzing Activity Areas: An Ethnoarchaeological Study of the Use of Space*. Albuquerque: University of New Mexico Press, 1984.

Kenyon, John P. *The History Men: The Historical Profession in England Since the Renaissance*. London: Weidenfeld and Nicolson, 1983.

Kidwell, Clara Sue. *Choctaws and Missionaries in Mississippi, 1818–1918*. Norman: University of Oklahoma Press, 1995.

———. *The Choctaw Indians of Oklahoma: From Tribe to Nation, 1855–1970*. Norman: University of Oklahoma Press, 2007.

Klein, Laura F., and Lillian A. Ackerman, eds. *Women and Power in Native North America*. Norman: University of Oklahoma Press, 1995.

Kleinfeld, J. "Visual Memory in Village Eskimo and Urban Cauasian Children." *Arctic* 24, no. 2 (1971): 132–38.

Klibansky, Raymond, and H. J. Paton, eds. *Philosophy and History: Essays presented to Ernst Cassirer*. New York: Harper and Row, 1936.

Klinck, C. F., ed. *Tecumseh: Fact and Fiction in Early Records*. Ottawa: Tecumseh Press,1978.

Kluckholn, Clyde, and Henry A. Murray, eds. *Personality in Nature, Society and Culture*. New York: Alfred A. Knopf, 1953.

Kramer, Carol, ed. *Ethnoarachaeology: Implications of Ethnography For Archaeology*. New York: Columbia University Press, 1979.

Krech, Shepard III. "The State of Ethnohistory." *Annual Review of Anthropology* 20 (1991): 345–75.

Kroeber, Alfred L. "The Culture-area and Age-area Concepts of Clark Wissler." In *Methods in Social Science*, ed. S. A. Rice, 248–65. Chicago: University of Chicago Press, 1931.

Kroeber, Alfred, Clyde Kluckholn, Wayne Untereiner, and Alfred G. Meyer. *Culture: A Critical Review of Concepts and Definitions*. New York: Vintage Books, 1952.

———. *The Nature of Culture*. Chicago: University of Chicago Press, 1952.

Kroeber, Theodora, ed. *Alfred L. Kroeber: An Anthropologist Looks at History*. Berkeley: University of California Press, 1963.

Krupat, Arnold. *Ethnocriticism: Ethnography, History, Literature*. Berkeley: University of California Press, 1992.

Kuhn, Thomas S. *The Structure of Scientific Revolutions*. Chicago: University of Chicago Press, 1970.

Laet, Sigfried J. de. *Archaeology and Its Problems*. New York: Macmillan, 1957.

Lame Deer, John Fire, and Richard Erodes. *Lame Deer, Seeker of Visions: The Life of a Sioux Medicine Man*. New York: Touchstone Books, 1972.

Lareau, Andrea, and Jeffrey Shultz. *Journeys through Ethnography: Realistic Accounts of Fieldwork*. Boulder: Westview Press, 1996.

Le Goff, Jacques, and Pierre Nora. *Constructing the Past: Essays in Historical Methodology*. London: Cambridge University Press, 1985.

Lee, Scout Cloud. *The Circle Is Sacred: A Medicine Book for Women*. Tulsa: Council Oak Books, 1995.

Lefebvre, Henri. *The Production of Space*. Oxford: Blackwell, 1991.

León-Portilla, Miguel. *Time and Reality in the Thought of the Maya*. 2nd ed. Norman: University of Oklahoma Press, 1988.

Levin, Michael D., ed. *Ethnicity and Aboriginality: Case Studies in Ethnonationalism*. Toronto: University of Toronto Press, 1993.

Lewin, Roger. *Complexity: Life at the Edge of Chaos*. New York: Macmillan, 1992.

Lewis, David R. *Neither Dog Nor Wolf: American Indians, Environment, and Agrarian Change*. New York: Oxford University Press, 1994.

Lewis, Oscar. "Manly-Hearted Women aong the North Piegan." *American Anthropologist* 43, no. 2 (April–June 1941): 173–87.

Li, Tania Murray. "Constituting Tribal Space: Indigenous Identity and Resource Politics in Indonesia." *Comparative Studies in Society and History* 42, no. 1 (January 2000): 149.

Linderman, Frank Bird, ed. *Old Man Coyote*. New York: John Day Company, 1931; Lincoln: University of Nebraska Press, 1996.

——— *Red Mother*. 1932; republished as *Pretty-Shield, Medicine Woman of the Crows*, Lincoln: University of Nebraska Press. 1972.

Lindford, Laurance D. *Navajo Places: History, Legend, Landscape*. Salt Lake City: University of Utah Press, 2000.

Linton, Ralph. *The Tree of Culture*. New York: Alfred A. Knopf, 1955.

Long, Roger D. "The Personal Dimension in Doing Oral History." *History Teacher* 24, no. 3 (May 1991): 307–12.

Lossiah, Lynn. *Cherokee Little People: The Secrets and Mysteries of the, Yunwi Tsunsdi*. Cherokee NC: Cherokee Publications, 1998.

Louch, A. R. *Explanation and Human Action*. Los Angeles: University of California Press, 1966.

Lowie, Robert H. *The History of Ethnological Theory*. New York: Farrar and Rhinehart, 1937.

———. *Primitive Society*. New York: Horace Liveright, 1920.

———. "Survivals and Historical Method." *American Journal of Sociology* 23, no. 4 (January 1918): 529–35.

Lowery, Malinda Maynor. *Lumbee Indians in the Jim Crow South: Race, Identity, and the Making of a Nation*. Chapel Hill: University of North Carolina Press, 2010.

Lowry, Laura M. "Differences in Visual Perception and Auditory Discrimination between American Indian and White Kindergarten Children." *Journal of Learning Disabilities* 3 (July 1970): 359–63.

Lowther, Gordon R. "Epistemology and Archaeological Theory." *Current Anthropology* 3, no. 5 (December 1962): 495–509.

Lurie, Nancy. "Ethnohistory: An Ethnological Point of View." *Ethnohistory* 8, no. 1 (1961): 78–92.

Lurie, Nancy Oestreich, ed. *Mountain Wolf Woman, Sister of Crashing Thunder: The Autobiography of a Winnebago Indian*. Ann Arbor: University of Michigan Press, 1961.

Magnaghi, Russell M. "Herbert E. Bolton and Sources for American Indian Studies." *Western Historical Quarterly* 6, no. 1 (January 1975): 33–46.

Mandelbaum, Maurice H. *The Anatomy of Historical Knowledge*. Baltimore: Johns Hopkins University Press, 1977.

Mannheim, Karl. *Ideology and Utopia: An Introduction to the Sociology of Knowledge*. London: Routledge and Kegan Paul, 1936; 4th printing, 1948.

Marquis, Thomas B. *Wooden Leg: A Warrior Who Fought Custer*. Lincoln: University of Nebraska Press, 1965.

Marshack, Alexander. *The Roots of Civilization: The Cognitive Beginnings of Man's First Art, Symbol, and Notation*. New York: McGraw-Hill, 1972.

Marshall, Humphrey. *The History of Kentucky*. Vol. 2. Frankfort: n.p., 1824.

Martin, Calvin. "Ethnohistory: A Better Way to Write Indian History." *Western Historical Quarterly* 9, no. 1 (January 1978): 41–56.

———. *In the Spirit of the Earth: Rethinking History and Time*. Baltimore: Johns Hopkins University Press, 1992.

———. "The Metaphysics of Writing Indian-White History." *Ethnohistory* 26, no. 2 (Spring 1979): 153–59.

Martin, Calvin, ed. *The American Indian and the Problem of History*. New York: Oxford University Press, 1987.

Matthews, Washington, ed. *Navajo Legends: Collected and Translated*. Boston: Houghton, Mifflin and Company, 1897.

McClelland, Peter D. *Causal Explanation and Model Building in History, Economics, and the New Economic History*. Ithaca NY: Cornell University Press, 1975.

McGaa, Ed. *Native Wisdom: Perceptions of the Natural Way*. Minneapolis: Four Directions Publishing, 1995.

McNab, David. *Circles of Time: Aboriginal Land Rights and Resistance in Ontario*. Waterloo, Ont., Canada: Wilfrid Laurier University Press, 1999.

McNeill, William H. *Mythistory and Other Essays*. Chicago: University of Chicago Press, 1986.

———. "Mythistory, or Truth, History, Historians." *American Historical Review* 91, no. 1 (February 1986): 1–10.

McTaggart, Fred. *Wolf That I Am: In Search of the Red Earth People*. Norman: University of Oklahoma Press, 1984.

Merrell, James H. *The Indians' New World: Catawbas and Their Neighbors from European Contact through the Era of Removal*. Chapel Hill: University of North Carolina Press, 1989.

———. "Some Thoughts on Colonial Historians and American Indians." *William and Mary Quarterly* 46, no. 1 (January 1989): 94–119.

Meyerhoff, Hans. *The Philosophy of History in Our Time: An Anthology*. Garden City NY: Doubleday, 1959.

Middlekauff, Robert. "Narrative History and Ordinary Life." *Pacific Historical Review* 60, no. 1 (February 1991): 3–13.

Miller, Dorcases S. *Stars of the First People: Native American Star Myths and Constellations*. Boulder: Pruett Publishing Company, 1997.

Miller, Jay. *Earthmaker: Tribal Stories from Native North America*. New York: Perigee Books, 1992.

Milne, Courtney. *Sacred Places in North America: A Journey into the Medicine Wheel*. New York: Stewart, Tabori and Chang, 1994; also published as *Spirit of the Land*, Toronto: Penguin, 1994.

Mintz, Steven, ed. *Native American Voices: A History and Anthology*. St. James NY: Brandywine Press, 1995.

Mischke, James A. *Circles, Consciousness and Culture*. Tsaile AZ: Navajo Community College Press, 1984.

Mithun, Marianne. *The Languages of Native North America*. New York: Cambridge University Press, 1999.

Montgomery, David H. *An Elementary American History*. Boston: Ginn and Company, 1904.

Mooney, James. *Myths of the Cherokee*. New York: Dover Publications, 1995.

Moore, Harvey C. "Cumulation and Cultural Process." *American Anthropologist* 56 (1954): 347–57.

Moore, John H. "Cheyenne Names and Cosmology." *American Ethnologist* 11, no. 2 (May 1984): 291–312.

Moran, Emilio F. *Human Adaptability: An Introduction to Ecological Anthropology*. Boulder: Westview Press, 1982.

Morgan, Lewis Henry. *Houses and House Life of the American Aborgines*. Contributions to North American Ethnology, vol. 4. Washington DC: U.S. Department of the Interior, 1881.

Munslow, Alun. *Deconstructing History*. London: Routledge, 1997.

Murdock, George Peter. *Social Structure*. New York: Macmillan, 1949.

Nabokov, Peter. *A Forest of Time: American Indian Ways of History*. Cambridge: Cambridge University Press, 2002.

Nabokov, Peter, ed. *Native American Testimony: A Chronicle of Indian-White Relations from Prophency to the Present, 1492–1992*. New York: Penguin, 1992.

Nadel, Siegfried Frederick. *The Foundations of Social Anthropology*. New York: Free Press, 1951.

Nagel, Ernest. *The Structure of Science: Problems in the Logic of Scientific Explanation*. Glencoe IL: Free Press, 1951.

Nash, Gary B. "Whither Indian History?" *Journal of Ethnic Studies* 4, no. 3 (Fall 1976): 69–76.

Nash, Roderick. *Wilderness and the American Mind*. New Haven: Yale University Press, 1982.

Nazarea, Virgina Dimasuay, ed. *Ethnoecology: Situated Knowledge/Located Lives*. Tucson: University of Arizona Press, 1999.

Neihardt, John Gneisenau, ed. *Black Elk Speaks: Being the Life Story of a Holy Man of the Oglala Sioux*. 1932; New York: Pocket Books, 1973.

Norton, Mary Beth, David M. Katzman, Paul D. Escott, Howard P. Chudacoff, Thomas G. Paterson, and William M. Tuttle Jr. *A People and a Nation: A History of the United States*, vol. 1, to 1877. Boston: Houghton Mifflin, 1982.

O'Danachair, Caoimhin. "Oral Tradition and the Printed Word." *Irish University Review* 9, no. 1 (Spring 1979): 31–41.

Olafson, Frederick A. "Narrative History and the Concept of Action." *History and Theory* 9 (1970): 265–89.

Olson, James C. "Some Reflections on Historical Method and Indian History." *Ethnohistory* 5, no. 1 (Winter 1958): 48–59.

O'Neil, Floyd. "Commentary" on "Perspectives on the Writing of Indian History from the Indian Point of View." In *Breaking Barriers*, ed. David L. Beaulieu, Newberry Library Center for the History of the American Indian, Occasional Paper Series, no. 1. December 1974.

Pagden, Anthony. *The Fall of Natural Man: The American Indian and the Origins of Comparative Ethnology*. Cambridge: Cambridge University Press, 1982.

Parsons, Jeffrey R. "Archaeological Settlement Patterns." *Annual Review of Anthropology* 1 (1972): 127–50.

Payne, Kenneth W., and Stephan O. Murray. "Historical Inferences from Ethnohistorical Data: Boasian Views." *Journal of the History of the Behavioral Sciences* 19 (October 1983): 335–40.

Pearce, Roy Harvey. "From the History of Ideas to Ethnohistory." *Journal of Ethnic Studies* 2, no. 1 (Spring 1974): 86–92.

Perdue, Theda. *Cherokee Women: Gender and Culture Change, 1700–1835*. Lincoln: University of Nebraska Press, 1998.

———. *Nations Remembered: An Oral History of the Five Civilized Tribes, 1865–1907*. Westport CN: Greenwood Press, 1980.

Perry, Barbara. *Silent Victims: Hate Crimes against Native Americans*. Tucson: University of Arizona Press, 2008.

Pesantubbee, Michelene E. *Choctaw Women in a Chaotic World*. Albuquerque: University of New Mexico Press, 2003.

Pitt, David C. *Using Historical Sources in Anthropology and Sociology*. New York: Holt, Rinehart and Winston, 1972.

Price, John. "The Native American Family." In *Ethnic Families in America*, ed. Charles H. Mindel, Robert W. Habenstein, and Roosevelt H. Wright, 248–70. New York: Elsevier, 1976.

Quam, Alvina, trans. *The Zunis: Self-Portrayals, by the Zuni People*. Albuquerque: University of New Mexico Press, 1972.

Radcliffe-Brown, Alfred Reginald. *Structure and Function in Primitive Society: Essays and Addresses*. New York: Free Press, 1965.

Radcliffe-Brown, Alfred Reginald, and M. N. Srinivas, eds. *Method in Social Anthropology: Selected Essays*. Chicago: University of Chicago Press, 1958.

Radin, Paul. *Primitive Man as Philosopher*. New York: Appleton and Company, 1927.

———. *The Trickster: A Study in American Indian Mythology*. New York: Schocken Books, 1971.

Rasnake, Roger Neil. *Domination and Cultural Resistance: Authority and Power among an Andean People*. Durham: Duke University Press, 1988.

Redman, Charles L., ed. *Research and Theory in Current Archeology*. New York: Wiley, 1973.

Reid, John Phillip. *A Law of Blood: The Primitive Law of the Cherokee Nation*. New York: New York University Press, 1970.

Rees, Martin. "The Anthropic Universe." *New Scientist* 115, no. 1572 (August 6, 1967): 44–47.

Richter, Daniel K. *Facing East From Indian Country: A Native History of Early America*. Cambridge, MA: Harvard University Press, 2001.

Ritchie, Donald A. *Doing Oral History*. New York: Twayne Publishers, 1995.

Rogers, John, Chippewa Chief. *Red World and White: Memories of a Chippewa Boyhood by John Rogers (Chief Snow Cloud)*. Norman: University of Oklahoma Press, 1974.

Rogers, J. Daniel, and Samuel M. Wilson, eds. *Ethnohistory and Archaeology: Approaches to Postcontact Change in the Americas*. New York: Plenum Press, 1993.

Romein, Jan. "Theoretical History." *Journal of the History of Ideas* 9, no. 1 (January 1948): 53–64.
Roosevelt, Theodore. *A Book Lover's Holiday in the Open*. New York: Charles Scribner's Sons, 1916.
Rouse, Irving. "The Strategy of Culture History." In *Anthropology Today*, ed. A. L. Kroeber, 57–76. Chicago: University of Chicago Press, 1953.
Sahlins, Marshall David. *Tribesmen*. Englewood Cliffs NJ: Prentice-Hall, 1968.
Sahlins, Marshall David, and Elman R. Service, eds. *Evolution and Culture*. Ann Arbor: University of Michigan Press, 1960.
Said, Edward. *Orientalism*. New York: Vintage Books, 1978.
Salisbury, Neal. "The Indians' Old World: Native Americans and the Coming of Europeans." *William and Mary Quarterly* 53, no. 3 (July 1996): 435–58.
Salmon, Merrilee H. *Philosophy and Archaeology*. New York: Academic Press, 1982.
Salmon, Wesley C. *Scientific Explanation and the Causal Structure of the World*. Princeton NJ: Princeton University Press, 1984.
Sando, Joe S. *The Pueblo Indians*. San Francisco: Indian Historian Press, 1976.
Schapera, I. "Should Anthropologists Be Historians?" *Journal of the Royal Anthropologocal Institute of Great Britain and Ireland* 92, no. 2 (July–December 1962), 143–56.
Schlelsier, Karl H. "Action Anthropology and the Southern Cheyenne." *Current Anthropology* 15, no. 3 (1974): 277–83.
Schmidt, Wilhelm. *The Culture Historical Method of Ethnology: The Scientific Approach to the Racial Question*. Trans. S. A. Sieber. New York: Fortuny's, 1939.
Scott, Gavin. "I Can't Cry Anymore." *Time Magazine*, February 22, 1993.
Sears, J. F. *Sacred Places: American Tourist Attractions in the Nineteenth Century*. New York: Oxford University Press, 1989.
Sears, William H. "The Study of Social and Religious Systems in North American Archaeology." *Current Anthropology* 2, no. 3 (June 1961): 223–46.
Seligman, Haim. "Is Oral History a Valid Research Instrument?" *International Journal of Oral History* 10, no. 3 (November 1989): 175–82.
Service, Elmer Rogers. *Primitive Social Organization: An Evolutionary Perspective*. New York: Random House, 1975.
"The Shadow Catcher: The Uses of Native American Photography." Special issue, *American Indian Culture and Research Journal* 20, no. 3 (1996).

Shafer, Boyd C. "History Not Art, Not Science, but History: Meanings and Use of History." *Pacific Historical Review* 29, no. 2 (May 1960): 159–70.

Shanks, Michael, and Christopher Tilley. *Re-Constructing Archaeology: Theory and Practice*. Cambridge: Cambridge University Press, 1987.

Sheehan, Bernard W. *Seeds of Extinction: Jeffersonian Philanthropy and the American Indian*. New York: W. W. Norton, 1973.

Shotwell, James Thomson. *The History of History*. New York: Columbia University Press, 1939.

Shumaker, Peggy. *The Circle of Totems*. Pittsburgh: University of Pittsburgh Press, 1988.

Silko, Leslie Marmon. *Ceremony*. New York: Penguin, 1977.

Slickpoo, Allen P. *Noon-Nee-Me-Poo (We, the Nez Perces): Culture and History of the Nez Perces*. Lapwai ID: Nez Perce Tribe of Idaho, 1973.

Smart, John Jamieson. *Philosophy and Scientific Realism*. London: Routledge and Kegan Paul, 1963.

Spicer, Edward Holland. *Cycles of Conquest*. Tucson: University of Arizona Press, 1962.

Spicer, Edward Holland, ed. *Perspectives in American Indian Culture Change*. Chicago: University of Chicago Press, 1961.

Spivak, Gayatri Chakravorty. *Can the Subaltern Speak?* New York: Columbia University Press, 2010.

Spores, Ronald. "New World Ethnohistory and Archaeology, 1970–1980." *Annual Review of Anthropology* 9 (1980): 575–603.

Standing Bear, Luther. *Land of the Spotted Eagle*. 1933; Lincoln: University of Nebraska Press, 1978.

Stansky, Peter. "The Crumbling Frontiers of History or History and Biography: Some Personal Remarks." *Pacific Historical Review* 59, no. 1 (February 1990): 1–14.

Stauss, Joseph H. (Jay). "The Study of American Indian Families: Implications for Applied Research." *Family Perspective* 20, no. 4 (1986): 337–50.

Steinberg, Ted. *Down to Earth: Nature's Role in American History*. New York: Oxford University Press, 2002.

Steward, Julian Haynes. *Basin-Plateau Aborginal Sociopolitical Groups*. Bulletin 120. Washington DC: Bureau of American Ethnology, 1938.

———. "Ecological Aspects of Southwest Society." *Anthropos* 32, no. 1 (1937): 87–104.

———. *Theory of Cultural Change: The Methodology of Multilinear Evolution*. Urbana IL: University of Illinois Press, 1955.

Stipe, Claude E. "Eastern Dakota Clans: The Solution of a Problem." *American Anthropologist* 73, no. 5 (October 1973): 1031–35.

Stoler, Ann Laura. *Carnal Knowledge and Imperial Power: Race and the Intimate in Colonial Rule*. Berkeley: University of California Press, 2002.

Sturtevant, William C. "Anthropology, History, and Ethnohistory." *Ethnohistory* 13, nos. 1–2 (Winter–Spring 1966): 1–51.

Susman, Warren I. *Culture as History: The Transformation of American Society in the Twentieth Century*. New York: Pantheon Books, 1973.

Swanton, John R. *Early History of the Creek Indians and their Neighbors*. Washington DC: Government Printing Office, 1922.

———. *Notes on the Creek Indians*. Bulletin 123. Washington DC: Bureau of American Ethnology, 1939.

———. "Social Organization and Social Usages of the Indians of the Creek Confederacy." In *Forty-Second Annual Report*. Washington DC: Bureau of American Ethnology, 1928.

Tainter, Joseph A., and Bonnie Bagley Tainter, eds. *Evolving Complexity and Environmental Risk in the Prehistoric Southwest*. Reading MA: Addison-Wesley, 1996.

Tedlock, Barbara, and Dennis Tedlock. *Teachings from the American Earth: Indian Religion and Philosophy*. New York: Liveright, 1975.

Teggart, Frederick John. *Theory of History*. New Haven: Yale University Press, 1925.

———. *Theory and Processes of History*. Los Angeles: University of California Press, 1941.

Terkel, Studs. *The Good War: An Oral History of World War Two*. New York: Ballantine Books, 1984.

———. *Hard Times: An Oral History of the Great Depression*. New York: Pantheon, 1970.

Thelen, David, ed. *Memory and American History*. Bloomington: Indiana University Press, 1990.

Thompson, James Westfall. *A History of Historical Writings*. 2 vols. New York: Macmillan, 1942.

Thornton, Russell. *American Indian Holocaust and Survival: A Population History Since 1492*. Norman: University of Oklahoma Press, 1987.

Thurman, Melburn D. "Plains Indian Winter Counts and the New Ethnohistory." *Plains Anthropologist* 27, no. 96 (May 1982): 173–75.

Tindall, George Brown. *America: A Narrative History*, vol. 1. New York: W. W. Norton, 1984.

Tinker, George. "An American Indian Theological Response to Ecojustice." In *Defending Mother Earth: Native American Perspectives on Environmental Justice*, ed. Jace Weaver, 153–76. Maryknoll NY: Orbis Books, 1996.

Tomlinson, John. *Cultural Imperialism*. London: Pinter Publishers, 1991.

Trigger, Bruce G. "Archaeology and the Image of the American Indian." *American Antiquity* 45 (1980): 662–76.

——— "Ethnohistory and Archaeology." *Ontario Archaeology* 30 (1978): 17–24.

———. "Ethnohistory: Problems and Prospects." *Ethnohistory* 29, no. 1 (1982): 1–19.

———. *A History of Archaeological Thought*. Cambridge: Cambridge University Press, 1989.

———. *The Huron: Farmers of the North*. 2nd ed. New York: Holt, Rinehart and Winston, 1990.

———. *Time and Traditions: Essays in Archaeological Interpretation*. New York: Columbia University Press, 1978.

Tweedie, M. Jean. "Notes on the History and Adaptation of the Apache Tribes." *American Anthropologist* 70, no. 6 (December 1968): 1132–42.

Tylor, Edward Burnett. *The Origins of Culture*. New York: Harper Torchbooks, 1958.

———. *Religion in Primitive Culture*. New York: Harper Torchbooks, 1958.

———. "The Science of Culture." In *Readings in Anthropology*, vol. 2, ed. Fred Merton, 1–18. New York: Thomas and Crowell, 1968.

Underhill, Ruth. ed. *Papago Woman, Maria Chona*. 1936; repr. New York: Holt, Rinehart and Winston, 1979.

Usner, Daniel H. *Indians, Settlers, and Slaves in a Frontier Exchange Economy: The Lower Mississippi Valley before 1763*. Chapel Hill: University of North Carolina Press, 1992.

Valandra, Edward Charles. *Not Without Our Consent: Lakota Resistance to Termination, 1950–59*. Champaign: University of Illinois Press, 2006.

Vanderwerth, W. C., ed. *Indian Oratory: Famous Speeches by Noted Indian Chieftans*. Norman: University of Oklahoma Press, 1971.

Vansina, Jan. *Oral Traditon as History*. Madison: University of Wisconsin Press, 1985.

Vanstone, James W. *Athapaskan Adaptations: Hunters and Fishermen of the Subartic Forests*. Chicago: Aldine Publishing Company, 1974.

Vaughan, Alden T. "From White Man to Redskin: Changing Anglo-American Perceptions of the American Indian." *American Historical Review* 87, no. 4 (October 1982): 917–53.

Vogel, Virgil J. *American Indian Medicine*. Norman: University of Oklahoma Press, 1970.

Voget, Fred W. *A History of Ethnology*. New York: Rinehart and Winston, 1975.

Wagner, Roy. *The Invention of Culture*. Englewood Cliffs NJ: Prentice-Hall, 1975; Chicago: University of Chicago Press, 1981.
Walker, James R. *Lakota Belief and Ritual*, ed. Raymond J. DeMallie and Elaine A. Jahner. Lincoln: University of Nebraska Press, 1980.
Walker, Kenneth. *The Circle of Life: A Search for an Attitude to Pain, Disease, Old Age and Death*. College Park: McGrath Publishing Company, 1970.
Wallace, Anthony F. C. *Culture and Personality*. New York: Random House, 1961.
Walsh, William Henry. *Philosophy of History: An Introduction*. 3rd ed. London: Hutchinson University Library, 1967.
Washburn, Wilcomb. "Ethnohistory: History in the Round." *Ethnohistory* 8, no. 1 (Winter 1961): 31–48.
———. "A Moral History of Indian-White Relations: Needs and Opportunities for Study." *Ethnohistory* 4, no. 1 (Winter 1957): 47–61.
———. "Ethical Perspectives in North American Ethnology." In *Social Contexts of American Ethnology, 1840–1984*, 1984 Proceedings of the American Ethnological Society, ed. June Helm, 55–64. Arlington VA: American Anthropological Association, 1985.
Watson, Patty Jo, Steven A. LeBlanc, and Charles L. Redman. *Archaeological Explanation: The Scientific Method in Archaeology*. New York: Columbia University Press, 1984.
Wax, Murray L. "The Ethics of Research in American Indian Communities." *American Indian Quarterly* 15, no. 4 (Fall 1991): 431–56.
Weaver, Jace, ed. *Defending Mother Earth: Native American Perspectives on Environmental Justice*. Maryknoll NY: Orbis Books, 1996.
Webb, George W., ed. *Chronological List of Engagements between the Regular Army of the United States and Various Tribes of Hostile Indians Which Occurred during the Years 1790–1895*. New York: AMS Press, 1976.
Welch, James. *Fools Crow*. New York: Penguin, 1987.
Wheeler, Robert E. M. *Archaeology from the Earth*. Oxford: Clarendon Press, 1954.
White, Leslie A. *The Concept of Cultural Systems: A Key to Understanding Tribes and Nations*. New York: Columbia University Press, 1975.
———. *The Science of Culture: A Study of Man and Civilization*. New York: Farrar, Strauss, 1949.
White, Morton Gabriel. *The Foundations of Historical Knowledge*. New York: Harper and Row, 1965.
White, Richard. "Discovering Nature in North America." *Journal of American History* 79, nos. 3–4 (December 1992): 874–91.

———. *The Roots of Dependency: Subsistence, Environment, and Social Change among the Choctaws, Pawnees, and Navajos*. Lincoln: University of Nebraska Press, 1983.
Whorf, Benjamin Lee. "An American Indian Model of the Universe." In *Teachings from the American Earth: Indian Religion and Philosophy*, ed. Dennis and Barbara Tedlock, 121–29. New York: Liveright, 1975.
Wickman, Patricia Riles. *Osceola's Legacy*. Tuscaloosa: University of Alabama Press, 2006.
Wiget, Andrew O. "Truth and the Hopi: An Historiographic Study of Documented Oral Tradition concerning the Coming of the Spanish." *Ethnohistory* 29, no. 3 (Summer 1982): 181–99.
Willey, Gordon Randolph, and Phillip Phillips. *Method and Theory in American Archaeology*. Chicago: University of Chicago Press, 1958.
Williamson, Ray. *Living the Sky: The Cosmos of the American Indian*. Norman: University of Oklahoma Press, 1984.
Wissler, Clark. *The Relation of Nature to Man in Aboriginal America*. New York: Oxford University Press, 1926.
———. *Man and Culture*. New York: Thomas Y. Corwell Company, 1923.
Woody, Elizabeth. "Earth Is Richer for This Voice." In E. K. Caldwell, *Dreaming the Dawn: Conversations with Native Artists and Activists*. Lincoln: University of Nebraska Press, 1999.
Wright, James V. "A Regional Examination of Ojibwa Culture History." *Anthropologica* 7 (1965): 189–227.
Wright, J. Leitch Jr. *Creeks and Seminoles: Destruction and Regeneration of the Muscogulge People*. Lincoln: University of Nebraska Press, 1986.
Young Bear, Severt, and R. D. Theisz. *Standing in the Light: A Lakota Way of Seeing*. Lincoln: University of Nebraska Press, 1994.

Index